Tourism, Ethnicity, and the State in Asian and Pacific Societies

Edited by Michel Picard and Robert E. Wood

University of Hawai'i Press

Honolulu

02 01 00 99 98 97   5 4 3 2 1

Library of Congress Cataloging-in-Publication Data
Tourism, ethnicity, and the state in Asian and Pacific societies /
   edited by Michel Picard and Robert E. Wood.
      p.   cm.
   Includes bibliographical references and index.
   ISBN 0–8248–1863–6 (cloth : alk. paper). – ISBN 0–8248–1911–X
(pbk. : alk. paper)
    1. Tourist trade—Asia.   2. Tourist trade—Pacific Area.
I. Picard, Michel.   II. Wood, Robert Everett, 1944–   .
G155.A74T66   1997
338.4'791504429—dc21   96–53034
                                              CIP

Book design by Omega Clay

Contents

Preface

The theme of identity is omnipresent within discourse about tourism (Lanfant 1995, 30).

In a study widely seen as inaugurating contemporary tourism studies in the social sciences, Dean MacCannell (1976, 5) counseled his readers to "follow the tourists" to understand the nature of modern identity. "By following the tourists," he suggested, "we may be able to arrive at a better understanding of ourselves."

For MacCannell, "ourselves" were the middle-class residents of the modern, Western societies who constituted the vast bulk of tourists, both international and domestic. But a number of anthropologists and sociologists were soon drawn to what tourism meant for the identities of others—most notably those people in non-Western societies who were increasingly becoming tourist objects themselves. In particular, the fate of *ethnic* identities and cultures in developing countries became a focus of debate in a fast-growing research literature. *Hosts and Guests: The Anthropology of Tourism,* edited by Valene L. Smith (1977), was an important early contribution to this literature. A year earlier, UNESCO (1976, 75) had proclaimed—perhaps prematurely but certainly presciently—that tourism, "more than an economic phenomenon with social and cultural effects, has become a phenomenon of civilization."

Despite tourism's global reach and economic significance, its importance for the understanding of ethnicity in the modern world has been generally neglected within the field of ethnicity studies, with a few major exceptions such as the work of Pierre van den Berghe and Charles Keyes (see their jointly edited issue of *Annals of Tourism Research* on ethnicity and tourism in 1984). Tourism is rarely mentioned in most of the major journals on race and ethnicity or in the periodic literature reviews of the field, apart from an occasional dismissal as an agent of the commoditization and, therefore, the degradation of ethnic culture.

Yet just as MacCannell suggested that tourism provided a way of understanding the modern identity of tourists, so it may be suggested that tourism provides a way of understanding what has been happening to ethnicity. With the proliferation of ethnic tourism, of ethnic museums and theme parks around the world, and of ethnic artifacts consumed not only by tourists but also by members of ethnic groups as assertions of their ethnic identities, ethnicity itself has become increasingly commoditized in specifically touristic ways. Indeed, one observer has gone so far as to suggest that:

> Cultures of all types—ethnic, national, regional, and the like—that are able to translate their qualities into marketable commodities and spectacles find themselves maintained, experienced, and globalized. Cultures that cannot or do not (re)present themselves in terms of marketable qualities, simulated instances, experiences, and products are finding themselves divested of members. In particular, traditional cultures . . . find that the way to keep their members interested in maintaining their culture is to involve the young people in the marketization of the culture, especially as touristic spectacle, through their music, dances, food, clothing, and ornamental items. This allows the youths to have incomes and, thereby, the ability to participate in the larger global market. . . . Cultures that cannot succeed in translating some of their qualities into spectacles or commodities seem to vanish only to become museum items (Firat 1995, 118).

This provocative analysis certainly challenges many presumptions about ethnic culture and commoditization and points to one of the central paradoxes of modern ethnicity—that its ability to facilitate participation in the global market may provide its appeal. However, Firat's analysis, like much of the earlier literature on tourism and ethnic identity, does not sufficiently consider the distinctively *political* sources of ethnic identity, particularly in terms of state policies and access to state resources. This consideration seems especially important in those societies where, on the one hand, states are striving to foster new national identities and to reconcile ethnic diversity and modern nationhood and, on the other hand, local people are finding they must increasingly negotiate their identities in arenas of intrusive state control.

The already complex task of reconciling ethnic and national identities has often been further complicated by the development of tourism. State elites have been primarily drawn to tourism for its economic benefits, although, as Richter (1989) and Leong (1989) have emphasized, there is an affinity between nationalism, regime interests, and the touristic promotion of a place as uniquely attractive. The marketing of ethnic diversity for tourism poses complex issues for states, however. How are ethnic divisions, symbolized by ethnic markers selected for tourist promotion, reconciled with national integration and the assertion of a national identity? Will ethnic tourism bind ethnic groups more tightly to the national political economy or will it reinforce their sense of separateness and potentially provide them with resources to resist integration? How will interethnic relations on local, regional, and national levels be affected?

These issues are particularly salient in many parts of Asia and the Pacific Islands, where ethnic diversity is pronounced and where ethnic identities have long been recognized as being particularly fluid. The region has the fastest growing tourism industry—both domestic and international—in the world. The interplay between the region's rapidly growing tourism development and its ongoing processes of ethnic construction in new and evolving political contexts is the central focus of this book.

Four of the chapters in this volume (by Adams, Michaud, Picard, and Wood) are updated versions of papers presented at the World Congress of Sociology in Bielefeld, Germany, in July 1994, at a session entitled "Tourism, the State, and Ethnicity," organized by Michel Picard under the auspices of a working group of the International Sociological Association (ISA), which has since been upgraded to the ISA Research Committee on International Tourism. While a number of individuals have been instrumental in securing this official recognition of tourism studies within both sociology and anthropology, the editors particularly want to acknowledge the important organizational and intellectual contributions of Marie-Françoise Lanfant and Krzysztof Przecławski.

In deciding to make these papers the nucleus of a book, we chose to focus on Asian and Pacific societies, partly because of our own research interests and partly because of the ways in which the nature of ethnicity in these societies poses particularly interesting and instructive questions about the intersection of the international tourism industry, state policies, and ethnic identities and relationships. Given this context, we solicited four additional chapters (by Kahn, Leong, Linnekin, and Oakes) to expand coverage of the region. We are aware that a number of interesting and important cases are not included, but we believe that the case studies in this volume provide a basis for significantly advancing our understanding of the dynamics of tourism, states, and ethnicity in the region.

It is commonplace to observe that it is an extremely difficult task to sort out the "impact" of international tourism from the many other sources of change in rapidly modernizing Asian and Pacific societies. But perhaps the more fundamental observation is that tourism does not do its work primarily from the outside. As an important part of broader processes of globalization, tourism has become an integral part of virtually all national societies, as the UNESCO statement quoted earlier implies. It no longer makes sense to conceive of tourism as a force external to contemporary societies, impacting them from the outside. What needs to be studied is how tourism has become institutionalized in different states and societies and how tourism alters incentives and opportunities for local actors in ways that unleash new and unique processes of change. As the case studies in this volume demonstrate, the responses of local actors to tourism have often been energetic, shrewd, and unpredictable. The often unintended results have included significant changes in the conceptions and markers of ethnic identities and in the relations between ethnic groups themselves and between ethnic groups and the state. These findings convince us that attention to both international and domestic tourism must be part of any adequate analysis of ethnicity and politics in the contemporary world.

Michel Picard
Robert E. Wood

References

Firat, A. Fuat
  1995 Consumer Culture or Culture Consumed? In *Marketing in a Multicultural World: Ethnicity, Nationalism, and Cultural Identity*, ed. Janeen A. Costa and Gary J. Bamossy, 105–125.

Lanfant, Marie-Françoise
  1995   International Tourism, Internationalization, and the Challenge to Identity. In *International Tourism: Identity and Change,* ed. Marie-Françoise Lanfant, John B. Allcock, and Edward M. Bruner, 24–43. London and Thousand Oaks, Calif.: Sage Studies in International Sociology.

Leong, Wai-Teng
  1989   Culture and the State: Manufacturing Traditions for Tourism. *Critical Studies in Mass Communication* 6:355–375.

MacCannell, Dean
  1976   The Tourist: A New Theory of the Leisure Class. New York: Schocken.

Richter, Linda K.
  1989   *The Politics of Tourism in Asia.* Honolulu: University of Hawai'i Press.

Smith, Valene L., ed.
  1977   *Hosts and Guests: The Anthropology of Tourism.* Philadelphia: University of Pennsylvania Press.

UNESCO
  1976   The Effects of Tourism on Socio-Cultural Values. *Annals of Tourism Research* 4:74–105.

van den Berghe, Pierre L., and Charles F. Keyes
  1984   Tourism and Ethnicity. *Annals of Tourism Research* 11:3.

ROBERT E. WOOD

» 1

Tourism and the State: Ethnic Options and Constructions of Otherness

Tourism is the world's largest industry. The travel and tourism industry is the largest employer in the world and is expected to account for more export earnings than any other industry by the turn of the century (Garrison 1989, 4). Recognition of these economic facts has led to increasing scholarly and professional interest in tourism, with a proliferation of journals, scholarly associations, and tourism studies programs. Yet it is possible that tourism's *cultural* importance is as great as its economic importance, partly because tourists are reaching, in ever increasing numbers, virtually every corner of the globe and partly because tourism as a mode of perception and experience—what John Urry (1990) has called the "tourist gaze"—has become increasingly "dedifferentiated" from other spheres of social life, making its influence almost universal. Tourism has become an intrinsic part of both global and local culture.

As tourism has grown, its product has become increasingly diversified. An increasingly significant market segment has come to be known as ethnic or cultural tourism, characterized by the tourist's interest in being exposed to and experiencing some form of cultural otherness.[1] Tourism entrepreneurs, indigenous groups, states, municipalities, multinational corporations, and a variety of other actors have scrambled to promote and market ethnicity and culture to tourists, both domestic and international. Inevitably, this promotion has led to the extension of commodity relationships into new areas of social life along with the intrusion of the tourists themselves.

The significance of this development for the general phenomena of ethnicity and ethnic relations has been obscured by the tendency of many observers to reject touristic ethnicity as unauthentic, unworthy of anything more than exposé. Several recent surveys of the race and ethnicity literature, for example, make no mention of tourism whatsoever. To the degree that most scholars of ethnicity have paid any attention to tourism, it has usually been in the form of exposing and (implicitly or explicitly) condemning the "bastardization" and "commoditization" of previously authentic ethnic cultures for the purpose of touristic display. Touristic ethnicity, in other words, is phony ethnicity.

Recent shifts in our understandings of both culture and ethnicity —as fluid, constructed, always changing, and always contested—have undermined such objectivist notions of authenticity, however, and studies of touristic ethnicity have shown that its influence on other ethnic arenas can be substantial. The role of tourism has to be considered in order to arrive at an adequate understanding of the construction of ethnicity and of culture in the contemporary world.[2]

The relationship between tourism and ethnicity is mediated by various institutions, but none more important in most instances than the state. For reasons explored more fully below, states have deep interests in both tourism and ethnicity. The relationship between tourism, states, and ethnicity is dynamic and ongoing, with highly variable outcomes. It is a basic thesis of this book that all three arenas are importantly affected by this interaction.

These three interacting processes of change may be seen as parts of a broader process of globalization. Perhaps even more than the ubiquitous McDonald's, international tourism symbolizes globalization not only in its massive movement of people to virtually every corner of the world but also in its linkage of economic, political, and sociocultural elements. Ethnicity is also increasingly recognized as shaped by contemporary global processes, rather than by residue from parochial pasts. States as well are partly created by international institutions and processes, although they may also be subverted by them. Indeed, the frequently contradictory implications of globalization are highlighted in the interactions of tourism, ethnicity, and state policies.

The Asia-Pacific region is the world's fastest growing tourist destination. Its share of international tourist arrivals increased from 3 percent in 1970 to 11.5 percent in 1991, and is expected to reach 18 percent in the year 2000 (Hall 1994, 11, 198).[3] An increasing majority of these international tourists are from other Asian countries, particularly Japan—reminding us that international tourism in the developing world can no longer be analyzed as a West to East phenomenon. The Asia-Pacific region includes two areas, Southeast Asia and Melanesia, that have been particularly prominent in the ethnicity literature for the fluid and interactional nature of their ethnic identities. As a whole, the region is a particularly valuable area in which to examine the dynamic construction of ethnic identities and relations in the dual context of a rapidly growing tourism industry and intrusive but sometimes contradictory state policies.

The Coming of Age of Tourism Studies

Despite tourism's undisputed economic importance, serious scholarship has been held back by two main factors. The first has been the concern of scholars that work in this field would not be taken seriously. Studying tourism may appear too much like taking a vacation and getting paid for it. And to be identified with one group of subjects—the tourists themselves—would constitute the ultimate disgrace. Gradually, however, the field has gained respectability as the scale and importance of the subject has become increasingly evident to all.

The second problem has been more internal to the field of tourism studies itself and has taken longer to rectify. It is the tendency to frame research questions in a simplistic, normative manner. Explicitly or implicitly, a great deal of the early research on tourism asked, Is tourism good or bad? Or, in only slightly more sophisticated form, Do its benefits outweigh its costs?

It has become increasingly evident that tourism's significance in the modern world transcends this narrow normative framework. Research has shown such questions to be both normatively arbitrary and deeply constraining in developing an adequate understanding of tourism's place in the contemporary world.[4] Researchers are increasingly setting aside simplistic normative questions in favor of analyses of the complex interaction of tourism and other major institutions and social processes. In such analyses the normative judgments of actors are a subject to be explored and explained, not simply assumed or rolled into the authoritative voice of the writer. This book is intended to be part of this "postnormative" trend in tourism studies.[5]

Tourism studies, then, has belatedly come of age as tourism's importance has gained wider appreciation and as the field's claims to scientific status have gained a more solid basis. Somewhat ironically, however, the field's traditional insularity and relative autonomy have been undermined by its own success. Tourism is increasingly recognized as something that cannot be conceptualized as an isolated phenomenon, defined and researched as a separate field of study. While in some ways representing a limiting case, Michel Picard's (1990) insistence that we stop seeing international tourism as something external to Balinese culture, impacting upon it from the outside, but rather as an integral part of that culture, holds in varying degrees for all cases. As Allcock (1995, 110) states, "Tourism does not stand apart from host cultures as a kind of obtrusive appendage. . . . The forms and rhetorics of tourism stand on all fours with the other resources" that form culture.

In a similar vein, Pierre van den Berghe's (1980, 1992b) reminders that tourism does not just affect ethnicity but is itself a set of ethnic relations, suggest that tourism has to be seen as one element of the global phenomenon of ethnicity, not something appended to it. The boundaries between international tourism and such social forces as migration, the movement back and forth of guest workers, domestic tourism, exposure to the mass media, formal education, and even literacy itself are increasingly fuzzy (see MacCannell 1992, 1–6, for a similar point). And as Urry's (1990) and similar analyses (for example, Sorkin 1992) suggest, the tourist gaze has been incorporated into an ever wider range of social life.

These brief observations suggest that while tourism studies will continue as a separate field of study, its boundaries will become increasingly permeable, much like the study of religion or development. We can expect more scholars to become "accidental" tourism researchers as they stumble onto tourism's expanding significance in the course of pursuing other agendas.

Another change associated with tourism's coming of age relates to the geographical focus of study. Recognition of the embeddedness of tourism in societal and global processes has produced a shift away from the almost exclusive focus on sites of direct host-guest interaction, characteristic of the early literature, and toward an interest in how the encounter between tourists and locals is profoundly structured by other, often "invisible" actors, including the host state, and toward a realization that many consequences of tourism occur in sites institutionally and geographically removed from the immediate

sites of tourist-local interactions. Tourism is shaped by societal structures and processes and its consequences are often found at these
levels. The key impacts of tourists are often on people they never see,
in places they never go.[6]

In the Asian and Pacific societies considered in this volume, the
state plays a central role not only in structuring the tourist encounter
but also in shaping and controlling the visible contours of ethnicity.
As the case studies show, the state's roles in these two areas can both
reinforce and conflict with each other. While tourism may not often
be a sufficient force to determine ethnic or political outcomes, its
presence may alter opportunity structures so that completely new
outcomes may be produced.[7]

The final point regarding the coming of age of tourism studies
involves the issue of agency and relates back to the worries that motivated much of the normative preoccupation of early tourism studies,
with titles such as *The Golden Hordes* (Turner and Ash, 1976). Clearly tourism—whatever we may think of it—is not a universal jugger-
naut, flattening everything in its path in the intentional or uninten-
tional service of global homogeneity and uniformity. Study after
study has documented how individuals and groups have responded
actively to both the constraints and the opportunities brought by
tourism development. Outcomes have been extremely varied and
often unpredictable.

From a normative perspective, this variability in outcomes
has meant that many of the fears voiced by early critics of tourism
have been unfounded.[8] From a scientific perspective, the open-ended-
ness of tourism's effects means that a cautious approach to theory
construction is definitely warranted. As with other forms of globalization, the local manifestations of tourism development are enor-
mously varied; local uniqueness and complexity reign supreme. In a
particularly useful survey of the anthropological tourism literature,
Malcolm Crick (1994, 3) has suggested that "the most pressing need
at the moment is for detailed ethnographic studies" rather than for
premature theoretical syntheses, a need that this book addresses.

The remainder of this introductory chapter offers a conceptual
framework for identifying key issues involved in the intersection of
international tourism, ethnic identity, and state policies. The goal is
to identify key issues, not to propose any kind of theoretical closure.
These issues involve (1) the interacting roles of tourism and the state
in diffusing particular concepts of ethnicity and culture; (2) the official sanctioning of particular ethnic labels and identities in the con-

text of tourism development; (3) the emergence of tourism as a resource and a prize in interethnic relations and competition, within the context of ethnic management by the state; and (4) the ways in which the intersection of state policies, tourism development, and ethnic politics shapes the range of ethnic options available to groups and the constructions of otherness produced by a variety of actors.

Tourism, the State, and the Definition of Ethnicity and Culture

In *The Politics of Tourism in Asia,* Linda Richter (1989, 2) observes that "tourism is a highly political phenomenon, the implications of which have been only rarely perceived and almost nowhere fully understood." In this book and elsewhere (for example, 1982, 1993), Richter has explored the dominant state role in early tourism development and how new political claimants emerge in the process. As Richter suggests (1992, 44), Asia and the Pacific contain "the classic case of using tourism development politically, that of the Philippines under Marcos," which is also "the classic case of tourism undoing a regime."

Wai-Teng Leong (1989) has observed that a natural affinity exists between the nation-state and tourism in terms of a shared interest in presenting a place as unique and distinctive. Because of this affinity, the state's interest in tourism is as much political as economic. But as Richter's example of the Philippine case indicates, the state's political interest in tourism is potentially fraught with contradictions and unintended consequences.

On the one hand, multiethnic states in an era of nation-states have a strong interest in asserting and creating unique national cultures. Concern with national culture and political stability has often led such states to be hostile to expressions of ethnic identity and solidarity. (Indeed, Pierre van den Berghe [1992a, 191] has suggested that modern nationalism is a "blueprint for ethnocide.") In reality, the national cultures may be little more than an official abstraction, as in the case of "Malaysian culture" marketed to tourists (King 1993, 103). (It seems revealing that the relevant government office is the Ministry of Culture and Tourism.) On the other hand, the most evident and most easily marketed forms of cultural uniqueness are often the lifestyles and artifacts of subnational ethnic groups—which are often considered "backward" by the dominant ethnic majority. Indeed, even the ethnic markers touristically identified with majority ethnic groups are often marginal or premodern. States everywhere attempt to resolve these tensions through discourses and practices aimed at reconciling nationhood and ethnic diversity, generally by subordinating or domesticating the latter in some way. However, such state attempts may inadvertently empower ethnic groups to assert their interests and identities in new ways.

Two levels of this process of defining ethnicity and culture may be distinguished. The first involves the diffusion and institutionalization of the concepts of ethnicity and culture. The second, to be discussed in the next section, involves state sanctioning of particular ethnic labels and markers and of particular discourses of ethnic diversity and nationhood.

There is a long history of debate among social scientists about how the closely related concepts of ethnicity and culture—generally assumed to apply to social phenomena that are essentially universal —are best defined. As Jocelyn Linnekin and Lin Poyer (1990) point out, however, these concepts are also part of popular discourse and represent a popular theory of group identity particularly rooted in Western societies. They, and the contributors to their *Cultural Identity and Ethnicity in the Pacific,* counterpose Oceanic concepts of group identity to Western conceptions of ethnicity. They argue that Western conceptions assume "that people can be classified into mutually exclusive bounded groups according to physical and behavioral differences," based on a putative shared ancestry. Oceanic ethnic identity, on the other hand, is seen as much more fluid, nested, and changeable and is based heavily on voluntary identification. Scholars in Africa and Asia have also asserted that indigenous conceptions of ethnicity and culture were significantly different from the conceptions diffused through Western ideologies and social science and that many of the ethnic groups politically and touristically evident today are essentially creations of either colonial rule or postcolonial decay. Without getting into the debate about the primordial assumptions of contemporary ethnic identities or how instrumentally manipulative they have been, it can be asserted that an international discourse has evolved that shapes contemporary manifestations of ethnicity. Ethnicity is more than a neutral social scientific term; it has become part of the way people factually and prescriptively see themselves and others. Indeed, Joel Kahn (1993, 18–19; 1992, 160–163) has suggested that both ethnicity and culture need to be seen above all as "folk concepts," historically constructed and reconstructed.

While the diffusion and institutionalization of this discourse of ethnicity has many sources, international tourism is a means by which particular conceptions of ethnicity and culture are spread today. Ethnic tourism is drawn to those groups that are most clearly bounded and culturally different. An intriguing example is how Western anthropologists, who have played a large role in elaborating a concept of culture as something unique and bounded, can themselves function as "markers of authenticity" for ethnic tourists. In a wonderful account of her experience observing tourism among the Toraja in Indonesia, Kathleen Adams (1991, 5) reports that:

> Tour guides soon recognized this and added me to their itinerary of touristic objects, stopping to knock at my door and introduce me to their guests as they ushered them through the village. On one occasion, while documenting a funeral ritual, I encountered a tour group and was chided by the local guide for not being outfitted in khaki. As he put it, "I wear my uniform and you must wear yours, otherwise they won't believe me when I tell them you're an anthropologist—they'll think you're just another tourist!"

Ironically, Adams was studying the tourists as well as their Toraja hosts.

Tourism reinforces the associated process of the objectification of culture in the form of concrete emblems of ethnic identity. As Linnekin (1990, 151, 164) observes:

> Categories that objectify culture . . . can usually be traced to Western concepts, but they have been incorporated into the conceptual framework of non-Western peoples. . . . The objectification of culture in Oceania today reflects shared premises about what constitutes culture and cultural identity; the diversity of indigenous paradigms appears to be giving way to a single mode of self-perception. Invocations, reenactments, and recreations of the cultural past are catching, which is to say that they represent an evolving global system of categories and distinctions.

An interesting and much discussed example of this process involves the widespread but diverse uses of the concept of *kastom* in southern Pacific societies. While in principle not different from other processes of cultural construction, *kastom* is particularly striking in its combination of self-consciousness, variation, and valorization of the local and indigenous (Lindstrom and White 1993) and in the way in which it functions within Western discourse while often purporting to oppose it. As Foster (1991, 240) comments, the various ideologies of *kastom* "exhibit aspects of a counterhegemonic discourse pervaded by the categories and premises of hegemonic discourse."

Few concepts have traveled so widely and with such effect as the anthropological concept of culture. Yet as Kahn (1993, 14) observes: "It might be argued that the very birth of the modern anthropological idea of 'other cultures' coincided with the final demise of genuinely discrete cultures in the context of cultural 'globalization.' " Virtually all states in the Asia-Pacific region have made "culture" the focus of a government ministry, and domestic tourism is often encouraged as a way to learn about the national culture. While we will later examine the state's attempt to label and define the substance of particular cultures, the issue here is the sanctioning of a particular concept of culture.

Francesca Merlan (1989) provides a fascinating example of conflicting notions of culture in her case study of the conflicts that arose when various Australian government and quasi-government agencies concerned with aboriginal affairs sought to assist the revival of an aboriginal women's ritual known as the *jarrarda*. These agencies were delegated with the business of supporting (touristically important) aboriginal culture, but their definition of what was and what was not cultural led them to insist on a radical distinction between what government and foundation money could be used for (transportation, provisioning) and what it could not (direct payments to participants). This distinction proved alien to the perceptions of the aboriginal organizers of the event, and considerable conflict and misunderstanding ensued. Unlike similar situations elsewhere, tourism does not appear to have been a direct factor in this case, but the narrowing of the definition of culture in accordance with Western and touristic assumptions appears to parallel the diffusion of a distinctive discourse of ethnicity.[9]

In an important Indonesian case study, Rita Kipp argues that states strive to obtain the political advantages of some degree of ethnic communalism, which functions to obscure class boundaries, weaken class solidarity, and sow division among nonelite classes, by pursuing strategies that limit ethnic culture to harmless display, thus preventing communalism from getting out of hand. In this case the interests of the state and the needs of tourism often coincide neatly, as suggested in her following observation:

> State endorsed ethnicity, as performance and exhibit, is an increasingly visible strategy as the new states attempt to manage both the heterogeneity within their boundaries and the homogenizing threat of consumer goods and popular culture deriving from the West. . . . Reducing culture to performance and exhibit in heteroge-

neous societies comes to terms with ethnicity by appearing to embrace cultural differences as a source of strength, while actually delimiting carefully the public arenas (tourist shows, parades, museums, airline stewardess costumes) where "feathers and flourishes" are appropriate (1993, 74).

The dynamics of tourism appear to promote this narrowed concept of culture, which is significant partly because this concept then may become the basis by which local people themselves evaluate the impact of tourism. In another study, Picard (1995, 61) has shown how many Balinese have come to objectify their culture in terms of the arts and to evaluate tourism's impact in terms of whether the arts are flourishing or not. Picard notes (1993, 90), "Accordingly, 'culture' is not understood as the anthropologist's broadly defined conception of the 'total range of activities and ideas of a group of people with shared traditions,' but is narrowed down to those aspects of culture that are subject to aesthetic appreciation, namely artistic expressions."[10] Furthermore, both Picard, in his studies of Bali, and Deborah Gewertz and Frederick Errington, in their study of the Chambri in Papua New Guinea, find that local people may interpret the very presence of tourists as a sign of the authenticity and continuity of their culture. Picard (1995) reports that a *Bali Post* poll of its readers found 60 percent citing the growing number of tourists as *proof* that Balinese were not losing their "Balineseness." Gewertz and Errington (1991, 80) describe a Chambri initiation in which the young men are met with the challenge, "Are you [man] enough to make carvings and place them in the men's house for the tourists to buy?" They further observe that the acquisition of money through tourism was "regarded as requiring the exercise of ancestral knowledge to 'pull' tourists to Chambri and to impel them to purchase artifacts. Hence, the presence of tourists at Chambri was interpreted not as testimony to the transformation of Chambri tradition but to its persistence and strength" (Gewertz and Errington 1989, 47).

Picard (1990, 74) has proposed the term "touristic culture" to refer to such cases where tourism has become an integral part of culture and where the interaction with tourists is a central component in the definition of ethnic identity and authenticity. While the degree to which Asian and Pacific ethnic groups and societies have such touristic cultures is variable, it is clear that a process of "touristification of society" is widespread throughout the region.

Tourism and State-Sanctioned Identity

While all the states covered in the case studies in this volume are involved in promoting certain definitions of ethnicity and culture, the degree to which states formally sanction specific ethnic labels and officially promote or proscribe specific manifestations of ethnic culture varies considerably. Similarly variable is how these ethnic labels and cultural attributes are inserted into a discourse of nationality. Tourism provides both a medium for the communication of these messages and a set of interests and resources that both reinforce and challenge them.

The Asian and Pacific countries addressed in this volume range from one extreme where ethnic labels, ethnic cultural display, and tourist access are all tightly regulated by the state to the opposite extreme where state intervention is fairly minimal and tends to be overshadowed by market dynamics. Unquestionably, China represents the statist extreme. As Timothy Oakes discusses in this volume and elsewhere (Oakes 1992; see also Diamond 1993, and Swain 1990), Chinese government ethnic policy draws on both indigenous and imported notions of ethnicity, including the evolutionary ideas of the nineteenth-century American anthropologist Lewis Henry Morgan. The Chinese government officially recognizes fifty-five ethnic minority "nationalities," mostly residing in officially designated autonomous regions, which range in geographical scope from a village to a province. Most autonomous regions contain several ethnic minorities, and since all residents of such regions receive special privileges and benefits, even the dominant Han Chinese have an interest in the special ethnic status of the region. Indeed, ethnic groups that have largely been assimilated into Han culture still retain an interest in seeking ethnic status. State recognition is not automatic, however; the manifestations of distinctive ethnicity must be judged "healthy" in terms of the officially prescribed goal of "socialist transformation," applicable to all. The Chinese state also designates official tourist sites and determines whether specific areas are to be opened or closed to foreign tourism (a decision partly based on whether the ethnic group has the material resources to reconstruct ritual traditions for tourist consumption). Yet even in the Chinese case, Oakes' account makes clear that state-sponsored ethnic tourism has unleashed processes—including the "commerce of authenticity"—that have quickly spread beyond the grasp of the state and that enable active and often shrewd responses on the part of local people.[11]

While somewhat less extreme than its Chinese counterpart, the Singaporean government likewise both mandates through public policy and promotes through tourism an officially sanctioned set of ethnic categorizations. Leong notes in his chapter that while the residents of Singapore define their own identity in terms of more precise categories (Hokkien, Peranakan, Batak, Tamil, and others), both the Singaporean state and the tourism industry treat Singapore as having simply four categories of ethnicity: Chinese, Malay, Indian, and Other —known popularly as CMIO. (These groups are actually referred to as "races" in government legislation and tourist promotional materials.) The categories accord with neither the self-identity nor the lived experience of most Singaporeans, nor do they reflect any ethnic "tradition." But a combination of images and sites manufactured for tourists and other state practices reinforce these labels and pressure individuals to be more ethnic in newly invented, state-sanctioned ways, even as at another level the government exhorts its citizens to think of themselves as Singaporeans. For Leong, the ongoing legacy of the CMIO policy gives the lie to the government's ostensible shift toward a Pan-Asian policy in recent years. In any case, the substance of ethnic culture has been redefined in the process. As David Brown (1994, 92) explains:

> The ethnic cultures of Singaporeans have now been largely "sanitized" by the state so as to remove their politically destabilizing connotations. . . . Therefore the ethnic cultures can be employed as the distinct but compatible building blocks for the articulation of the new "umbrella" national culture of Asian values.

On the surface at least, the task of domesticating ethnicity has proven more complex and difficult in Singapore's northern neighbor, Malaysia. This difficulty partly reflects differences in ethnic arithmetic: whereas Chinese constitute over 75 percent of Singapore's population, Malays account for only 48 percent of Malaysia's population. In both countries, however, the state actively sanctions particular ethnic labels and makes them the basis for policies aimed at both citizens and foreign tourists. The government's effort to create in effect a new majority ethnic group combining the Malays and other "indigenous" peoples into a new category called the "Bumiputeras" (sons of the soil) has been largely unsuccessful, both culturally and politically. Yet, as Francis Loh Kok Wah and Joel Kahn (1992) have stressed, *all* the ethnic labels in Malaysian politics have been culturally constructed and are continuously reconstructed as rapid economic and political change transforms the country in what Kahn (1992) calls a "creative dialogue with modernity."[12] Of particular interest is the ongoing constitution of "Malayness" itself, achieved in part through the creation of tourist sites such as Mini-Malaysia, clearly modeled on the earlier Indonesian theme park, and the urban restoration project in Penang analyzed by Kahn in this volume.

In Thailand, on the other hand, with about 83 percent of its population Tai-speaking and about 10 percent of its population of Chinese origin relatively assimilated as Sino-Thais, the Thai state's interest in defining and dealing with ethnic diversity has focused on the Malay-speaking peoples in the south and the so-called hilltribes in the west and north. The Tai-speaking population, however, is not a unified ethnic group and has been characterized by "ethnoregional" movements against the dominance of Central Thais by Tai-speakers and others in the northeast (Isan), north, and south (Keyes 1987).

The hilltribe peoples of Thailand comprise less than 1 percent of its population, but they have drawn disproportionate (and often unwanted) attention from the Thai state because of border security concerns. Although the growth of hilltribe tourism appears to have developed completely outside official tourism planning, the Thai state now seems to regard it as a means of integrating and gradually assimilating the hilltribe ethnic groups—a policy the state had pursued, often with little success, via military and other means over the past several decades. But just as it has been reported that most foreign tourists who trek among the hilltribes are unable to recall the names of the ethnic groups they have visited within a few days of their visit (Dearden and Harron 1992, 100), so has neither the Thai state nor its tourist authority shown much interest in officially sanctioning—much less preserving—the distinctive ethnic diversity of its northern and northwestern regions.[13]

Interestingly, however, Jean Michaud's study in this volume of a Hmong village in northern Thailand, Ban Suay, finds that, after more than a decade, trekking tourism has had relatively little impact on the village. Ironically, according to Michaud, trekking tourism has brought into bolder relief the "frontiers of Hmong identity," thereby reinforcing values associated with "Hmongness" that have limited participation in the tourist trade. As a result, tourism seems to have resulted neither in the economic dependency nor in the "Thai-ization" predicted by some officials and other observers.[14]

In Indonesia, the politics of state-sanctioned identity is most apparent in issues of religion and region, rather than in ethnicity per se.

The Indonesian government is formally blind to ethnicity: it does not collect data on ethnicity in its census and it does not sanction particular ethnic labels. Religion is another matter, however. The Indonesian state officially recognizes only certain religions, basically the world religions, and requires that they engage in at least the pretense of monotheism. Indonesia is unique in having a Ministry of Religion (Departemen Agama) that rules on what does and does not meet the standard of religion. A nonrecognized religion is considered a "belief" by the Indonesian government and is given some degree of recognition and protection under the Joint Secretariat for Beliefs of the Ministry of Education and Culture. Under the secretariat, religious traditions of ethnic groups have roughly been accorded the status of *adat,* the Indonesian term for local custom or tradition. Indonesians who are *belum beragama* (not yet having an officially recognized religion) have, especially under the New Order regime, been targets for conversion, but in recent years the *adat* status of "belief" has given local religions an added degree of legitimacy. Interestingly, Aragon (cited in Kipp 1993, 119) quotes a missionary who complains, "When the government promotes *adat* even for the tourists, it makes a lot of trouble for us." Touristic recognition of *adat* can have consequences within missionary religions as well; for example, Adams (1993, 41–42) reports that Christian Toraja have used the touristic fame of *tau-tau*—effigies of the dead—to resist the Torajan church's condemnation of this "pagan" practice.[15]

The Indonesian state's discourse of nationhood has sought to downplay ethnicity in favor not only of religion but also of region.[16] This emphasis on region is visually evident at Beautiful Indonesia in Miniature Park, commonly known as Taman Mini Indonesia, opened in 1975 on the southern outskirts of Jakarta. Aimed mainly at domestic tourists and promoted through school textbooks as the place to learn about all of Indonesia, the park contains twenty-seven pavilions, each representing one of Indonesia's provinces, with a representative "customary house" as its centerpiece (for a description and analysis, see Pemberton 1994). The national government is also sponsoring the creation of regional museums in each of the provinces. Official Indonesian discourse speaks of "regional cultures," each with cultural "peaks" suitable for being a part of Indonesian national culture. Taylor (1994, 73) reports that "each provincial museum staff selects those elements of the province's culture [sic] that are worthy of exhibition within the centrally planned guidelines that shape every government museum." According to Picard (1993,

93), the discourse of regional culture implies "its decomposition into discrete cultural elements, to be sieved through the filter of the national ideology and sorted out: those deemed appropriate to contribute to the development of the [national culture] should be salvaged and promoted, whereas those deemed too primitive or emphasizing local ethnic identity should be eradicated."[17]

The state's role in defining and promoting ethnic labels and identities should not obscure the distinctive dynamics of markets. As Linnekin's chapter on Hawaii and Western Samoa reminds us, states expedite market processes but do not control the forms of commoditized ethnicity that result. The touristic commoditization of culture becomes a precursor for other venues of cultural representations, with potentially unintended results. Both tourists and locals begin to consume culture through ethnic merchandise and display, with results that are only minimally controlled by the state. As capitalist development elicits more autonomous and disembedded market processes elsewhere in the region, the importance of markets in shaping ethnic identity and display is likely to grow.

An undercurrent in each of the case studies in this book is the potential for resistance and subtle manipulation by subordinate ethnic groups. While local responses have varied greatly, nowhere have local people been powerless or passive. These responses, however, take place in a context defined by the structure and policies of the state, the preexisting field of interethnic relations, and the particular features of the tourism industry, most notably its preoccupation with authenticity. The contradictory interests of the states, partly rooted in their desire to promote ethnic tourism, provide room for creative maneuver by local ethnic groups and produce complex forms of mutual accommodation.

Tourism as a Resource in Intergroup Competition

International tourism, as van den Berghe has stressed, is itself a form of ethnic relations, often involving an ethnic division of labor within the host population in addition to the ethnic difference between tourist and "touree." In his study of Cuzco, Peru, van den Berghe (1980, 387) argues that "tourism superimposes itself on a preexisting, native system of ethnic relations," transferring a long-established unequal relationship between mestizos and Indians onto the new social and economic terrain of tourism. In his more recent study of the Mexican town of San Cristobal, van den Berghe (1992b, 1994) finds an identical ethnic division of labor, although he also contends that ethnic tourism has modified for the better the attitudes and behavior of the ladino middlemen toward the local Indians.[18] A similar conclusion about more appreciative attitudes among middlemen is found in Stanley Toops' (1992) analysis of the relationship between Han guides and minority peoples in Xinjiang, China. In both cases, however, direct economic benefits of ethnic tourism accrue disproportionately to the dominant ethnic group functioning as middlemen.

In the cases just cited, the objects of ethnic tourism are geographically and socially marginalized ethnic groups occupying a subordinate position to an overwhelmingly dominant majority ethnic group. A similar ethnic division of labor has been reported for the hilltribes of Northern Thailand (Cohen 1982, 1989, Dearden and Harron 1992, 1994, Michaud 1993), and Michaud's analysis in this volume documents in striking fashion how little of the trekkers' expenditures ends up in the hands of local villagers. Where the relations between ethnic groups are less unequal, however, the impact of tourism has often been more complex and less predictable. Tourism has on occasion become an important new resource in intergroup rivalry and status competition, sometimes modifying or reversing historic patterns.

An unusual and intriguing case involves firewalking displays for tourists in Fiji. Based on fieldwork carried out in 1975, Carolyn Brown reports that Indians in Fiji, drawing on both North and South Indian traditions, have sought to break the Fijian monopoly on this tourist attraction, promoted entirely as a "traditional Fijian" practice by the local tourist board. Brown downplays the economic motives behind this, seeing it as a contest over the assertion of spiritual and supernatural power between the two ethnic groups. According to Brown (1984, 223–224), the tourists unwittingly constitute "simply one more resource in the power struggle between the two ethnic groups which goes on all fronts, including symbolic ones." A more recent study of Fijian firewalking (Stymeist 1996) indicates the native Fijians have retained their touristic monopoly on the practice, despite the fact that historically it was extremely limited in its distribution on Fiji and is now rarely if ever performed outside the touristic context. Fijian firewalking in this context has acquired an "emergent authenticity" (see Cohen 1988): "Fijians are justifiably proud of their institutions, and this pride now extends to firewalking."

The impact of international tourism on ethnic relations in contexts of more than two rival ethnic groups is perhaps even more complex. An interesting case involves the Sherpa of Nepal, whose ethnic uniqueness has become an increasing component of trekking tourism in the Mount Everest region. Several studies attest to how tourism has intensified Sherpa ethnic identity and provided a new terrain for the extension of Sherpa traditions, such as a variety of historic patterns of reciprocity (Adams 1992) and a basis for the revitalization of Buddhism (Stevens 1991; for a somewhat less optimistic assessment, see Zurick 1992, 618). Most relevant here, however, is how the tourism-induced economic prosperity and the cultural pride of the Sherpas have affected their relations with others. James Fisher (1990, 137–140) reports that prosperity and pride have led to a significant rise in status of Sherpas residing in Kathmandu and that the long-standing process of sanskritization—the emulation of upper-caste Hindu practices—of Himalayan mountain groups is now being effectively countered by a process of "sherpaization," as culturally similar groups such as the Tamangs identify with and adopt key aspects of Sherpa culture and identity. Sherpa dress has in fact become "high fashion" in Kathmandu, worn in fashionable restaurants and by Royal Nepal Airlines flight attendants.

How we evaluate the apparent fate of Tamang ethnic separateness and identity in the previous case depends a great deal on our point of view, but a more unambiguously negative result is described by Sylvia Rodriguez in her analysis of the "tri-ethnic trap" of Hispanics in Taos, New Mexico. Rodriguez (1989, 87) shows how the growth of ethnic and arts-oriented tourism reinforced and enabled dominant Anglo views to be articulated through tourism—including the romanticization of traditional Native American culture—with the result that the Hispanics in Taos find themselves "conquered, dispossessed, dependent, ghettoized, and, above all, witness to the Indian's spiritual and moral elevation above themselves in Anglo eyes." While the situation described in Kathleen Adams' study of Toraja-Bugis relations in this volume is different, in that the Buginese, by virtue of their geographical position as "Gateway to the Toraja," have been able to reap many of the benefits of the middleman role, there is some similarity in the Buginese's sense that their own culture has been unfairly neglected by the tourists, who merely see Ujung Pandang as a place to make a flight connection to Tana Toraja or to hire a car to drive to the highlands. According to Toby Volkman (1982, 31), the Buginese "express the view that tourism has unjustly ignored their own gentle landscape, colorful marriage ceremonies, and, in their eyes, more sophisticated culture." Among Toraja, however, the view is commonly expressed that tourism has redressed the historic domination and exploitation of the highland Toraja by the coastal Buginese.

A contrasting account of how international tourism may promote both individual and ethnic group mobility is found in Bob Simpson's account of how members of a Sri Lankan quasi-pariah group, the Beravā, have exploited the opportunities created by tourism and used them to raise their status. The Beravā are ritual specialists in healing and exorcism, whose masks and "devil dance" have become major tourist attractions. Simpson (1993, 170) notes that their very unusualness makes them touristically attractive as emblems of Sinhalese culture.[19]

> Groups like the Beravā and the imagery they purvey are particularly apt to objectify culture in this way. They are socially marginal within Sinhalese society because they still retain vestiges of a caste identity that ranks them little better than out-castes. Their activities are viewed with ambivalence and disdain by middle-class Sinhalese Buddhists, for whom exorcism ceremonies and all they stand for are considered little better than primitive superstition. Yet the rich imagery that the Beravā generate through their ritual activity is the very imagery from which "cultural emblems" intended to signify tradition and antiquity are drawn.

In a richly textured and illustrated account, Simpson documents the economic prosperity mask-making has brought to a Beravā family and describes the family's effort to claim recognition of its new status through a religious housewarming ceremony full of symbolic paradoxes and contradictions.

In such cases we see clearly that international tourism has the potential to upset, as well as to reinforce, previously existing ethnic relations. Such changes are often reflected in politics and state policies. Touristic importance can be turned into claims on the state and give rise to new forms of competition with other ethnic groups.

Ethnic Options and the Construction of Otherness

Studies of tourism and ethnicity reinforce what is probably the central theoretical tenet in the ethnicity literature in recent years: that ethnic identity is not something fixed and bequeathed from the past, but rather is something constantly reinvented—or reimagined, if we adapt Benedict Anderson's felicitous term—symbolically constructed, and often contested. By its nature, tourism both elicits and illuminates new processes of cultural construction.

In his classic study, Fredrik Barth (1969, 15) proposed that the critical focus of ethnic study should be "the ethnic *boundary* that defines the group, not the cultural stuff that it encloses." As we have seen above, both the tourist industry and the state have become players in the processes of boundary determination and maintenance. But studies of tourism and ethnicity also suggest that the marketing of ethnicity to tourists tends to make people self-conscious and reflexive about the "cultural stuff," which, before, they may have taken more or less for granted. This tendency is partly generated by the demands of tourist marketing, of defining the ethnic product in competition with others. In addition, the very act of objectifying and externalizing ethnic culture makes it more visible and subject to reflection, debate, and conscious choice—the exercising of ethnic options.

I have taken the phrase "ethnic options" from Mary Waters' (1990) book on white ethnic identities in the United States. Waters' focus is clearly quite different from the one in this volume: she studied the individual choice of ethnic labels in a unique national context in which the choice for the white majority has a strong voluntaristic component and entails limited consequences. The case studies in this volume, on the other hand, observe contexts where individual choices of ethnic labels are much more constrained and examine manifestations of ethnicity that arise from a complex process of symbolic construction involving ethnic groups, the state, and the tourism industry. Nonetheless, Waters' term reminds us that the ethnic labels that enter the tourism arena are neither automatic reflections of some preexisting objective reality nor in themselves determinative of the "cultural stuff" that will be marketed to tourists. Both the labels and the definition of their cultural content involve the exercise of ethnic options by several different actors interacting with one another. Such a process of cultural construction is, as anthropologists such as Linnekin (1992), Errington (1989), and Keesing (1989) have emphasized, inherently political and contentious.[20]

In the context of tourism, ethnic options are exercised to construct the images of "otherness" marketed to tourists. While it is often assumed that tourists are attracted mainly to radical, exotically different otherness, it is not always the case. Adams (1991), for example, noting that four out of five tourists to the Toraja highlands in Sulawesi are fellow Indonesians, observes that domestic Indonesian tourism bears elements of a national pilgrimage, with an emphasis on cultural continuity as reflected in Indonesia's national slogan, "unity in diversity." As Adams notes, both Taman Mini Indonesia and state propaganda encourage domestic tourism as a means of consolidating the cohesion and unity of the nation.[21]

Unlike some postmodernist usages, otherness in this sense is defined by its specificity, not by some assumed generalized opposition to Western culture. There are various discourses of otherness: those of the state, the tourism industry, including middlemen culture brokers such as those discussed by Cohen (1982, 1989) and others, and the ethnic group itself—the latter sometimes a cacophony of separate voices. Furthermore, different constructions of otherness may be presented to different types of tourists. In principle, they are as capable of stressing similarity (including a similarity with the lost pasts of the tourists) as difference.[22]

By and large, apart from generalized assertions of the intensification of ethnic identity or the increase of ethnic pride, the issue of how the selection of ethnic options and the construction of specific forms of otherness for the tourism industry may affect local ethnic identity and culture has been more a matter of speculation than actual research. The studies in this volume begin to explore this issue in empirical detail.

Ethnic Options and the State: Unintended Consequences

The notion of ethnic options draws attention to the way active choices shape ethnic identity. These choices, however, are always constrained, and they are made by a range of actors—a range that increases as tourism enters the picture. The early literature on this subject tended to focus on how the tourism industry itself exercised these options, with local people portrayed as victimized and relatively passive. Even when later studies, for which Philip McKean's (1973, 1976, 1977a, 1977b) work on Bali was both pioneering and representative, stressed the active response of local people and generally regarded the outcomes as more positive, the analytic focus tended to remain solely on the interaction of "hosts and guests," as in the title of Valene Smith's (1977) important anthology.

The case studies in this book stress the need to place the construction of ethnicity in a broader context. Tourism always enters a dynamic process of historical change involving many actors. Tourism both introduces new actors and provides preexisting actors with a range of new opportunities and constraints.

The central role of the state has been given particular prominence in the ethnicity literature in recent years (for example, Brown 1994,

Toland 1993, Calhoun 1993, Williams 1989, Brass 1985). Tourism tends both to increase state intervention in the process of defining and regulating ethnicity and to provide locals with new resources for pursuing their own agendas. Hence it is not surprising that a theme in each of the chapters in this volume is the unintended consequences of state policies.

Oakes, for example, shows how Dong villagers have quickly learned to appropriate touristic discourse in defining local identities, asserting claims against the state, and resisting the adoption of Han characteristics. Oakes hastens to add that the lesson to be learned "is not so much the relatively benign role played by tourism in its earliest stages of development, but the way the experience of tourism becomes a fundamental component of people's sense of place and ethnic identity"—an observation that applies in unique ways to each of the cases in this volume.

Locally empowering unintended consequences are less evident in the Singaporean case, as analyzed by Leong. With its fabled technocratic efficiency, Singapore has erased most physical manifestations of history in both its general development policies and its tourism policies, which have focused on "reconstruction" and "adaptive reuse" rather than on preservation or restoration. The government's CMIO policy, discussed earlier, appears to be a classic case of a set of state-defined ethnic options seemingly overriding local definitions. The result, Leong fears, is a set of parallel processes of "cultural involution," in which individuals are pressured to identify with ethnic groups defined by the state and thus fossilized in their separateness.

Yet Leong's analysis also points to several contradictions. The most commonly cited one is that Singapore has erased most of what draws tourists, raising questions about its ability to draw tourists based on the allure of shopping alone. But Leong's analysis also raises deeper questions about ethnic relations and the future of Singaporean identity. He observes that while most individuals recognize the inadequacy of the CMIO labels as applied to their own ethnic group, there is evidence that *interethnic* perceptions and relations are increasingly structured along these lines. Furthermore, both tourism and other government policies raise questions about the sustainability of identities that fail to fit the model, such as the Peranakan, who are a hybrid of Chinese and Malay. Ironically, this simplification of ethnic topography could eventually work against the goal of national unity that Singapore's leaders have so assiduously pursued, even if the goal of CMIO policies has been to domesticate potential ethnic division.

Kahn's chapter on a historic restoration project in a district of Penang, Malaysia, highlights the importance of locating tourism policy within a larger cultural landscape. Tourism developers have not had a free hand in Penang, as evidenced in the defeat of a powerfully backed initiative to turn Penang Hill into a major resort. Kahn locates the Lebuh Acheen–Lebuh Armenian project—one with considerably more local support—within a broader process of culture-building in which the state participates but does not control: a modernist Malay cultural project that transcends significantly the limitations of the grand vision of the Mahatir government (Khoo 1992). Kahn also reminds us that an unintended consequence of globalization is the introduction of an international discourse of the global and the local, the universal and the particular, that increasingly shapes cultural projects, even when they are couched in local ethnic or regional terms.[23]

Among the cases in this volume, the Thai case is the one where the state has been most reluctant to embrace ethnic diversity for touristic purposes, although it appears that the government has begun to promote *regional* cultural identities for heritage and touristic purposes now that regionalism no longer seems a political threat (Peleggi 1996, 445). Michaud's analysis shows how a combination of Thai ethnic dominance and security concerns has largely kept the state from promoting the ethnic diversity of its northern highlands. The limited official interest in trekking tourism that has developed appears mainly linked to the anticipation that tourist contact is likely to accelerate assimilation into the Thai majority. But, at least in the village where Michaud carried out his fieldwork, the ironic consequence of tourism is that it appears to accentuate consciousness of the perceived fundamentals of Hmong identity, thereby limiting both participation in the tourist trade and its potentially assimilative effects.

Adams' chapter documents how tourism in South Sulawesi, Indonesia, has become a new arena of ethnic conflict. Although the Indonesian state has gone to considerable lengths to channel local identities along regional and religious lines, tourism has elicited assertions of subregional ethnic identity and rivalry. While the government has promoted both international and domestic tourism as a means of national integration, Adams finds diverse and complex interethnic consequences. She does note, however, following Kipp

(1993), that even if ethnic rivalry is an unintended consequence of state tourism promotion, it may benefit the Indonesian state by deflecting attention from both social class inequalities and issues of Javanese and Chinese political and economic domination.

In the Balinese case discussed by Picard, there is a unique correspondence of province and ethnic group. Picard's analysis suggests that tourism development in Bali has contributed significantly to the central government's effort to channel ethnicity in nonthreatening ways: first, to delimit the realm of ethnic culture to artistic display and, second, to subordinate ethnicity per se to regional and religious identity. In the process, Balinese culture—as constructed and understood by Balinese political, economic, and cultural elites—has been fundamentally transformed. Picard's analysis indicates that these developments have elicited a lively debate among Balinese intellectuals and the middle classes, although the defeat of local opposition to two recent controversial tourism projects and the increasing number of officially designated "tourist zones" on the island raise fundamental questions about the ability of the Balinese to maintain their distinctive cultural project.

In some ways, Linnekin's chapter on Hawaii and the Island Pacific points to the most extreme case of unintended consequences, in the sense that touristic ethnicity has largely escaped from both state control and the tourism industry. As with Bali, tourism has become such a part of local culture that its sphere is not easily delimited. Linnekin documents how a touristic discourse of essential ethnicity—originally in part derived from historic state policies—has spread through the consumer market. Ethnic representations in commodity form are increasingly consumed by locals in a market driven by profit seeking rather than by tourism or the state. Linnekin finds evidence of an increasingly hypermasculine ethnic assertiveness among subordinate groups, representing an unintended consequence of the state's marketing of cultural difference for tourism and a potential threat to its official policy of aloha multiculturalism.

Of course, these case studies also suggest that it is not only the state that faces unintended consequences in its linking of ethnicity and tourism. While these studies show local groups using tourism to respond actively to the state, the outcomes are anything but certain. Oakes' account shows that locals quickly master the discourse of authenticity and use it to service their own ends, but they are unable to control its logic once it becomes embodied in the tourism industry. And so it is with many other aspects of becoming objects of the tourist gaze. Both ethnic and national identities will continue to be contested in Asian and Pacific societies, and tourism will continue to be an important arena in which this contestation is played out.

Notes

I would like to acknowledge gratefully the assistance of Monika Deppen Wood, who coauthored an earlier paper that served as the basis for this chapter.

1. Tourism need not be ethnically focused in order to have ethnic consequences. Nonetheless, the major focus of this chapter and of the case studies that follow is cultural and ethnic tourism. While for some purposes a distinction between cultural and ethnic tourism may be useful (for attempts to define and refine the distinction, see Smith [1977], Wood [1984], and Harron and Weiler [1992]), it is not central for this discussion.

2. A pronounced emphasis on tourism's role is found in the writings of many postmodernist scholars, many of whom see tourism as symbolizing the ludic, semiotic, and patchwork quality of contemporary social life. However, it is certainly a great exaggeration to assert, as does one such scholar, that "Tourism is *the* primary mode of reciprocity between countries, ethnic groups, regions and classes" (Harkin 1995, 650, emphasis added).

3. The World Tourism Organization's definition of the Asia-Pacific region includes Southeast Asia but not South Asia. For a fine overview of the politics of tourism in the region, see Richter (1989).

4. For a more detailed exposition of this point, see Wood (1993).

5. More subtle normative biases still abound, however, especially in the literature on tourism and ethnicity, which almost universally assumes that the preservation of ethnic identities and cultures is a good thing and tends to look suspiciously at the state's attempt to build a national culture.

6. One version of this distant impact involves what has been called "indirect tourism," in which an ethnic group produces ethnically identified artifacts for tourists but refrains from direct contact with tourists, such as the Brazilian Mamainde, discussed by Aspelin (1977). However, globalization means that "local" handicrafts and souvenirs sold to tourists are often imported from Taiwan and other newly industrializing countries. In any case, even where contact with tourists is extensive, the most important consequences may involve altered relationships within the ethnic group or with other groups.

7. James Lett (1989, 277) has observed that early studies of tourism tended to attribute excessive causal importance to tourism and to neglect other sources of change. While this weakness is directly addressed by the chapters in this volume, I doubt it is helpful simply to conclude, as Valene Smith (1989, x) does in the second edition of *Hosts and Guests,* that "the

research undertaken in the intervening decade indicates overall that tourism is *not* the major element of culture change in most societies." In how many societies can any one factor be identified as *the* major element of culture change? The task is to assess how tourism interacts with other sources of change to produce outcomes different from those that most likely would have occurred in its absence.

8. Although these early fears are unfounded, such concerns are frequently reiterated in the popular press and are occasionally recycled in academic articles. For a recent example of the latter, see Munt (1994).

9. As Adams (in press) notes, the touristic commoditization of culture tends to promote a quantitative notion of culture, such that the Indonesian Torajans commonly say, "We Torajans have more culture here," implicitly suggesting that their tourist-deprived neighbors must have less culture. For further analyses of the commoditization of Toraja culture, see Volkman (1984, 1987, 1990).

10. A similar point is made by Vickers (1989, 195), who writes, "Culture, as it is talked about officially by Balinese, other Indonesians and tourists, is not about such things as fighting with one's relatives, making decisions about borrowing money, buying a motorcycle or listening to the radio, but wearing sarongs, holding cremations, or dancing in a manner prescribed by tradition." Customary land tenure in Asian and Pacific societies, viewed by many anthropologists as a central part of culture in agricultural societies, is seldom accepted as part of local culture to be preserved when it conflicts with the claims of the state.

11. Oakes' account demonstrates the importance of ethnic tourism in a general process of ethnic labeling and change, well summarized by Dru Gladney (1994, 265): "The ethnonyms of many of these groups existed before their recognition by the state, but the attachment of the term *minzu* by the state legitimates, objectifies, and in some cases invents these identities. . . . My argument is that the discursive categories of identity applied by the state have shaped the contours of this ethnogenesis. The state authorized and legitimated a defined set of categories—which would be accepted, and then used, in resistance to the state."

12. It is interesting to note Linnekin's similar observation later in this volume that Portuguese were considered a separate race in Hawaii until the 1930s, after which they were reclassified as Caucasians.

13. In 1990 I participated in an upcountry tour of Fulbright fellows led by distinguished Thai scholars from Chulalongkorn University in Bangkok. On the one day we were taken to a "hilltribe village," we first spent close to a full hour in Chiang Mai slowly circling the statue of an early Thai king so we could appreciate the view from each angle and hear the most intricate details of his life and times. When we asked our university guides about the ethnicity of the people in the village we were about to visit, however, they were unable to answer, apart from saying the people were a "hilltribe."

14. It is interesting to contrast the Thai case with that of Japan, which has resisted the concept of ethnic minorities even more vociferously. For the Ainu on the island of Hokkaido, however, domestic tourism has been the key mechanism by which they have reconstructed and asserted their ethnic identity against the Wajin majority. See Sjöberg (1993).

15. Several studies note that the privileged status of tourism can provide a safe haven for practices and lifestyles that are otherwise contested. A fascinating example involves the touristic display of old colonial and Maasai lifestyles on Mayers Ranch in Kenya. Bruner and Kirshenblatt-Gimblett (1994, 448) observe that "tourism is a safe place for practices that are contested in other spheres, for in tourism they function in a privileged representational economy." They conclude (467) that the Maasai and the Mayers are "in business together": both "get essentially the same thing from tourism—the ability to maintain a contested, some might say anachronistic and even reactionary, lifestyle in contemporary Kenya, a lifestyle at once signified and subsidized by the tourist production."

16. The deemphasis of ethnicity proper presumably serves to mask Javanese political dominance and Chinese economic dominance. It is interesting to observe that touristically, Indonesia's Chinese minority—the largest in Southeast Asia—is completely erased. It is not mentioned in government tourist promotion and not recognized at Mini-Indonesia or its regional imitations.

17. A particularly transparent example of this process was the publication by the Indonesian Ministry of Education and Culture in 1983–1984 of a series of books, one for each province, under the rubric, "Traditional Sayings Which Have a Connection with the Principles of *Pancasila*" (see Rodgers 1993). The "Tourism Consciousness Campaign," discussed by Adams in this volume, also appears to filter local cultures for tourism.

18. Speaking mainly but not exclusively of the Maya in Guatemala, Manning Nash (1989, 110) argues that the Maya have not yet become an "ethnic group" in the sense of any larger Mayan Indian identity and solidarity beyond the local community, which raises the interesting question of whether Mayan ethnic tourism is likely to be a vehicle for the importation of the ethnic concept.

19. Depending on the definition of ethnicity, caste groups may or may not be included. For a detailed discussion of caste that does consider it a form of ethnic stratification, see van den Berghe (1981, Chapter 8). It seems unlikely that ethnic tourists maintain a distinction.

20. It is important to stress the open-ended implications of the term "ethnic options" in contrast to the deterministic notion of "reconstructed ethnicity," defined by MacCannell (1984, 377, 388) as "the kinds of ethnic identities which have emerged in response to pressures from tourism." MacCannell argues that an ethnic group "ceases to evolve naturally" when it sells itself as a tourist attraction. This naturalistic image of culture and tradi-

tion has been effectively critiqued by Handler and Linnekin (1984). Mac-Cannell (1994) has recently offered a more positive view of changes in ethnic art.

21. Adams (1991) notes that Batak tourists from Sumatra are particularly attracted to the Toraja because of the similarities of their cultures. Others, particularly the Buginese, appear more likely to confirm previous negative stereotypes about others.

22. Indeed, as Australian tourism researcher, Brian King, has pointed out, one type of international ethnic tourism is specifically based on similarity and connection: VFR (visiting friends and relatives for purposes of ethnic reunion). King observes (1994, 176), "From an Australian perspective, there appears to be a mismatch between the preoccupation of the tourism literature with the search for the exotic and the need to gain a better understanding of the links between migration and travel for ethnic reunion purposes." For further analysis of some of the ambiguities of the VFR category, see Seaton (1994).

23. A similar point is nicely made and explored with respect to ethnic tourism in Oakes (1993).

References

Adams, Kathleen M.
  1991 Touristic Pilgrimages, Identity, and Nation-Building in Indonesia. Paper delivered at the Annual Meeting of the Association for Asian Studies, New Orleans.
  1993 Theologians, Tourists and Thieves. *Kyoto Journal* 22:38–45.
  (in press) Taming Traditions: Torajan Ethnic Imagery in the Age of Tourism. In *Traders, Travelers and Tourists in Southeast Asia,* ed. Christina Fink and Jill Forshee. Berkeley: Center for Southeast Asian Studies.
Adams, Vincanne
  1992 Tourism and Sherpas, Nepal: Reconstruction of Reciprocity. *Annals of Tourism Research* 19:534–554.
Allcock, John B.
  1995 International Tourism and the Appropriation of History in the Balkans. In *International Tourism: Identity and Change,* ed. Marie-Françoise Lanfant, John B. Allcock, and Edward M. Bruner, 100–112. London and Thousand Oaks, Calif.: Sage Studies in International Sociology.
Aspelin, Paul L.
  1977 The Anthropological Analysis of Tourism: Indirect Tourism and Political Economy in the Case of the Mamainde of Mato Grosso, Brazil. *Annals of Tourism Research* 4:135–160.

Barth, Fredrik
  1969   *Ethnic Groups and Boundaries: The Social Organization of Culture Difference.* Boston: Little, Brown.
Brass, Paul, ed.
  1985   *Ethnic Groups and the State.* Totowa, N.J.: Barnes and Noble.
  1991   *Ethnicity and Nationalism: Theory and Comparison.* New Delhi: Sage Publications.
Brown, Carolyn Henning
  1984   Tourism and Ethnic Competition in a Ritual Form: The Firewalkers of Fiji. *Oceania* 54:223–244.
Brown, David
  1994   *The State and Ethnic Politics in Southeast Asia.* New York: Routledge.
Bruner, Edward M., and Barbara Kirshenblatt-Gimblett
  1994   Maasai on the Lawn: Tourist Realism in East Africa. *Cultural Anthropology* 9:435–470.
Calhoun, Craig
  1993   Nationalism and Ethnicity. *American Review of Sociology* 19:211–239.
Cohen, Erik
  1982   Jungle Guides in Northern Thailand—the Dynamics of a Marginal Occupational Role. *Sociological Review* 30:236–266.
  1988   Authenticity and Commoditization in Tourism. *Annals of Tourism Research* 15:371–386.
  1989   Primitive and Remote: Hill Tribe Trekking in Thailand. *Annals of Tourism Research* 16:30–61.
Crick, Malcolm
  1994   *Resplendent Sites, Discordant Voices: Sri Lankans and International Tourism.* Chur, Switzerland: Harwood Academic Publishers.
Crystal, Eric
  1977   Tourism in Toraja (Sulawesi, Indonesia). In *Hosts and Guests,* ed. Valene L. Smith, 109–125. Philadelphia: University of Pennsylvania Press.
Dearden, Philip, and Sylvia Harron
  1992   Tourism and the Hilltribes of Thailand. In *Special Interest Tourism,* ed. Betty Weiler and Colin M. Hall, 95–104. London: Belhaven Press.
  1994. Alternative Tourism and Adaptive Change. *Annals of Tourism Research* 21:81–102.
Diamond, Norma
  1993   Ethnicity and the State: The Hua Miao of Southwest China. In *Ethnicity and the State,* ed. Judith D. Toland, 55–78. New Brunswick, N.J.: Transaction Publishers.

Errington, Frederick, and Deborah Gewertz
  1989   Tourism and Anthropology in a Post-Modern World. *Oceania* 60:37–54.

Errington, Shelly
  1989   Fragile Traditions and Contested Meanings. *Public Culture* 1:49–65.

Fisher, James
  1990   *Sherpas: Reflections on Change in Himalayan Nepal.* Berkeley and Los Angeles: University of California Press.

Foster, Robert J.
  1991   Making National Cultures in the Global Ecumene. *Annual Review of Anthropology* 20:235–260.

Garrison, Lloyd
  1989   Tourism—Wave of the Future? *World Development (UNDP)* 2:4–6.

Gewertz, Deborah, and Frederick Errington
  1991   *Twisted Histories, Altered Contexts: Representing the Chambri in a World System.* New York: Cambridge University Press.

Gladney, Dru C.
  1994   Salman Rushdie in China: Religion, Ethnicity, and State Definition in the People's Republic. In *Asian Visions of Authority: Religion and the Modern States of East and Southeast Asia,* ed. Charles F. Keyes, Laurel Kendall, and Helen Hardacre, 255–278. Honolulu: University of Hawai'i Press.

Hall, Colin Michael
  1994   *Tourism in the Pacific Rim: Development, Impacts and Markets.* Melbourne: Longman Cheshire/Halsted Press.

Handler, Richard, and Jocelyn Linnekin
  1984   Tradition, Genuine or Spurious. *Journal of American Folklore* 97:273–290.

Harkin, Michael
  1995   Modernist Anthropology and Tourism of the Authentic. *Annals of Tourism Research* 22(3):650–670.

Harron, Sylvia, and Betty Weiler
  1992   Ethnic Tourism. In *Special Interest Tourism,* ed. Betty Weiler and Colin M. Hall, 82–94. London: Belhaven Press.

Kahn, Joel S.
  1992   Class, Ethnicity, and Diversity: Some Remarks on Malay Culture in Malaysia. In *Fragmented Vision: Culture and Politics in Contemporary Malaysia,* ed. Joel S. Kahn and Francis Loh Kok Wah, 158–178. Honolulu: University of Hawai'i Press.
  1993   *Constituting the Minangkabau: Peasants, Culture and Modernity in Colonial Indonesia.* Providence, Rhode Island, and Oxford, U.K.: Berg Publishers.

Keesing, Roger M.
 1989 Creating the Past: Custom and Identity in the Contemporary Pacific. *Contemporary Pacific* 1:19–42.

Keyes, Charles F.
 1987 *Thailand: Buddhist Kingdom as Modern Nation-State.* Berkeley: University of California Press.

Khoo, Kay Jin
 1992 The Grand Vision: Mahathir and Modernization. In *Fragmented Vision: Culture and Politics in Contemporary Malaysia,* ed. Joel S. Kahn and Francis Loh Kok Wah, 44–76. Honolulu: University of Hawai'i Press.

King, Brian
 1994 What Is Ethnic Tourism? An Australian Perspective. *Tourism Management* 15:173–176.

King, Victor
 1993 Tourism and Culture in Malaysia. In *Tourism in South-East Asia,* ed. Michael Hitchcock, Victor King, and Michael Parnwell, 99–116. London and New York: Routledge.

Kipp, Rita Smith
 1993 *Dissociated Identities: Ethnicity, Religion, and Class in an Indonesian Society.* Ann Arbor: University of Michigan Press.

Leong, Wai-Teng
 1989 Culture and the State: Manufacturing Traditions for Tourism. *Critical Studies in Mass Communication* 6:355–375.

Lett, James
 1989 Epilogue. In *Hosts and Guests: The Anthropology of Tourism,* 2d ed., ed. Valene L. Smith, 275–279. Philadelphia: University of Pennsylvania Press.

Lindstrom, Lamont, and Geoffrey M. White
 1993 Introduction: Custom Today. *Anthropological Forum* 6:467–473.

Linnekin, Jocelyn
 1990 The Politics of Culture in the Pacific. In *Cultural Identity and Ethnicity in the Pacific,* ed. Jocelyn Linnekin and Lin Poyer, 149–173. Honolulu: University of Hawai'i Press.
 1992 On the Theory and Politics of Cultural Construction in the Pacific. *Oceania* 62:249–263.

Linnekin, Jocelyn, and Lin Poyer, eds.
 1990 *Cultural Identity and Ethnicity in the Pacific.* Honolulu: University of Hawai'i Press.

Loh Kok Wah, Francis, and Joel S. Kahn
 1992 Introduction: Fragmented Vision. In *Fragmented Vision: Culture and Politics in Contemporary Malaysia,* ed. Joel S. Kahn and Francis Loh Kok Wah, 1–17. Honolulu: University of Hawai'i Press.

MacCannell, Dean
  1984 Reconstructed Ethnicity: Tourism and Cultural Identity in Third World Communities. *Annals of Tourism Research* 11:375–391.
  1992 *Empty Meeting Grounds: The Tourist Papers*. London and New York: Routledge.
  1994 Tradition's Next Step. In *Discovered Country: Tourism and Survival in the American West,* ed. Scott Norris, 161–179. Albuquerque: Stone Ladder Press.
McKean, Philip
  1973 Cultural Involution: Tourists, Balinese, and the Process of Modernization in Anthropological Perspective. Ph.D. diss., Department of Anthropology, Brown University.
  1976 Tourism, Culture Change and Culture Conservation. In *World Anthropology: Ethnic Identity in Modern Southeast Asia,* ed. D. Banks. The Hague: Mouton.
  1977a Towards a Theoretical Analysis of Tourism: Economic Dualism and Cultural Involution in Bali. In *Hosts and Guests,* ed. Valene L. Smith, 93–107. Philadelphia: University of Pennsylvania Press.
  1977b From Purity to Pollution? A Symbolic Form in Transition. In *The Imagination of Reality: Symbol Systems in Southeast Asia,* ed. A. Becker and A. Yengoyan, 293–302. Tucson: University of Arizona Press.
Merlan, Francesca
  1989 The Objectification of "Culture": An Aspect of Current Political Process in Aboriginal Affairs. *Anthropological Forum* 6:105–116.
Michaud, Jean
  1993 Tourism as a Catalyst of Economic and Political Change: The Case of Highland Minorities in Ladakh (India) and Northern Thailand. *Internationales Asienforum* 24:21–43.
Munt, Ian
  1994 Eco-tourism or Ego-tourism? *Race and Class* 36:49–60.
Nash, Manning
  1989 *The Cauldron of Ethnicity in the Modern World.* Chicago and London: University of Chicago Press.
Oakes, Timothy S.
  1992 Cultural Geography and Chinese Ethnic Tourism. *Journal of Cultural Geography* 12:3–17.
  1993 The Cultural Space of Modernity: Ethnic Tourism and Place Identity in China. *Environment and Planning* 11:47–66.
Peleggi, Maurizio
  1996 National Heritage and Global Tourism in Thailand. *Annals of Tourism Research* 23(2):432–448.

Pemberton, John
  1994   Recollections from "Beautiful Indonesia" (Somewhere Beyond the Postmodern). *Public Culture* 6:241–262.
Picard, Michel
  1990   "Cultural Tourism" in Bali: Cultural Performances as Tourist Attraction. *Indonesia* 49:37–74.
  1993   Cultural Tourism in Bali: National Integration and Regional Differentiation. In *Tourism in South-East Asia,* ed. Michael Hitchcock, Victor King, and Michael Parnwell, 71–98. London and New York: Routledge.
  1995   Cultural Heritage and Tourist Capital: Cultural Tourism in Bali. In *International Tourism: Identity and Change,* ed. M. F. Lanfant, J. B. Allcock, and E. M. Bruner, 44–66. London: Sage Studies in International Sociology.
Richter, Linda K.
  1982   *Land Reform and Tourism Development: Policy-Making in the Philippines.* Cambridge, Mass.: Schenkman Publishing Company.
  1989   *The Politics of Tourism in Asia.* Honolulu: University of Hawai‘i Press.
  1992   Political Instability and Tourism in the Third World. In *Tourism and the Less Developed Countries,* ed. David Harrison, 35–46. London: Belhaven Press.
  1993   Tourism Policy–Making in Southeast Asia. In *Tourism in South-East Asia,* ed. Michael Hitchcock, Victor King, and Michael Parnwell, 179–199. London and New York: Routledge.
Rodgers, Susan
  1993   Batak Heritage and the Indonesian State: Print Literacy and the Construction of Ethnic Cultures in Indonesia. In *Ethnicity and the State,* ed. Judith D. Toland, 147–176. New Brunswick, N.J.: Transaction Publishers.
Rodriguez, Sylvia
  1989   Art, Tourism, and Race Relations in Taos: Toward a Sociology of the Art Colony. *Journal of Anthropological Research* 45:77–99.
Seaton, A. V.
  1994   Are Relatives Friends? Reassessing the VFR Category in Segmenting Tourism Markers. In *Tourism: The State of the Art,* ed. A. V. Seaton, 316–321. Chichester, U.K.: John Wiley.
Simpson, Bob
  1993   Tourism and Tradition: From Healing to Heritage. *Annals of Tourism Research* 20:164–181.
Sjöberg, Katarina V.
  1993   *The Return of the Ainu: Cultural Mobilization and the Practice of Ethnicity in Japan.* Chur, Switzerland: Harwood Academic Publishers.

Smith, Valene L., ed.

    1977   *Hosts and Guests: The Anthropology of Tourism,* Philadelphia: University of Pennsylvania Press.

    1989   Preface. In *Hosts and Guests: The Anthropology of Tourism,* 2d ed., ed. Valene L. Smith, ix–xi. Philadelphia: University of Pennsylvania Press.

Sorkin, Michael

    1992   *Variations on a Theme Park: The New American City and the End of Public Space.* New York: Hill and Wang.

Stevens, Stanley F.

    1991   Sherpas, Tourism, and Cultural Change in Nepal's Mount Everest Region. *Journal of Cultural Geography* 12:39–58.

Stymeist, David H.

    1996   Transformation of Vilavairevo in Tourism. *Annals of Tourism Research* 23(1):1–18.

Swain, Margaret Byrne

    1990   Commoditizing Ethnicity in Southwest China. *Cultural Survival Quarterly* 14:26–30.

Taylor, Paul Michael

    1994   The Nusantara Concept of Culture: Local Traditions and National Identity as Expressed in Indonesia's Museums. In *Fragile Traditions: Indonesian Art in Jeopardy,* ed. Paul Michael Taylor, 71–90. Honolulu: University of Hawai'i Press.

Toland, Judith, ed.

    1993   *Ethnicity and the State.* New Brunswick, N.J.: Transaction Publishers.

Toops, Stanley

    1992   Tourism in Xinjiang, China. *Journal of Cultural Geography* 12: 19–34.

Turner, Louis, and John Ash

    1976   *The Golden Hordes: International Tourism and the Pleasure Periphery.* New York: St. Martin's Press.

Urry, John

    1990   *The Tourist Gaze.* London and Newbury Park: Sage Publications.

van den Berghe, Pierre L.

    1980   Tourism as Ethnic Relations: A Case Study of Cuzco, Peru. *Ethnic and Racial Studies* 3:375–392.

    1981   *The Ethnic Phenomenon.* New York: Elsevier.

    1992a The Modern State: Nation-builder or Nation-killer? *International Journal of Group Tensions* 22:191–208.

    1992b Tourism and the Ethnic Division of Labor. *Annals of Tourism Research* 19:234–249.

    1994   *The Quest for the Other: Ethnic Tourism in San Cristobal, Mexico.* Seattle: University of Washington Press.

Vickers, Adrian
  1989 *Bali: A Paradise Created.* Berkeley: Periplus Editions.
Volkman, Toby Alice
  1982 Tana Toraja: A Decade of Tourism. *Cultural Survival Quarterly* 6:30–32.
  1984 Great Performances: Toraja Cultural Identity in the 1970s. *American Ethnologist* 11:152–169.
  1987 Mortuary Tourism in Tana Toraja. In *Indonesian Religions in Transition,* ed. R. Kipp and S. Rodgers, 161–167. Tucson: University of Arizona Press.
  1990 Visions and Revisions: Toraja Culture and the Tourist Gaze. *American Ethnologist* 17:91–110.
Waters, Mary
  1990 *Ethnic Options: Choosing Identities in America.* Berkeley and Los Angeles: University of California Press.
Weiler, B., and C. M. Hall, eds.
  1992 *Special Interest Tourism.* London: Belhaven Press.
Williams, Brackette F.
  1989 A Class Act: Anthropology and the Race to Nation across Ethnic Terrain. *Annual Review of Anthropology* 18:401–444.
Wood, Robert E.
  1984 Ethnic Tourism, the State, and Cultural Change in Southeast Asia. *Annals of Tourism Research* 11:353–374.
  1993 Tourism, Culture and the Sociology of Development. In *Tourism in South-East Asia,* ed. Michael Hitchcock, Victor King, and Michael Parnwell, 48–70. London and New York: Routledge.
Zurick, David N.
  1992 Adventure Travel and Sustainable Tourism in the Peripheral Economy of Nepal. *Annals of the Association of American Geographers* 82:608–628.

TIMOTHY S. OAKES

≫ 2

Ethnic Tourism in Rural Guizhou: Sense of Place and the Commerce of Authenticity

In a recent review of scholarship on the relationship between tourism, culture, and development, Robert Wood (1993, 48) posed the question: "Do the processes of modernization and development necessarily entail the 'passing' of the 'traditional' societies of Asia, Africa, and Latin America and a global process of cultural homogenization in the direction of the West?" Countering the assumption—most often heard among Western tourists themselves—that tourists are the "shock troops" of Western modernity as it steamrolls across the world's remaining areas of cultural diversity, Wood argues that tourism is often appropriated by locals in their symbolic constructions of culture, tradition, and identity. As he explains, this conceptualization of tourism as a dynamic social ingredient of a local culture, not as an outside force that "flattens" the culture, represents an important shift in tourism studies. Wood's question can also be asked in geographical terms: Does modernization necessarily result in a placeless landscape, where place-based community identities once thrived? In these terms, some writers have noted that tourism can destroy an authentic sense of place, alienating people from an identity with the landscape in which they live (for example, Relph 1976, 117). Britton (1991,465–466) noted that the "commodification of place" associated with tourism "generates a 'flatness' where depth of appreciation, understanding, and especially meaning, is replaced with a new kind of superficiality in the most literal sense: a loss of depth of feeling, meaning or understanding is compensated for with transitory exhilaration, glitter, particular kinds of euphoria, and intensities of feelings." While this flatness may not necessarily lead to "cultural homogenization in the direction of the West," Britton clearly assumes a loss of authentic place identity associated with commercial tourism development.

This chapter suggests that the process of commercial and cultural integration associated with tourism does not necessarily break down a place-based sense of identity or render it flat and inauthentic; instead, it becomes an important factor in the ongoing construction of place identity. Place-based identity is built according to a broader set of political, economic, and cultural processes rather than in relative isolation from those processes. In many places in Asia, tourism has rapidly become a powerful example of these broader processes, injecting a new set of conditions into local expressions of identity and sense of place. Even on the frontiers of tourism in Asia, locals have quickly learned to appropriate the tourist experience in their claims of place identity. This appropriation is not necessarily because tourism is such a powerful social and cultural force, but because local actors have always been conditioned by broader historical processes—such as commercial trade, military campaigns, state revenue collection or political campaigns, and foreign missionaries—in constructing their senses of place.

To support these claims, I draw on the experience of two ethnic tourist villages in China's southwestern province of Guizhou. Both sites, situated deep in the mountains of Guizhou's Qiandongnan autonomous prefecture, have only recently been opened to international tourism and, in 1994, together received fewer than thirty-five foreign tour groups. Yet already, ethnic tourism has become an important factor in how locals express who they are and where they live. Indeed, villagers are accustomed to carving a space of identity within the broader political economy in which they live. In China, that political-economic context is overwhelmingly defined by the state. In this case, the state is the sole purveyor of tourism development. State-sponsored ethnic tourism combines two very different processes to influence significantly local place identity. One is the process of commercial, economic, and social integration inherent in tourism development. The other involves state policies regarding ethnic minority culture and its preservation, in which ethnic identity becomes officially associated with certain standardized cultural forms and unambiguous symbolic markers. These state-mediated processes provide much of the raw material—along with factors historically specific to the places themselves—that locals use to claim a distinct place identity. Even as tourism introduces processes that increasingly link villagers to the outside world, threatening to dislocate and alienate them, it simultaneously allows them to continue the ongoing redefinition of place in new terms. It is the Chinese state that clearly arbitrates this dynamic relationship between tourism, development, and place identity.

Before discussing each village specifically, it is important to review the three broader historical and geographical processes that have conditioned local place identity: historical conflicts and rebellions as direct administration was asserted over a frontier region, a state-sponsored project of ethnic minority identification in which ethnicity is defined according to cultural distance from the Han Chinese, and a commercial ethnic tourist industry based on the ideal of cultural authenticity. Given the importance of these three processes in conditioning the prevailing sense of place in each village, a considerable portion of the chapter is devoted to their analysis.

Frontier Geography and History

Qiandongnan Miao and Dong Autonomous Prefecture occupies the southeastern corner of Guizhou. Unlike the rest of the province, Qiandongnan is not a karst landscape of eroded limestone mounds, but a rumpled mass of folded clastic mountains incised by deep river valleys. While the soils are generally the most fertile in the province and rainfall is abundant and relatively consistent from year to year, the vertical terrain has always made agriculture difficult. The mountains, which reach their peak at the 2,178 meter summit of Leigongshan, are locally known as the Miaoling and form the watershed dividing the drainages of the Changjiang (Yangzi) and the Zhujiang (Pearl) Rivers. Thus straddling the frontier between China's two primary transportation networks, the region has historically been a remote hinterland to the downstream civilizations in Hunan and Guangxi and a refuge for those who refused to assimilate as Han Chinese culture began to predominate in the valleys, plains, and along the waterways of southern China. Chinese migration into the region did occur, though, especially during the eighteenth and nineteenth centuries, along the two primary waterways draining the region, the Qingshui and Duliu Rivers. The trading ports that arose along these rivers became Han Chinese enclaves, while the rest of the region was dominated by tribespeople, commonly referred to by the Chinese as Miao, "sprouts" or "weeds," the uncivilized aboriginals.

As early as the Han Dynasty (206 B.C.–A.D. 220), the Chinese government maintained a policy of indirect rule in the empire's frontier regions. This rule became formalized as the *tusi* system of native chieftainship, in which local chiefs were invested with hereditary titles, allowed to collect their own taxes, and able to keep their own armies. In exchange, most *tusi* paid a nominal land tax to the government. By the late Ming (1368–1644), however, the government regarded the *tusi* system as a source of instability and disorder and began eradicating *tusi* leaders and implementing direct administration. This policy, known as *gai tu gui liu,* was accompanied by the intensification of government sponsored military-agricultural colonies *(tuntian),* in which soldier-settlers were stationed in remote frontier settlements as the vanguards of Chinese civilization. Although frontier regions farther west in Yunnan and Sichuan remained immune to these developments well into the Qing (1644–1911), Guizhou was subjected to early attempts at direct imperial control. Direct administration was first implemented during the Yuan (1271–1368), when an imperial edict ordered that all tribespeople living north of the Wu River, which roughly bisects Guizhou, relocate to lands south of the river. After becoming a province in 1413, more and more of Guizhou was placed under direct administration. But *gai tu gui liu* engendered stiff resistance from local *tusi,* while indigenous farmers were increasingly alienated from productive land by *tuntian* colonies. The countryside erupted in rebellion on an average of one every three and a half years during the Ming period (Jenks 1985, 80). Because of its terrain, the Qiandongnan region was the most difficult area of Guizhou for the government to control. It became a refuge of powerful *tusi,* who had long been exempt from paying any tax to the government. In the late Qing, during what became known as the Miao Rebellions (1854–1872), local rebels successfully held all major towns in the region for nearly twenty years.

The nineteenth-century rebellions were, according to Robert Jenks (1985), motivated less by ethnic hostility than by land alienation, onerous taxation, and administrative abuses—factors that crossed ethnic lines. As Jenks points out, however, branding the rebellions as ethnic conflict brought about by immutable cultural differences (that is, between the civilized and the uncivilized) absolved the government from responsibility for inherent political and economic causes. "The

Qing were well aware that the Han played a major role in the rebellion. By labeling it a Miao rebellion in official historiography, the stigma of having rebelled and caused vast destruction and misery was attached squarely to the Miao and not the Han" (1985, 3). "Miao" was a Han Chinese term for a whole array of people in the region, defined according to their collective distance from Chinese culture. The Miao were those who renounced Chinese civilization, who practiced unusual agriculture such as shifting cultivation, and who did not adhere to Confucian morality (Diamond 1995). In reality, of course, the region was a complex mix of social classes and cultural economies. But the mystique of the rugged Miaoling as the isolated home of rebellious and exotic natives has remained in popular Chinese culture and has become an important feature of contemporary ethnic tourism in the region.

Today, 40 percent of Qiandongnan's population is comprised of those officially classified as Miao. Another 35 percent are Dong, and most of the remainder are Han Chinese, who are concentrated in the region's towns and cities. The Miaoling tends to divide the region into two different cultural landscapes. Belonging to the Sino-Tibetan language family, the Miao are mostly concentrated in the upper elevations of the mountains and throughout the valleys draining northward into the Qingshui. South of the divide, the topography loses elevation quickly and deep gorges give way to the broad valleys of the Duliu River. This region, considerably lower and warmer than the rest of Qiandongnan, is dominated by the Dong, a group belonging to the Tai language family. Historically favoring settled valley rice cultivation, the Dong in this region were less at odds with en-croaching Chinese culture as the Han established outposts along the river. Perhaps because of their similar cultural economies and because of the area's greater accessibility via the broad, placid Duliu River, the Dong were less subject to repressive Chinese efforts to assimilate "uncooked" tribespeople like the Miao. Whereas the Miao to the north were divided into a great diversity of socioeconomic and cultural groups with little interconnection between them, the Dong of the Duliu basin maintained a tight social organization based on a representative system of traditional law and order known as the *kuan* and political-administrative units of territory known as *dong*. Chinese references to *dong* regions date to the Yuan Dynasty, and it is perhaps from this term that the Chinese began to refer to these people as "Dong" (they refer to themselves with a variety of names, most of which sound something like *gaeml*).

Table 2.1 Comparison of Grain Production and
Peasant Income in Dong and Han Villages, Liping
County, 1987 (in Percentages)

Grain Production	*Dong*	*Han*
Contributing villages	28.7	47.0
Self-sufficient villages	19.6	24.2
Grain deficit villages	51.7	28.8
Net Peasant Income Per Capita (nongmin chunshouru)		
Over 300 *yuan*	0.4	
251–300	12.0	21.2
201–250	15.4	34.8
151–200	20.8	34.8
101-150	40.0	5.3
100 and below	1.3	1.5

Source: Liping Xianzhi 1989.

The Duliu River basin is the most sparsely populated region in
Guizhou. It also contains the least amount of cultivated land, only
4.3 percent (the average for Guizhou as a whole is 10.5 percent). But
the vast majority is irrigated paddy, and grain yields tend to be some
of the highest in the province. The region is still relatively well for-
ested and timber is the primary industry. Large log rafts can still be
seen floating down the Duliu to be processed at mills in Guangxi.
The majority of productive agricultural land tends to be farmed by
Han Chinese. A comparison of Dong and Han villages in Liping
County, one of the three that make up the region, reveals a significant ethnic income division, even among farmers (Table 2.1). Although land in the subtropical valleys can be quite productive, it is
extremely scarce and significant capital investments are required to
put it into production. All three counties in the region are officially
classified as "impoverished counties" *(pinkunxian),* qualifying them
for state assistance, generally in the form of low-interest loans or
grants for land engineering projects or for diversification schemes
such as planting fruit orchards on marginal slope land.

The two villages with which this chapter is ultimately concerned—Zhaoxing and Gaozeng—are both Dong villages situated in the Duliu basin, not far from the Guangxi border. Both are recognized as important centers of Dong culture, and each has been a *dong* seat for hundreds of years. They also serve as administrative village seats *(xiang)*, representing the lowest level of state bureaucracy in the rural administrative hierarchy. They thus maintain a direct link to the governments in their respective counties. Historically, both have been relatively prosperous agricultural communities, enjoying a subtropical climate, abundant rain, and convenient nearby transportation along the Duliu. Today, however, they are regarded as two of the most inaccessible tourist sites in the province. Once the railroad and major highways (which pass through the northern part of Qiandongnan only) rendered river transport relatively obsolete, Qiandongnan's Miao regions became, ironically, the most accessible in the prefecture. As will be discussed below, this shift in transportation reversed the historical situation and enabled the local tourism industry to portray these Dong villages as the most remote, mysterious, and authentic in the province. This distinction has not been lost on the villagers as they begin to adjust their sense of place in light of their new situation.

Chinese Modernity, Theme Parks, and State Cultural Policy

Since the initiation of economic reforms and the open-door policy, China has experienced an unprecedented degree of exposure to the West, which has been accompanied by an intense collective inquiry into Chinese national culture and identity (see Schein 1993). Much of the discourse of nationalism in China seeks to articulate a contradiction between an avowed desire for modernity and a desire to maintain continuity with a traditional past. As Anagnost (1993) has suggested, anxiety over this contradiction is perhaps related to the popularity of Shenzhen's Splendid China (Zhenxiu Zhonghua) tourist park as well as to the proliferation of "old towns" *(fangujie)* throughout urban China.

Splendid China comprises over thirty hectares of miniaturized national landmarks. Especially intriguing, Anagnost notes, is the juxtaposition of this miniaturized landscape of ancient Chinese cultural traditions set within that most modern and transient of all Chinese cities, Shenzhen. This juxtaposition is a compelling expression of modernity and nationalism in China. Shenzhen is the site of China's latest revolutionary rupture: the dramatic upheaval of market capitalism. "Shenzhen hurtling toward the telos of modernity *is* the present 'time' of the nation, but one that all the more requires the calming certainty of a timeless identity residing within" (Anagnost 1993, 590). For Anagnost, Splendid China serves as that calming certainty, and its position within China's earliest and most successful Special Economic Zone indicates, perhaps, a collective ambivalence over the destabilizing openness that has only intensified since 1989.

The construction of Splendid China signifies a general trend in China in which tourism and intensified market commercialism and commodification have collaborated to invent a landscape of nostalgia on which to build a sense of national identity. Another example discussed by Anagnost is the proliferation of the old towns *(fangujie)* throughout many urban centers in China. These spectacles of commodity consumption are at once a rejection of the socialist architectural legacy, an invention of traditional Chinese urbanity, and an affirmation of "market socialism" in which commodity exchange has seemingly replaced industrial production as the driver of history. Modernity, tradition, socialism: in the old town you can have it all. Tourism in China, in other words, is thriving on the experience of anxiety, ambivalence, and disorientation brought by modernity.

Perhaps the most profound aspect of this experience has been a popular fascination with ethnic minority culture as an exotic and primitive source of vitality for modern China as it faces the cool onrush of global capitalism and the McWorld. Tourism has been crucial in directing China's gaze toward minority culture and in standardizing that culture into a set of "authentic" markers easily recognizable for public consumption. Thus, shortly after the opening of Splendid China, work began next door on a 180,000 square meter China Folk Culture Villages (Zhongguo Minsu Wenhuacun) tourist park. Opened on October 1, 1991, the Villages unambiguously situates ethnic minority culture within a comprehensive definition of the modern Chinese nation (note, for example, the opening date: China's National Day). Featuring "authentic replicas" (that wonderful oxymoron of tourism) of "typical" dwellings for twenty-one of China's fifty-six officially recognized *minzu* groups,[1] the park domesticates and displays ethnic culture to modern Chinese, who find themselves whirling in the maelstrom of Shenzhen and in need of the "calming certainty" of folk tradition (Figures 2.1 and 2.2). As if to heighten the juxtaposition between transnational modernization and Chinese national identity, a McDonald's restaurant has been placed directly outside the gate of the Villages. Emerging from this collection of

Figure 2.1. Cover for souvenir book from China Folk Culture Villages. (Photo from Shen and Cheung 1992, Courtesy of China Travel Advertising)

exotic and colorful ethnic spectacles, the arresting and universal vision of the Golden Arches is perhaps all it takes to convince the visitor that modern China's identity rests squarely on the shoulders of its ethnic minorities.

China Folk Culture Villages traffics in the selective cultural essence of a particular ethnic group, "weeding out" those qualities that might detract from a vision of multinational unity. In visiting the Villages, tourists are supposed to collect carefully crafted images and experiences that together convey a sense of the wholeness that pervades and surrounds the park: modern China (Figure 2.3). A souvenir book illustrates this sense quite explicitly. Written in English and Chinese, it states that, "Guided by the principle of 'originating from real life but rising above it, and discarding the dross and selecting the essential' [*yuan yu shenghuo, gao yu shenghuo, huiji jingcui, you suo qushe*], the Villages attempts to reflect from various angles the folk customs and cultures of China's nationalities" (Shen and Cheung 1992, 4). The book entices the visitor with descriptions of the vari-

Figure 2.2. One big, happy (multi)national family at the Villages. (Photo from Shen and Cheung 1992, Courtesy of China Travel Advertising)

ous festival activities regularly performed at the Villages and even prescribes the visitor's reaction: "Grand, romantic, rejoicing and auspicious, these festivals will enable visitors to take in the happy atmosphere of the magnificient occasions and to feel the poetic quality of the life of the Chinese nation" (Shen and Cheung 1992, 4). The touristic vision of the Chinese nation, in other words, is of a poetic and colorful mosaic, a distinctive tapestry woven by the happy and servile minorities.

This is not, however, simply a touristic vision of nationalism, but a fundamental legacy of Chinese modernity. During the New Culture Movement of the 1920s and 1930s, writers such as Wen Yidou and Shen Congwen valorized minority culture as a source of vitality to which China should turn in casting off its subjugation and reclaiming its identity in the modern world (see Kinkley 1987).[2]

With the ethnic identification project *(minzu shibie)* under the communists after 1949, this turn to the non-Han periphery was institutionalized and rendered scientific. The communists instituted a

Figure 2.3. Tradition juxtaposed with modernity at the Villages. The nightly laser folk music fountain performance provides a modern technological spectacle, which situates China's ethnic traditions, symbolized in structures such as the Dong drum tower, within the modern space of the Chinese nation-state. (Photo from Shen and Cheung 1992, Courtesy of China Travel Advertising)

policy of regional autonomy, along the Stalinist lines developed in the Soviet Union, in which minority nationality areas *(shaoshu minzu diqu)* were allowed some leniency in the implementation of socialist transformation. Unlike the Soviet prototype, however, Chinese autonomy policy explicitly declared minority areas to be an inseparable part of the People's Republic (Conner 1984, Dreyer 1976). Policies concerning minority nationalities were primarily governed by a desire to establish Chinese national unity and the ultimate goal of socialism. These issues, in turn, conditioned the Party's subsequent project of ethnic identification, in which over four hundred groups claiming separate ethnic identity were classified into fifty-five *minzu* categories (Fei 1981). Ethnic identification and regional autonomy were not about self-determination but about defining regions and their inhabitants according to their backwardness and need for economic, cultural, and social development (Solinger 1977, Hsieh 1989). Stalin's criteria were ostensibly used in categorizing ethnic groups, but the more fundamental issue was the extent of sociocultural distance from the Han Chinese.[3] Theoretically, this identification was important because certain groups had some "catching up" to do in achieving the ultimate goal of socialist transformation. In order to recognize them and grant them territory where their "special characteristics" would temper the speed of their transformation, they needed to be scientifically identified. In this the Chinese relied heavily on the stages of development model attributed to Lewis Henry Morgan (1877), a model that had inspired Marx and Engels (see Engels 1884). As China's preeminent ethnologist Fei Xiaotong (1981, 65) commented, "The state of the nationalities in China in the early post-liberation years provided researchers with a living textbook on the history of social development."

Morgan's evolutionary framework became important not only for identifying where a particular group stood along the path of social development but also for providing the state with a standard set of cultural markers that would indicate a group's stage of development. These cultural markers became the primary determinants of *minzu* status since few groups consistently exhibited Stalin's other characteristics. *Minzu* categories came to be defined primarily according to cultural criteria (Harrell 1990), which established a very important aspect of state-sanctioned ethnicity in China, especially in the southwest. Because Chinese people had historically "seeped" into the various tribal domains of southwest China over an extended period of time, the cultural traditions of that region have long been influenced by Han Chinese culture. Although Barth reminds us that the "sharing of a common culture should not be constructed as the essential definitional criterion of ethnic groups" (cited in Okamura 1981, 457), the Chinese state proceeded from the assumption that *minzu* groups could be identified according to essential non-Han cultural markers. Fei (1981) notes that the major problem confronted by *minzu shibie* was the separation from everyone else those who, despite claiming otherwise, were really Han. These were generally groups who could not claim sufficient cultural distinctiveness from dominant Chinese markers. Thus, more than anything, *minzu* groups were defined according to cultural distance from the Han.

Norma Diamond illustrates this search for cultural distance from the Han in her analysis of how the Miao were classified during *minzu shibie:*

That the Miao were initially identified as an example of primitive communal society is somewhat surprising, since the bulk of the survey work on the Miao was carried out in Guizhou. It was the absence of clear-cut class stratification within many Miao communities, the absence of "big landlords," full-time artisans, and merchants; and the existence of communal lands that were the basis for viewing Miao populations as representative of an early stage of society. The investigators underplayed Miao involvement in local marketing systems and their use of currency, stressing instead the self-sufficiency of the household economy (Diamond 1995, 108–109).

Given the contentious history of Chinese-Miao relations, it is not surprising that investigators would be looking for certain cultural markers that indicated the Miao were a primitive people.

On this linear scale of social development, the Dong were located, according to the state, somewhere between the Miao and the Han (who, of course, were the farthest along this scale and thus most qualified to lead the country's socialist transformation). Settled agriculturalists, the Dong had also been known to prosper from commercial cash crop production, especially during the late nineteenth and early twentieth centuries when industrialism along the coast created a great demand for cotton (Jiang 1991). Unlike the primitive Miao, the Dong had flirted with capitalism. Cultural markers of Dong identity focused on those visible artifacts of the social organization that had enabled the Dong to become more socially developed. These artifacts included magnificent drum towers *(gulou)*, covered wind and rain bridges *(fengyuqiao* or *huaqiao)*, and large barnlike post-pile houses *(diaojiaolou)*, all evidence of the peculiar sociocultural organization of Dong village and family life. Also emphasized were social activities, like intervillage singing performances, which reflected the alliance networks that defined the Dong.

State ethnic identification was initially carried out under the theoretical assumption that socialist modernization would produce an end to national (that is, ethnic) distinctions. During the Cultural Revolution, this assumption was put forcefully into practice, and the whole institution of *minzu shibie* was demolished as a remnant of "local nationalism." With the reforms initiated in 1978, however, not only did *minzu shibie* return but there also was a significant cultural revival that increased interest in the distinctive cultural features of minority groups. While it is still assumed that modernization will lead to the transformation of all society, the state now supports the idea that cultural distinctiveness, at least on a symbolic level, should be maintained among the different *minzu* groups. In promoting a largely symbolic cultural diversity, the state hopes to establish an environment conducive to national economic integration, geopolitical security, and patriotism.

The equating of ethnicity with essential non-Han cultural markers thus remains the central feature of state-sanctioned ethnic identity in China today. *Minzu* groups like the Dong are identified according to increasingly standardized markers. Many books on Dong culture and customs begin with such lines as "the most representative features of the Dong are the drum tower and the covered bridge" (Wang Shengxian 1989, 1). The "distinctive architecture" represented at China Folk Culture Villages is only the most obvious example of these markers. Since its 1991 opening in Shenzhen, similar parks have opened in Qingdao, Kunming, Guilin, and Beijing. In the four theme parks I've visited, the Dong villages all feature identical drum towers, covered bridges, waterwheels, and post-pile houses, despite a great variety of forms and styles throughout regions populated by Dong.[4] Filtered by representations in tourist theme parks and by images in television, film, and other media, *minzu* groups are associated with very specific and delimited cultural markers that are standardized and circulated in China's burgeoning industry of cultural commodity production.

Michel Picard has documented a similar situation concerning Balinese culture in Indonesia. Exemplified in Asia's original miniaturized theme park, the Beautiful Indonesia in Miniature Park, the Indonesian state promotes a "national culture" composed of many "regional cultures," each identified by specific cultural symbols. Picard notes that

> the conception of Balinese culture as *kebudayaan daerah* [regional culture] implies its decomposition into discrete cultural elements, to be sieved through the filter of national ideology and sorted out: those deemed appropriate to contribute to the development of the *kebudayaan nasional* [national culture] should be salvaged and promoted, whereas those deemed too primitive or emphasizing local ethnic identity should be eradicated (1993, 93).

This selective preservation and discarding of local culture has been the pervasive approach to promoting cultural diversity and multiethnic unity in China (see also Heberer 1989, 47).

Ethnic theme parks are probably the most visible manifestation of such state cultural policy. As we shall see below, they also play a significant role in defining as authentic the more remote villages that display the cultural forms selected by the state as representing particular *minzu* groups. The state thus plays an active role in historical preservation in the remote places where local architecture and customs have served as the model for ethnic theme parks in China's modern cities. A combination of state agencies determines what is to be preserved, the most significant being the Nationalities Affairs Commission *(minwei)* and the Cultural Relics Division of the State Cultural Bureau *(wenwuchu)*. Whereas the *minwei* is concerned with all aspects of nationality affairs and is the major source of funding in the promotion of ethnic tourism in Guizhou, the *wenwuchu* is more specifically responsible for selecting and preserving cultural artifacts. These include temples and pavilions, houses and guild halls, tombs and graves, bridges, city walls, and revolutionary sites. Recently, entire villages have been selected if they represent a well-preserved example of typical *minzu* architecture and customs. When a *minzu* village gains status as a *wenwu baohu danwei* (literally a "protected cultural relic unit"), it qualifies for certain state funds to maintain its traditional character; locals then must abide by a code preventing new "modern" buildings from being built or traditional buildings from being altered. In such cases, state cultural preservation seeks to "fossilize" certain aspects of cultural tradition, drawing distinct boundaries around local customs, fixing them in time and space, and ensuring that they remain encased as exhibits for the modern metropolitan world to observe and appreciate. As will be discussed below, such preservation, and the access to the state it affords, plays a significant role in shaping a local discourse of place identity, in which groups claim status as the most authentic representatives of a particular *minzu*.

The state's sanctioning and promoting of an ethnic cultural revival has had a significant impact on the identity of *minzu* groups. Stevan Harrell (1990, 545) claims that while the state "recognizes cultural criteria for ethnicity pure and simple," the groups themselves "operate from the kind of primordial-instrumental dialectic described by so many ethnicity theorists." It is true that the Dong in the villages featured here display this primordial-instrumental dialectic, but their situation as tourist sites has also provided them with a state-sanctioned battery of symbolic markers that can be used to measure their authenticity as Dong. Harrell states that "when primordial sentiments cannot be converted into culturalist claims because of a lack of evidence . . . the state and the local people will be at odds; and ethnic identity is likely to be a matter of dispute" (1990, 545). Although Harrell's case deals with a group disputing its state-assigned *minzu* status, rather than, as in the present study, a group's qualifications as the most authentic representative of a particular *minzu,* the situation is similar enough to warrant comparison. The additional factor of tourism provides locals with materials to create culturalist claims when previous claims of authenticity become jeopardized and to transform a possible dispute with the state into a means of building a sense of place in keeping with the broader context of state cultural policy and economic development.

Ethnic Tourism Development in Qiandongnan

In 1982 the Guizhou Tourism Bureau (GTB) was established and began promoting two separate tourist routes out of Guiyang. The western route emphasized lakes, caves, waterfalls, and other scenic attractions peculiar to karst landscapes, all within easy access of Guiyang. The eastern route, in Qiandongnan, was to emphasize both scenery and *minzu* customs. Developments in Qiandongnan did not really get under way until 1985, with the opening of Kaili (the prefectural capital), Shibing, and Zhenyuan to foreign tourists and with the establishment of a prefectural tourism bureau in Kaili (Qiandongnan's most well-known scenic sites—Yuntai Mountain and the Wuyang Gorge—are located in Shibing and Zhenyuan). More remote from Guiyang, with poorer roads and fewer financial resources, Qiandongnan lagged considerably behind the western route in terms of investments and numbers of tourists (Table 2.2).[5] The majority of tourists who did visit, however, tended to be foreigners or compatriots from Hong Kong who stayed longer and spent more money than their counterparts along the western route (Table 2.3). From 1985 to 1990, roughly 60 percent of the foreign tourists in Qiandongnan were from Japan. In the early 1980s teams of Japanese ethnographers visited Qiandongnan and published books with observations on Miao customs and dress that were similar to those found in ancient feudal Japan, thus popularizing the idea that the Miao and the Japanese have the same origins. Soon many Japanese tourists were coming to Qiandongnan to look for their roots.

Local officials quickly recognized *ethnic* tourism as the main attraction to foreigners in Qiandongnan. Higher level tourism planners in the State Tourism Administration (STA) in Beijing and in the GTB were relatively slow to recognize the potential of ethnic tourism

Table 2.2 Foreign Tourists Received in Qiandongnan, 1984–1993

Year	Number	Percent of Guizhou Total	Estimated Revenues* (in U.S.$)
1984	71	0.69	
1985	206	1.83	
1986	430	3.07	8,000
1987	864	4.59	9,900
1988	1,071	4.53	20,700
1989	920	6.73	9,950
1990	1,174	4.87	20,930
1991	1,414	3.77	38,100
1992	2,096	2.75	53,000
1993	3,951	3.86	80,500

*Revenues based on food, lodging, and official fees for tour groups only.
Source: Qiandongnan Tourism Bureau, Guizhou Tourism Bureau.

Table 2.3 Comparison of Guizhou's Eastern (Qiandongnan) and Western Tourist Routes, 1985–1990

	Eastern Route	Western Route
Average length of stay		
Foreign tourists	2.84 days	0.76 days
Hong Kong, Taiwan tourists	6.06 days	1.22 days
Average expenditures per foreign tourist	106.53 *yuan*	11.94 *yuan*
Tourism investments (to 1989)	500,000 *yuan*	8,550,000 *yuan*

Source: Yang et al. 1991, 60.

in Guizhou. In part, this slow response reflects Chinese assumptions about tourism in general, in which natural and historical landscapes —not exotic customs—have been the most highly valued tourist reources (Yang-Peterson 1995). Despite state inaction at higher levels, however, the Qiandongnan prefectural tourism bureau began to establish a number of ethnic tourist villages around Kaili. By 1987,

Figure 2.4. Welcoming ceremony at a Miao ethnic tourist village near Kaili. (Photo by Timothy S. Oakes)

seven villages—all Miao but one—had been selected where tour groups were treated to elaborate welcoming ceremonies, song and dance performances, and crafts demonstrations (Figure 2.4). These villages generally charge a fee (determined by the tourism bureau) for receiving tour groups, and in most cases tourism brings a substantial change to a village's economic situation (Table 2.4). Ironically, reception activities in these villages tend to be modeled on the ethnic theme parks, which mark the activities as authentic.

Table 2.4 Selected Characteristics of Three Ethnic Tourist Villages in Guizhou, 1993

	Western Route		Qiandongnan
	Changlinggang	Heitu	Langde
Total tourists received	4,063	1,343	3,945
Foreign	2,324	801	530
Domestic	1,739	542	3,415
Fees paid to village *(yuan)*	68,090	22,878	43,103
Fees per tourist *(yuan)*	16.76	17.03	10.67
Fees per village household *(yuan)**	1,745.89	571.95	399.10
Fees per villager *(yuan)**	362.18	103.99	81.33
Net peasant income in county *(yuan* per capita 1990)	528	528	209

*Actual figures will vary since not all fees are distributed to households and not all households participate in tourist receptions. Some households earn substantially more (up to 150 percent of the basic per household fees) by selling handicraft souvenirs.
Source: Guizhou Xianqing 1992, Qingzhen *minwei*, village secretaries.

There were basically three reasons for Qiandongnan's locally initiated emphasis on ethnic tourism. First, foreign tourist demand, especially from the Japanese, was crucial. Specifically, guides at China International Travel Service (CITS) in Guiyang played an important role in directing Qiandongnan toward ethnic tourism promotion.

A second reason involves local control over tourist resources and returns on investments. The director of the prefectural tourism bureau, Pan Xinxiong (1994b), stated that he had no interest in investing precious capital in yet another cave, waterfall, or canyon: "Developing scenic sites requires much more money than developing an ethnic village; it takes a long time to realize any returns. And now, with so many scenic sites already being developed in western Guizhou, there's no point in trying to compete." More importantly, the prefectural tourism bureau has virtually no say in the development of Qiandongnan's major scenic sites, as they fall under the jurisdiction of state organs, which have the capital necessary to develop them. Yuntai Mountain is being developed by the ministries of construction and forestry, while most of the money for the Wuyang Gorge is from the hydroelectric bureau. These large, state-level units basically bypass

Qiandongnan's local tourism authorities. In the current economic environment in which local units are expected to be fiscally responsible and in which Qiandongnan's tourism bureau is expected to fund its own projects by expanding tourist revenues, there is little incentive for Pan to encourage tourists to visit scenic areas. Indeed, he actively discourages tours to the Wuyang Gorge, claiming it is a boring trip in a noisy motor boat on an artificial reservoir. Ethnic tourist villages, on the other hand, are directly administered by the prefectural tourism bureau, which sets the fees to be paid to the villages. Although most investments for these villages actually come from the *minwei,* the tourism bureau administers their use and distribution. The *minwei,* claimed Pan, do not know anything about tourism, "so they just let us take care of it." Thus, the tourism bureau and the local branch of CITS realize direct returns from ethnic village tourism.

Finally, according to Pan (1994b), ethnic tourism offers locals direct benefits that scenic tourism does not. Although scenic sites offer places for locals to sell souvenirs and other services, they also encumber large amounts of land and resources in areas where land is a precious source of livelihood, which is the situation at the large cave and waterfall sites along the western route. In Qiandongnan, at the Wuyang Gorge and Yuntai Mountain, local peasants are prohibited from cutting trees for firewood, but they do it anyway, especially on the steep slopes above the gorge where erosion is defacing the hillsides and muddying the river. This action places them in direct conflict with the government and alienates them from tourism. Such environmental conflicts with the state are not likely to happen in ethnic tourist villages (Pan). More important, while rural incomes derived from tourism remain rather limited (that is, beyond the actual tourist villages), tourism is regarded by local officials as a force that can break through the isolation still pervading the Miaoling. According to Pan:

> It all has to do with transportation. Rivers, roads, or railroads, it's all the same; this area has always been extremely difficult to get to and get around in. Why don't the Han have the hundreds of festivals which people in this region take part in each year? Because they've never had to come up with an excuse to bring people in neighboring areas together. Here, because of the difficulty of transport, local villages have always kept to themselves; but they need occasions for trade, social interaction, and particularly, opportunities to get their youth

married. That is the main purpose of the local festivals. Why have minority people here been getting shorter and shorter? Because they never go more than a few kilometers to get married. And this kind of local breeding causes other shortcomings as well; they have little ambition to broaden the horizons of their world. The most important thing tourism is doing here is changing everyone's perspective. It's not important they learn about America or France or even Hong Kong and Taiwan; but what they *are* learning about is what the people in the next valley over are doing, and particularly, what's going on in the towns and in the city of Kaili (1994a).

The idea that tourism ultimately broadens local horizons has encouraged the prefectural tourism bureau to develop ethnic tourist resources throughout the region. By 1994, over fifty different villages had been selected as meeting the criteria for ethnic tourist sites.[6] This expansion has also resulted from the tourism bureau's increased awareness of how the concept of authenticity drives the foreign market in ethnic tourism, particularly among Westerners. As suggested by Table 2.4, western route ethnic tourist villages (which have been opened more recently than those in Qiandongnan) receive only slightly more tourists than those in Qiandongnan, but they now earn significantly higher revenues. As a result, the more remote villages of Qiandongnan have maintained a greater degree of authenticity in the eyes of Guiyang tour guides. According to one guide (Oakes 1994), "Those villages [along the western route near Guiyang] are way too commercial, too close to the city; they don't have very traditional lives, and their values are oriented toward money, they always want money for everything." She said she preferred taking tour groups to the villages in Qiandongnan, which were "much less spoiled, more traditional." Whether a village satisfies Western tourists, apparently, is seen as the best indicator of authenticity. Travel agencies in Guiyang are thus more likely to take Western tour groups to Qiandongnan because Westerners are known to appreciate "more traditional villages."

Even within Qiandongnan, the original seven tourist villages are now often regarded as "too commercial," and so Western groups these days are steered toward more remote places where the customs are "still authentic." Domestic Chinese tourists now predominate in these original seven villages, of which Langde, in Table 2.4, is the most popular. Given this situation, the Dong villages of the Duliu basin have achieved somewhat special status in Guizhou's ethnic tourism. The region was only officially opened to foreign tourists in 1993. Since then, the Duliu basin has been promoted, by both the prefectural tourism bureau and travel agencies in Guiyang, as the "authentic frontier" of ethnic tourism: Zhaoxing and Gaozeng are not yet commercialized, are remote, and are said to offer examples of "pure" Dong culture. More important, opening the Duliu basin has enabled tourists to travel directly to Qiandongnan from the popular tourist city of Guilin, in Guangxi to the south. This change gives the prefectural tourism bureau direct access to tourists entering the province, whereas previously they had to deal with Guiyang travel agencies, which meant losing a significant share of the revenues. Pan Xinxiong was thus eager to exploit this new route to secure Qiandongnan's independence from Guiyang.

Aside from their relative accessibility, Zhaoxing and Gaozeng were selected as ethnic tourist villages because of their status as "preserved cultural relics" under the provincial *wenwuchu*. The typical pattern in Qiandongnan has been for protected villages to later become tourist sites. That this has become a source of some tension between the *wenwuchu* and the tourism bureau reflects an area of potential conflict between state cultural policy and commercial tourism development. The head of the prefectural cultural bureau told me he resented how the tourism bureau always took advantage of *wenwuchu* "discoveries," capitalizing on *minwei* and *wenwuchu* investments and reaping all the benefits. He did not appreciate that the efforts of the *wenwuchu* to protect cultural relics were often undermined by the tourism industry. "The needs of tourism development," he said, "often puts the *wenwuchu* at odds with the tourism bureau over what changes should be allowed to occur in a protected village" (Oakes 1994).

Villagers occupy an ambiguous space between these broader contending forces of cultural preservation and commercial tourism development. The state has established a framework that encourages both market-oriented economic development and the preservation of symbolic cultural diversity. Because the idea of ethnic authenticity based on cultural distance from the Han has been sanctioned and institutionalized by the state's ethnic identification project, agencies such as the *wenwuchu,* the metropolitan tour guides, and many tourists themselves are likely to see a contradiction between commercialism and the preservation of ethnic cultural authenticity. Villagers are not unaware of the need to meet the expectations of their visitors, but to them the idea of a contradiction between authenticity and economic development is generally incomprehensible. Villagers thus tend to promote their own commercial tourism development quite vigorously. In Langde, Qiandongnan's most visited ethnic tourist site, villagers have initiated several schemes, such as a handicraft shop and a parking lot, with the goal of retaining more control over tourism revenues.[7] These schemes have been resisted by both the prefectural tourism bureau (which seeks to maintain its own control over revenues) and the *wenwuchu* (which sees the plans as compromising the village's authenticity). The head of the prefectural cultural bureau thus makes frequent trips to Langde, reminding villagers of Langde's enviable position as an open-air museum and a preserved relic.

As has already happened in Langde, once villagers begin to initiate their own commercial tourism ventures they also run into conflicts with the *wenwuchu* over the protected status of their village. The loss of protected status, however, can dramatically alter a village's tourism prospects. A village not only loses access to state investments that help it to develop tourist resources but also, and more importantly, loses its authenticity as a true *minzu* village in the eyes of the broader industry—the county and prefectural tourism authorities and the tourist agencies in Guiyang.

The cases of Gaozeng and Zhaoxing represent two different versions of how villagers occupy and appropriate this space between state-sanctioned expectations of cultural authenticity and state-encouraged development of a commercially viable tourist industry. The two villages have had contrasting experiences: one lost its status as a protected relic and has subsequently sought to reclaim its authenticity, while the other has effectively exploited its status as an authentic village by maintaining key ties with the broader tourism industry. Both, however, are similar in that villagers are clearly articulating local tradition with extralocal processes as they reproduce their senses of place identity.

Gaozeng: Place Identity and the Loss of Authenticity

Gaozeng is a large village at the upper end of a narrow plain of good paddy land extending south to the Duliu River and bordered by mountains rising eight hundred meters above the valley floor. Formerly a *dong*, the seat of Gaozeng commune, and now an administrative *xiang*, the village has a history of at least six hundred years. While the village itself has a population of 1,825 (1993), it is the administrative and economic center for an area that includes thirty-eight natural villages and nearly 14,000 people, of whom approximately 90 percent are Dong. Incomes are derived almost entirely from rice cultivation and timber processing. Villagers throughout the region produce household wood products and sell them in the county town, only eight kilometers from Gaozeng. The village actually consists of three clan-based natural villages, each with its own drum tower. Historically, drum towers have served as gathering sites for village defense, clan meetings, and festival events. Because of its collection of three towers, hundreds of *diaojiaolou* houses, and a picturesque setting, Gaozeng was designated a *wenwu baohu danwei* in 1982, the first village in Qiandongnan to be granted such status. In 1984 Gaozeng received a grant from the *minwei* to renovate the drum towers, repair houses and bridges, and otherwise beautify the village. Although the region was not officially open to foreign tourists until 1993, a few tour groups were granted special permission to go there as early as 1982. By 1988 the village received a regular flow of about twenty tour groups a year, most of them Japanese.

Gaozeng's early rise in Qiandongnan's fledgling ethnic tourist industry was partly due to the efforts of Wang Shengxian, who grew up in the village and became a Dong scholar at the Qiandongnan Nationalities Research Institute in Kaili. During the 1980s he wrote eight books on various aspects of Dong culture, and through his positions in different prefectural propaganda and research organs he promoted Gaozeng as an example of ancient Dong culture and civilization. Because of Wang's initiative and influence, groups of *minzu* scholars began to visit the village and many of Gaozeng's youth received jobs in performance troupes in Guiyang and other parts of China. Many of the tour groups who visited during the 1980s were led by Wang and stayed in his family's house, which subsequently became the richest in the village.

Gaozeng's prospects as a center of Dong ethnic tourism were dramatically altered in 1988, however, when a fire destroyed two-thirds of the village and two of the three drum towers. With the fire, Gaozeng's privileged position in the hierarchy of state recognition and cultural preservation was lost. According to the director of the prefectural cultural bureau (Oakes 1994), "That village is now ruined *(pohuaile)*. The villagers may rebuild the drum towers, but they will no longer be authentic cultural relics *(zhenshi wenwu)*." The state saw no point in providing funds to rebuild the towers as they would have no value as traditional antiques. The county did cancel Gaozeng's taxes and grain quotas, but no relief funds were distributed to help rebuild the village; the drum towers themselves were regarded as a clan responsibility. Unfortunately, wood had grown scarce and the old-growth logs necessary to build new towers would have to be purchased from a neighboring *xiang*. By 1994, only about half of the needed money had been raised.

It was particularly difficult for villagers to raise money because tourism quickly dwindled to three or four groups per year. Travel agencies and tourism authorities no longer promoted the village, and attention began to focus, instead, on Zhaoxing. Meanwhile, the village's advocate, Wang Shengxian, became an entrepreneur, investing in local timber and mining schemes. Wang became less concerned with promoting the village as an authentic spectacle and started funding development projects, such as a new school, to get the people on their feet again. Within the tourism industry, it became common to refer to Gaozeng as "ruined." Along with this, the village earned the label of being too "Hanified" *(hanhuale)*: it was no longer an authentic Dong village. Tourism officials and guides began to steer visitors who wanted to learn about the true Dong not to Gaozeng but to the more remote mountain village of Xiaohuang, three hours by foot from Gaozeng. In addition to the absence of two drum towers, the loss of authenticity was visible in that many of the houses were rebuilt with brick instead of wood; wood was scarce and expensive, and brick had the advantage of being fireproof. Wang Shengxian's family, for their part, built a new cement house, the largest in the village. But the loss of authenticity was especially visible in the new rural credit association building, a large, incongruous white cement structure built outside the village gate (Figure 2.5). Such a building would never have been permitted if the village had remained a *wenwu baohu danwei*.

County officials and leaders in the *xiang* government (most of whom were not from Gaozeng but had been assigned there) claimed that such changes were inevitable in Gaozeng, which was, after all, only eight kilometers from the county town. "Gaozeng is becoming modern," the *xiang* secretary told me (Oakes 1994). He referred to the fact that billiards and smoking cigarettes had replaced music and singing as the main activities of village youth. "Most of the village girls no longer learn how to weave; they want to buy modern clothes in town." But he also claimed that the villagers liked the new credit association building, that it symbolized modernity and progress for them. If tourists wanted to see the authentic Dong, he said, they could hire a jeep to take them to Xiaohuang, but it was important and desirable for Gaozeng to become a developed, modern village.

Figure 2.5. Gaozeng in 1994 with the new rural credit association, *xiang* government building, and forestry offices visible at the lower end of the village (far left). (Photo by Timothy S. Oakes)

According to this official, such a development necessarily entailed "Hanification."

Among villagers, however, there was a great deal of ambivalence about Gaozeng's loss of protected status and consequent "modernization." Villagers I interviewed could not understand why tourists would want to go to Xiaohuang instead of Gaozeng. "Those people," one told me, referring to Xiaohuang, "they're not clean *(tamen bujiang weisheng)*, they're uncivilized; Gaozeng is over six hundred years old! Why would tourists want to go there instead of here?" Most were acutely aware that after the fire Gaozeng had lost something in the eyes of the *guojia,* the state. The village's status as a *wenming baohu cunzhai* (civilized preserved village), enjoyed during the 1980s, had become an important aspect of their place identity, and "modernity" was a poor substitute for the loss of that status. "This place is becoming just like the county town," one woman told me, "the new buildings, the restaurants, the pool tables; these aren't

Dong." In 1984, the state had erected two tablets in the village, declaring it a *wenming baohu cunzhai*. These were destroyed in the fire, and where the drum towers had once stood, villagers had defiantly made their own signs with little white rocks set in the hard ground: *wenming gulao cun,* "ancient civilized village." For villagers, the loss of identity as a civilized place was symbolically found not only in the absence of the two drum towers but also in the fact that the village had never rebuilt its splendid covered bridge, which had burned down in 1911. Rebuilding these and initiating a new era of tourism was thus seen as the key to reclaiming their status as a civilized place in the eyes of the state and outside visitors.

The campaign to rebuild the drum towers and bridge was being spearheaded by the village elders association *(laonian xiehui),* who considered the villagers the key to promoting Gaozeng. In 1993, the association petitioned the provincial government for 200,000 *yuan* to fund a tourism development project, which included rebuilding the bridge and the road into the village and developing a nearby scenic waterfall. As the petition made clear, rebuilding the bridge was the most pressing need of the villagers: "The hearts of the masses of Gaozeng all want to restore the covered bridge to their lives, to preserve their heritage" (Gaozeng Village 1994). Gaozeng, the petition went on to claim, "has been the cultural hearth of the Dong people since ancient times." Its early status as a "village of ancient civilization" was a recognition of this tradition. The association has also served as the primary fund-raiser for the drum towers and has organized singing and dancing lessons for village youth to prepare them for the return of tour groups. To the association's leader, the 1988 fire initiated Gaozeng's decline. After the fire, village youth started playing pool and people no longer built traditional houses, not caring how the village looked. The new credit association building, a *yangfangzi* (Western building), was a "disgrace" to the village. The association's petition thus proposed rerouting the road into the village and building a new gate so that tourists would not see the *yangfangzi* as they entered Gaozeng.

The activities of the elders association represented an effort by villagers to reclaim the ingredient of authenticity that had been such an important aspect of their place identity. Their sense of place had been conditioned by the broader processes of state cultural policy and commercial tourism, processes in which the concept of authenticity was highly valued. When the village's link to those processes was jeopardized by the fire, villagers began taking initiatives to reclaim it.

The issue was not tourist dollars, for these had never been significant, but identity as a civilized place, a traditional hearth of Dong culture. Modernity was regarded as a threat only after the village's secure place-identity was lost in the fire, and tourism, which didn't even exist officially until 1993, was already regarded as the necessary medium with which to reestablish Gaozeng's place as a village of ancient civilization. With drum towers and covered bridges promoted as the "crystals of the Dong people"—valuable capital in China's new cultural economy—tourism development becomes the clearest means by which Gaozeng can reclaim its cultural heritage and express its identity to the outside world. To illustrate further the importance of those links to the commerce of authenticity afforded by tourism, we turn to the second case, the village of Zhaoxing.

Zhaoxing: Home of the "True Dong"

Like Gaozeng, Zhaoxing has long been an established local political and cultural center. Now a *xiang* seat administering a region of twenty-nine natural villages and just over ten thousand people, it occupies a position identical to Gaozeng in China's rural administrative hierarchy. But with a population of over 3,500, the village of Zhaoxing proper is nearly twice the size of Gaozeng and boasts not three clans but twelve. It is recognized by county and prefectural officials as the largest and most ancient Dong village in China. The village sits at the bottom of a deep, three-sided basin, with the surrounding ridges rising nearly one thousand meters, giving the place an enclosed and hidden quality. It has five drum towers (some of the smaller clans share a drum tower) and five covered bridges (one, washed away in a flood in July 1994, was recently rebuilt) (Figure 2.6). The drum towers were all destroyed during the Cultural Revolution, but since being rebuilt they have been given county-level protected status. Three hundred meters up the mountainside in the village of Jitang, a half-hour's walk from Zhaoxing (still within Zhaoxing *xiang*), are three more drum towers, each at least 150 years old. Two of these were given provincial-level protected status in 1982, and by 1985 all of Jitang was recognized as a protected village, an "open-air museum" *(lutian bowuguan).*

Although during the 1980s Zhaoxing was not promoted as a place of authentic culture to the same extent as Gaozeng, it nevertheless developed important connections with the broader commercial industry of *minzu* culture. Because of the density of drum towers and covered bridges in the area, peasants from Zhaoxing were recruited

Figure 2.6. Drum tower and covered bridge in Zhaoxing. (Photo by Timothy S. Oakes)

to build replica drum towers in the county town and in Kaili. They were also recruited to build entire replica villages (complete with drum towers, waterwheels, covered bridges, and *diaojiaolou* houses) in the ethnic theme parks in Shenzhen, Guilin, and Beijing. Perhaps more than any other factor, the theme park industry helped secure Zhaoxing's eventual status as a place of authentic Dong tradition. The local builders who traveled to these cosmopolitan cities gained status as the bearers of an ancient architectural art. They learned that tourists would pay as much as 150 *yuan* (U.S. $17.50) per ticket to see their structures. They returned to Zhaoxing with the knowledge that their village was the "most representative" *(zuiyou daibiaoxing)* of all the Dong villages.

Song and dance troupes recruited to perform at the Dong villages in these ethnic theme parks were sent to Zhaoxing to learn authentic Dong songs and dances. While I stayed in Zhaoxing, such a troupe from Guilin spent three weeks there. The members of the troupe, all Dong, were mostly from villages closer to Guilin, in Guangxi. Each brought the distinctive clothing and styles of his or her native village. But they had come to Zhaoxing to learn the kinds of songs and dances performed in this, the most authentic of Dong villages. When

I asked villagers why they thought Zhaoxing had become so well known for its cultural traditions, most simply answered that it was "the most cultured and civilized" *(zui you wenhua, zui you wenming)* of the Dong villages. Several times I was told the story of a professor from Beijing who came to study the Dong. He had first gone to Guangxi, because "Guangxi is more developed and they are better at propaganda *(xuanchuan)* than Guizhou." When he was about to return to Beijing, it was suggested that he visit Zhaoxing. He did and was so overcome that he exclaimed to the leader of the local cultural bureau, "The Dong of Zhaoxing are the true Dong; the Dong of Guangxi are fake *(jiade).*"

Through a combination of broader industry and local initiatives, the pattern of tourism development in Zhaoxing has been clearly driven by this ideal of authenticity. In 1994 the STA sent an investigative team to Qiandongnan to formulate a new comprehensive tourism development plan. Although the team visited Gaozeng, its tour of the Dong areas emphasized Zhaoxing as the comprehensive site of Dong ethnic tourism. Plans called for nearby Jitang to be maintained as an open-air museum where tourists could be treated to an authentic Dong experience. The jeep trail to the village was to be improved, a reception house in traditional style would be built, and homestays for tourists arranged. In Zhaoxing proper, the several Western buildings that had already been built (the bank, theater, school, and old guesthouse) were to be renovated in the traditional architectural style of the *diaojiaolou*. While it was recognized that Zhaoxing itself had become more modern and somewhat "Hanified," state funds would help restore a traditional look to the place, while the nearby village of Jitang would be promoted as the "authentic Dong village." The head of the Zhaoxing cultural bureau told me that locals also planned to promote other nearby villages to tourists who were "looking for an even more authentic village" (Oakes 1994). These villages required several hours of hiking to reach. "Those who want to see the *real* Dong will be willing to endure some hardship." He also expressed confidence that if the state failed to supply funding for the plan, locals would pay for it somehow, since "everyone recognizes how important this is for Zhaoxing's future."

Tourism, though just getting under way in Zhaoxing, was already encouraging locals to express a sense of place that incorporated this ideal of authenticity, an ideal conditioned by Zhaoxing's links to the broader commercial tourism and culture industries. One result was a popular confidence that the Dong of Qiandongnan were more civi-

lized than the Miao. A retired cadre, living in one of Zhaoxing's out-
lying villages, expressed this confidence quite lucidly:

> It's because of history. If you don't understand history, you can't
> understand the differences between the Dong and the Miao. It all has
> to do with transportation. Back when there were no roads or rail-
> roads, only rivers, transportation to the Dong areas was more conve-
> nient than in the Miao areas. The Duliu River was our link to Guangxi
> and Guangdong. And even though it was hard to get to a place like
> Zhaoxing, it was easier than getting to Kaili or any of the other Miao
> places. That's why the Dong are still more civilized than the Miao. It's
> funny, because now the situation is reversed. Now transportation to
> the Miao areas is more convenient, because of roads and railroads.
> Kaili has become a big, culturally developed city. But in the country-
> side, the Miao are still uncivilized because of their history (Oakes
> 1994).

This cadre's attitude had been supported not only by state policy,
which defines *minzu* categories according to cultural distance from
the Han, but also by the tourism industry, which legitimized Zhaoxing's claim as a civilized place.

Tourism had also become a factor in building a sense of place for
Zhaoxing that set it apart from other Dong villages in the region.
Several villagers claimed, for example, that in terms of customs and
traditions, there was little difference between Zhaoxing and Gaozeng, but that since the fire in 1988, Gaozeng had become more like
the Han. One went further, saying that Gaozeng was culturally backward compared to Zhaoxing and that many of Gaozeng's musicians
and dancers had learned their art in Zhaoxing. "Historically, it has
always been this way, so it makes sense that Zhaoxing has become
the more important tourist site. Zhaoxing is the true heart of Dong
culture" (Oakes 1994).

Most important, though, tourism had given village leaders a way
to embrace modernity without losing their traditions, a way to ensure that Zhaoxing remain authentically Dong. I asked the head of
the cultural bureau whether village youth were becoming more interested in traditional songs and dances. He told me:

> As this place progresses and becomes more developed, people learn
> the value of their traditions, and they work harder to support them.
> There is no contradiction between progress and preserving tradition.
> On the contrary, modernization will help us keep our *minzu* customs,

because our development plan is now based on our traditions. Tourism is a very big part of this. It has encouraged us to work with the elders in the village, the elders association, to relearn the old ways which were almost forgotten. This makes the elders very happy; they support this kind of development. They support the tourism plan for Zhaoxing (Oakes 1994).

And did the youth support it? I asked. Are they itching for change? He said that although that was true in many places like Gaozeng, tourism had taught the youth of Zhaoxing to respect their traditions. Although I noticed a certain degree of ambivalence regarding this last point among the young people with whom I spoke, they at least seemed more conscious of the issue than their counterparts in Gaozeng.

Tourism and Local Identity

Obviously, tourism in Zhaoxing, not to mention Gaozeng, has not reached the commercial level necessary to commoditize place or ethnicity in the manner discussed by Britton (1991) and MacCannell (1984). It remains to be seen what increased numbers of tourists, revenues, and the potential intrusion of outside opportunists will bring. It may be premature to conclude that the secure sense of place expressed in Zhaoxing will not become displaced with the intensified commercialism tourism is capable of generating. But it seems equally premature to assume that tourism leaves in its wake a placeless landscape. The cases of Gaozeng and Zhaoxing illustrate not so much the relatively benign role played by tourism in its earliest stages of development, but the way the experience of tourism becomes a fundamental component of people's senses of place and ethnic identity. By providing a sketch of the broader historical processes in which these villages have been situated—namely a frontier history of conflict with the imperial Chinese administration, a *minzu* identity defined according to cultural distance from the Han Chinese, and a commercial tourist industry driven by the ideal of cultural authenticity—I have tried to argue that local identity is always conditioned by a dynamic tension between extralocal forces and local traditions. Tourism is the latest (and probably most intense) manifestation of these broader forces to become appropriated by a local cultural discourse of identity and meaning. Conceiving of tourism as an adopted component of a local culture's internal dynamics of ongoing change, rather than as an uncontrollable force bearing down upon locals, yields a more accurate view of the situation and urges a reevaluation of the belief that tourism is simply another cog in the wheel of modernization's steamroller.

Despite the obvious difficulties villagers face in gaining both fair economic compensation for their participation in tourist activities and inclusion in the broader administrative decision-making process, tourism plays an important social and cultural role that cannot be dismissed as purely negative. In China, where the central state remains overly sensitive to the unhealthy vestiges of "local nationalism" or to any challenges to its definitions of *minzu* status or the virtues of modernization and cultural development in the direction of the Han, tourism provides local minority groups with a forum for making claims about themselves and their villages. That has certainly been the case in Gaozeng as villagers attempt to reject "Hanification" and to regain a lost sense of authenticity. And in Zhaoxing, a similar attitude was expressed that Dong places were still more civilized, despite the increased infrastructural integration in the Miao areas. Similar situations can be found in other parts of Guizhou. I would not doubt they exist throughout the rest of China. Clearly, as Gaozeng's experience also illustrates, villagers are highly vulnerable to the whims of the commerce of authenticity. That does not mean, however, they do not themselves participate in this commerce and understand that, even amid the risks, they stand to benefit from it a great deal.

Notes

Field work for this study was conducted in 1993–1994. The author gratefully acknowledges the financial support of the National Science Foundation and the Committee on Scholarly Communication with China, and the assistance of Guizhou Normal University and the Qiandongnan Tourism Bureau. Thanks also to James Bell, Stevan Harrell, Michel Picard, and Robert Wood for comments on earlier versions of this chapter.

1. *Minzu* may be translated as either "nationality" or "ethnic group," but has no real equivalent in English. In this chapter I have chosen to follow a growing convention among those studying ethnicity in China and leave the term untranslated.

2. Wen Yidou, introducing a collection of folksongs from Hunan, Guizhou, and Yunnan, wrote: "You say these [poems] are primitive and savage. You are right, and that is just what we need today. We've been civilized too long, and now that we have nowhere left to go, we shall have to pull out the last and purest card, and release the animal nature that has lain dormant

in us for several thousand years, so that we can bite back" (cited in Spence 1981, 317).

3. Stalin's four criteria for nationality identification were "common language, common territory, common economic life, and a typical cast of mind manifested in a common culture" (Heberer 1989, 30).

4. Most Chinese ethnic theme parks contain only a selection of China's fifty-six *minzu* groups. According to Harrell (personal correspondence), the major factor determining a group's inclusion in these parks is the visual distinctiveness of their architecture.

5. For a more complete account of tourism development in Guizhou, see Oakes (1995).

6. These criteria are (1) convenient transportation; (2) distinctive architecture, unique customs, and picturesque landscape; (3) ability of villagers to accommodate tourists at any time; (4) recognition as an important site for local festivals; and (5) support of village leadership.

7. These schemes are often initiated with the aid of metropolitan advocates who, after having visited the village as tourists, become involved with village development projects.

References

Anagnost, Ann
   1993   The Nationscape: Movement in the Field of Vision. *Positions: East Asia Cultures Critique* 1(3):585–606.
Britton, Stephen
   1991   Tourism, Capital, and Place: Towards a Critical Geography of Tourism. *Environment and Planning D: Society and Space* 9:451–478.
Conner, Walker
   1984   *The National Question in Marxist-Leninist Theory and Strategy.* Princeton: Princeton University Press.
Diamond, Norma
   1988   The Miao and Poison: Interactions on China's Southwestern Frontier. *Ethnology* 27(1):1–25.
   1995   Defining the Miao: Ming, Qing, and Contemporary Views. In *Cultural Encounters on China's Ethnic Frontiers,* ed. S. Harrell, 92–116. Seattle: University of Washington Press.
Dreyer, June
   1976   *China's Forty Millions: Minority Nationalities and National Integration in the People's Republic of China.* Cambridge: Harvard University Press.
Engels, Friedrich
   1884   *The Origin of the Family, Private Property, and the State.* London: Lawrence and Wishart.

Fei, Xiaotong
  1981 *Toward a People's Anthropology.* Beijing: New World Press.
Gaozeng Village People's Government, People's Committee, and Ethnic Affairs Commission
  1994 *Report Requesting Support to Rebuild Gaozeng Dong Village's "Hua Qiao."* 4 April.
Guizhou Xianqing Editorial Committee
  1992 *Guizhou Xianqing 1949–1990* (Guizhou county summary). Beijing: Statistical Publishing House.
Harrell, Stevan
  1990 Ethnicity, Local Interests, and the State: Yi Communities in Southwest China. *Comparative Studies in Society and History* 32(3): 515–545.
Heberer, Thomas
  1989 *China and Its National Minorities: Autonomy or Assimilation?* Armonk, N.Y.: M. E. Sharpe.
Hsieh, Shih-chong
  1989 On the Dynamics of Dai-Lue Ethnicity: An Ethnohistorical Analysis. Ph.D. diss., Department of Anthropology, University of Washington.
Jenks, Robert
  1985 The Miao Rebellion, 1854–1872: Insurgency and Social Disorder in Kweichow During the Taiping Era. Ph.D. diss., Department of History, Harvard University.
Jiang, Daqian
  1991 Lun Dongzu Fangzhi Wenhua (A discussion of Dong textile culture). In *Dongzu Wenhua Xinlun* (New theories of Dong culture), ed. Wang Shenxian et al., 34–50. Guiyang: Renmin.
Kinkley, Jeffrey
  1987 *The Odyssey of Shen Congwen.* Stanford: Stanford University Press.
Liping Xianzhi Editorial Committee
  1990 *Liping Xianzhi 1989* (Liping gazetteer). Guiyang: Renmin.
MacCannell, Dean
  1984 Reconstructed Ethnicity. *Annals of Tourism Research* 11:375–391.
Morgan, Lewis Henry
  1877 *Ancient Society.* Cambridge: Harvard University Press.
Oakes, Timothy
  1994 Field notes. Guizhou Province, China.
  1995 Ethnic Tourism in Guizhou: The Legacy of Internal Colonialism. In *Tourism in China: Geographical, Political, and Economic Perspectives,* ed. A. Lew and L. Yu, 203–222. Boulder, Colo.: Westview.
Okamura, Jonathan
  1981 Situational Ethnicity. *Ethnic and Racial Studies* 4(4):452–465.

Pan Xinxiong
  1994a Interview with author. Kaili, Guizhou. 18 April.
  1994b Interview with author. Kaili, Guizhou. 28 April.
Picard, Michel
  1993 Cultural Tourism in Bali: National Integration and Regional Differentiation. In *Tourism in South-East Asia,* ed. M. Hitchcock et al., 71–98. London: Routledge.
Relph, Edward
  1976 *Place and Placelessness.* London: Pion.
Schein, Louisa
  1993 Popular Culture and the Production of Difference: The Miao and China. Ph.D. diss., Department of Anthropology, University of California, Berkeley.
Shen, Ping, and Yuet-Sim Cheung, eds.
  1992 *China Folk Culture Villages.* Hong Kong: China Travel Advertising.
Solinger, Dorothy
  1977 *Regional Government and Political Integration in Southwest China, 1949–1954.* Berkeley: University of California Press.
Spence, Jonathan
  1981 *The Gate of Heavenly Peace.* New York: Penguin.
Wang, Shengxian
  1989 *Dongzu Wenhua Yu Xisu* (Dong culture and customs). Guiyang: Minzu.
Wood, Robert
  1993 Tourism, Culture, and the Sociology of Development. In *Tourism in South-East Asia,* ed. M. Hitchcock et al., 48–70. London: Routledge.
Yang, Guanxiong, et al., eds.
  1991 *Xinan Luyou Ziyuan Kaifa Yu Buju* (Development and distribution of tourism resources in the southwest). Beijing: Chinese Academy of Sciences.
Yang-Peterson, Yin
  1995 The Chinese Landscape as a Tourist Attraction: Image and Reality. In *Tourism in China: Geographic, Political, and Economic Perspectives,* ed. A. Lew and L. Yu, 141–154. Boulder, Colo.: Westview.

≫ 3

Commodifying Ethnicity:
State and Ethnic Tourism in Singapore

Any travel brochure invariably promises potential tourists a variety of sensory pleasures in the sights, smells, food, people, and geography of a particular place. It acts as a cultural broker that eases the foreigner's visit, offering solutions to the mundane hassles of travel: accommodation, money exchange, appropriate clothing, visa requirements, customs regulations, and so on. However, travel brochures generally leave out information such as internal conflicts that may plague a country, communication difficulties, intercultural misunderstandings, health hazards, traffic snarls, and tourist traps.

In similar ways, the state represents the repressed in tourism. Tourists are seldom aware of the agency of the state in structuring the images and the experiences of travel. Travel is perceived as a phenomenology of space and an encounter with the "other" and is seldom thought to be an encounter between individuals and the state or a society-state relationship. Nevertheless, the state lurks as an invisible presence in tourism. By providing infrastructural support for services, a state can determine the direction of growth of a tourist industry, and it can shape the package of images that have a cultural impact on the experience of travel.

Tourism is primarily an industry that generates foreign exchange.

Given its economic importance, the state has a stake in the business of providing services for tourists and overseeing private tourism enterprises. Most nations promote tourism and, in the process, they become planners of tourist development, marketers of cultural meanings, and arbiters of cultural practices (Wood 1984).

Tourism has international and national political implications. States exist in relation to other states. More specifically, a given nation-state seeks to be a cultural and political entity, distinct and separate from other nation-states, and tourism presents images of the distinctiveness of a particular nation-state to the international polity. The marketing of tourism is not unlike international diplomacy, a field that involves national image-management. States are concerned with projecting wholesome and "politically correct" images. Thus, travel brochures rarely reveal the endemic tensions and squalid sides of a given country.

The cultural identity that tourism projects to the international market simultaneously relates to the process of nation-building. Elements of tourism are at the same time the ingredients of nationalism: the identification with a place, a sense of historical past, the revival of cultural heritage, and the national integration of social groups. While tourism advances an awareness of the national entity, it also confers privileges on some local or specific groups. From a multitude of cultural, historical, and geographical forms, the state singles out a few for tourism. Such selectivity has implications for internal struggles whereby one cultural group appears to be sponsored or favored while other groups are forgotten or ignored.

Cultural diversity can be either a boon or a bane for the state. More often than not, government officials perceive ethnic differentiation as a constant source of headaches. Ethnic groups not only compete for scarce resources but also make claims and demands on state actors. Moreover, ethnic loyalties threaten to undermine the nationalist project of cultural unity within a given territory.

In a different context, ethnic diversity is seen as a blessing. Most of the time, the positive valorization of ethnic differentiation is based not on anthropological concerns for humanism or the survival of cultural groups but on largely monetary motives. Tourism in particular harnesses ethnicity as a resource to generate income and foreign exchange. States that have previously considered ethnic minorities as an embarrassment (minorities perceived as primordial "primitives"), as an alien nation (minorities refusing to assimilate to the dominant culture), as an anathema (minorities contesting the state over land rights and indigenous entitlements) now find that these same minorities may contribute to the economy via tourism.

As the globe becomes smaller and the areas left to be discovered are fewer, and as the demand for travel increases because of affordability and affluence, the frantic search for exotica leads the tourist industry to seek out neglected aborigines in China, Taiwan, and Australia, disenfranchised natives in America and Canada, and rejected outcasts such as the Ainu of Japan. In these ways, tourism brings to the forefront the complex relations between ethnicity and the state (Wood 1984, 1994, van den Berghe 1992).

This chapter examines the complex relationship between state, ethnicity, and tourism in Singapore. After describing the economic aspects of tourism in Singapore, I will examine the political foundations of tourism by discussing the role of the state in Singapore, its concern with international imaging, and its technocratic vision that led to the dismissal of history as nostalgia. Then I will discuss tourism as a cultural industry that commodifies ethnicity and the consequent tenuous links between ethnicity and the state.

Tourism as an Industry

Instituted in 1964, the Singapore Tourist Promotion Board (STPB) is a state organization that actively seeks to draw tourists from the international market. This organization sells Singapore overseas through fifteen regional offices in Frankfurt, London, Zurich, Paris, New York, Los Angeles, Chicago, Toronto, Sydney, Perth, Tokyo, Osaka, Seoul, Hong Kong, and Taipei. In addition to these specialist tourist bases, there are offices of the Singapore Economic Development Board and the Singapore Trade Development Board in India, China, the Middle East, and Northern Europe. These trade missions, as representatives of the STPB, connect potential tourists or business visitors with Singapore as a destination.

These offices not only provide beautiful travel literature but also undertake extensive foreign advertising that appears in major newspapers and broadcast media in many foreign countries. The STPB actively participates in international trade fairs and oversees domestic arrangements and ancillary services like hotels, tour operations, and leisure industries. Its activities highlight the fact that tourism in Singapore is a big business (Table 3.1).

The growth in Singapore tourism as indicated by the number of visitors and estimated tourism earnings is often touted as part of Singapore's economic success as a newly industrialized country, one

Table 3.1 Tourist Arrivals and Spending in
Singapore

	Number of Visitors	*Tourism Receipts**
1979	2.25 million	S$2.4 billion
1980	2.56 million	S$3.1 billion
1981	2.83 million	S$3.8 billion
1982	2.96 million	S$4.0 billion
1983	2.85 million	S$4.2 billion
1984	2.99 million	S$4.0 billion
1985	3.03 million	S$3.7 billion
1986	3.19 million	S$4.0 billion
1987	3.68 million	S$4.6 billion
1988	4.19 million	S$5.1 billion
1989	4.83 million	S$6.4 billion
1990	5.32 million	S$7.61 billion
1991	5.41 million	S$8.67 billion
1992	5.99 million	S$8.45 billion
1993	6.42 million	S$9.36 billion
1994	6.89 million	S$10.93 billion
1995	7.14 million	S$11.65 billion

*U.S.$1 = S$1.45.
Source: Singapore Tourist Promotion Board, Arrival Reports;
Singapore Annual Report on Tourism Statistics, 1995.

of the four dragons in the Pacific Rim. The figures are phenomenal
on two counts. First, there is a steady progression in the number of
visitors to Singapore despite global recession in major markets like
the United States, Japan, and Australia in the late 1980s and early
1990s. Large increases in tourists from Korea, Taiwan, Hong Kong,
China, and the Association of Southeast Asian Nations (ASEAN)
more than offset the impact of economic slowdown of major industrialized countries. In this respect, the tourist industry in Singapore is
gaining from the economic expansion in the Asia-Pacific region. Its
growth depends not so much on the internal efforts of the STPB's
marketing strategies as on the external changes in neighboring Asian
societies, particularly the high consumption patterns of an emerging
middle class.

Second, Singapore is one of the few countries in the world that receive visitors numbering more than twice the national population. In 1984, the population of Singapore was 2.4 million people and there were 2.99 million visitors. In 1993, the 6.4 million visitors more than doubled the size of the population of 3.1 million. Although Singapore is the smallest nation in ASEAN, it has the largest number of visitors, followed by Malaysia, Thailand, Indonesia, the Philippines, and Brunei. Each year, more than 80 percent of the visitors are tourists, while the remainder are business and convention travelers.

The growth of the tourist industry in Singapore can be understood in the broader context of a state apparatus that is efficient both economically and politically. For the past three decades, Singapore has been ruled by a dominant political party of elites, the People's Action Party, without any significant countervailing center of power. This one-party supremacy has meant that government, public bureaucracies, and political party are virtually synonymous institutions or categories. When there is no separation of powers and when external opposition and internal dissent are effectively handicapped, the state eventually dominates every institutional sphere of social life.

The state in Singapore has a virtual monopoly on education, social services, and public utilities. It is the major landlord, with more than 80 percent of the population living in state housing. Television, radio, telephone, and new communication technologies are state owned, while the new media and entertainment machinery of film and popular music are state controlled through licensing, censorship, and import restrictions. State involvement in every institutional area facilitates the coordination of plans and execution of policies. Thus, the tourist board can expect the cooperation of the Ministry of Environment, the Urban Redevelopment Authority, the Economic Development Board, the Ministry of Transportation, the television network, and other bodies in implementing its tourist campaigns.

The Singapore state operates its agencies as if they were economic enterprises: minimizing costs and maximizing returns, producing results and consumer satisfaction. "The STPB adopts a forward-looking strategic approach in planning for the future and in the use of technology to promote sustainable growth and enhance visitor satisfaction" (MITA 1993, 101). Most state agencies, including the STPB, are called statutory boards. Distinct from the civil service, which is concerned with mundane state administration, statutory boards are expected to be proactive in marketing strategies, in upgrading skills and technology, and in making profits. All the key statutory boards in Singapore—the Telecommunications Authority, the Housing Development Board, the Urban Redevelopment Authority, the Port of Singapore Authority, the Public Utilities Board, the Television Corporation, and others—have operated as enterprises that generate revenue and surplus. Collectively, they confer political legitimacy to the ruling party, which can then boast of successfully delivering economic goods to the electorate.

The state in Singapore can thus be characterized as authoritarian paternalism that works. By monopolizing institutions and stymieing opposition, it can effectively devise and implement policies despite the will or discontent of segments of the populace. At the same time, the state promises economic growth, efficiency, and security. One indication of the wealth and efficiency of the state is its net foreign reserves, comprising gold, foreign exchange assets, and special drawing rights. In 1988, Singapore had net foreign reserves worth S$33 billion (Sullivan 1991, 159). By the end of 1995, these had increased to S$97.3 billion.

Tourism as International Image-Making

Just as individuals in daily life attempt to control impressions others form of them (Goffman 1959), politicians and nation-states employ artifice and ritual to project favorable images to their constituencies or audience (Adatto 1993). The proverbial example of image-making is the wall built in Manila when the Philippines hosted an International Monetary Fund meeting and international beauty pageant. This wall was intended to shield foreign visitors from the slums and squatters that not only constituted an eyesore but also revealed a symptom of national neglect. The front stage of touristic spectacle and the back stage of harsh facts of daily life are instances of impression management (MacCannell 1989).

The state in Singapore is particularly obsessed with images presented both to its citizens and to the international audience, and its program of image management involves the control of the mass media wherein negative commentaries or unflattering reports on Singapore are forbidden. When the foreign media covers such information, the state will restrict its circulation in Singapore, enforce censorship, or impose a fine for defamation (Parker 1988, Hachten 1993, Lent 1984). Major news sources such as *Newsweek, Time,* the *Economist, Far Eastern Economic Review, Asiaweek,* the *Asian Wall Street Journal,* and the *International Herald Tribune* have suffered the brunt of state censorship and restriction in Singapore.

The management of information is part of a wider network of social control whereby the state intervenes in the minutiae of private life, engineering the citizen's family, morality, education, housing, work, personal finances, and pattern of consumption. State regulation of everyday life, however, is a relatively recent phenomenon. In the colonial era, the British administrators treated their subjects essentially as self-contained communities. To avoid potential ethnic tensions, the British created geographical divisions for various ethnic and dialect groups (Hodder 1953). These divisions, however, did not inhibit social interaction. The diverse communities mingled, especially in the context of the marketplace of trade and commerce, developing a *lingua franca* called "bazaar Malay" as a means of communication (Furnivall 1948).

The relative autonomy of communities under colonial administration was eclipsed when power was transferred from the British to the new, local elites. In other words, the omnipotence of the state began in the early 1960s when the dominant political party saw itself as architect of a new nation, principally in charge of economic and urban development. In its role as economic planner and developer, broad and sweeping changes transformed the place and the people.

Before political independence in 1965, Singapore was like any other Southeast Asian city, an apparently haphazard maze and mix of diverse land uses (McGee 1967). There were no zoning laws; the central business district was the hub of day and night life; high-rise multinational commercial buildings stood beside low-rise merchant shops of the local petty bourgeoisie; hawkers and peddlers sold fish, vegetables, meat, and general produce on the street pavements. On the coast were fishing villages where huts, crudely built but functionally adequate, stood on stilts *(kelongs),* with little river boats (sampans and bumboats) tottering along with the waves and tides. Beginning in the late 1960s, urban and industrial development progressively bulldozed such landscapes and living traditions (Gamer 1972).

Two mass campaigns instituted at this time were Keep Singapore Clean and Towards a Green Garden City—self-conscious efforts of the new nation-state to construct and transform a new environment for tourism and urban development. Streets and roads were rebuilt, as far as possible, according to the American grid pattern, thus replacing the British style of winding, unplanned streets. Parks and open spaces were landscaped with new forms of greenery. A September date was officially proclaimed as annual tree-planting day, and ministers of state visited schools, government offices, and community centers for a ceremonial ritual of tree planting. Fruit trees were replaced by decorative trees to avoid the sight of rotten fruits dropping from the branches. Shop owners were told to tidy their frontages. Littering on the streets became a public offense punishable by a S$500 fine, while spitting was liable to a S$100 fine.

As early as 1965, the tourism authority enlisted the Ministry of Health in an "island-wide campaign to stimulate public interest to 'Keep Our City Clean,' especially in places frequented by tourists" (Singapore Tourist Association 1966/1967, 7). Buildings and gas stations along Orchard Road, the heart of the tourist belt, were "encouraged to set up small gardens that would make their frontages more attractive." October was the month of Keep Singapore Clean, and cleanliness competitions were organized in subsequent years to award shops with neat and tidy decor (Singapore Tourist Association 1968/1969).

These campaigns included the cleansing of cultural forms that were considered unappealing to tourists. Thus, the ingredients of what urban economists call the "informal sector" of economic production, consisting of labor-intensive but low-capital inputs—hawking, petty commodity production, cottage industries, and night bazaars on street pavements *(pasar malam)*—progressively faded from the urban scene. Street hawking became illegal.

The cleaning and the cleansing of the city-state have been so successful that foreign travel guidebooks and foreign observers have commented on the tidiness and cleanliness of the city, observations that suggest the city is antiseptic and the culture sterile. It was first started in 1965, and the cleanliness campaign continues today. Recalcitrant litterbugs must spend a day picking up trash in public spaces, wearing a vest with the words "corrective work order" printed in neon colors to catch the attention of passersby—reminiscent of prisoners toiling in a chain gang.

Social historians have proposed that matters of cleanliness are social codes that reveal information about how people conduct their everyday lives and how they perceive themselves and others (Wilkie 1994, 144). In Singapore, the role of the state in instituting cleanliness campaigns is congruent with the political dramaturgy and image management of Singapore as a nation-state.

Between 1963 and 1965, Singapore was part of Malaysia (including Malaya, Sarawak, and Sabah). Ousted by Malaysia in 1965, the Singapore state defined itself against its neighboring countries. Massive restructuring of economic and social institutions occurred, and cleanliness was a metaphorical corollary of such social transformations. Today, cleanliness makes Singapore remarkably distinct from neighboring countries.

Beyond the health correlate, cleanliness represents aspirations of upward social mobility and the "civilizing process" of taming those habits that are deemed boorish and backward (Elias 1978). Many state officials in Singapore were educated in England and America. Westernized and upwardly mobile, these state authorities chose to spruce up the city in the clean-green campaigns instead of encouraging the blossoming of street life.

According to Mary Douglas (1966), the obsession with cleanliness and dirt is symbolic of larger concerns with order and chaos, conformity and deviance. A tightly controlled society, as symbolized by cleanliness and orderliness, is particularly intolerant of deviance and divergence, which threaten the symbolic order and taint its image. The case of Bugis Street illustrates this point. Although not advertised in any official and commercial tourist literature, for a long time Bugis Street had been a popular haunt that attracted tourists who learned of its existence through word of mouth and cabdrivers.

After midnight, glamorous transsexuals from all over the world paraded in stunning and provocative garb, selling pictures of themselves to amused tourists or offering sundry services to the lonely. This exotic and seamy place of drag queens had a long history in Singapore: during the period of British rule, these transsexuals and transvestites catered to the sexual and entertainment needs of British soldiers, officials, and male immigrants. Bugis Street outlived the British withdrawal of military troops by drawing interested tourists, locals, and military men from Australia and New Zealand (ANZAK forces). And Singapore became an Asian capital for sex-change surgery (Ratnam 1991).

Although a popular tourist spot, Bugis Street represented all that the state authorities in Singapore wished to eradicate. It was at odds with the orderliness and control that the authorities sought to project as an image of the nation-state in the clean-green campaigns. The cleanliness movement involved efforts to cleanse the city of the "dirt" in social life, symbolized by informal economic activities that included prostitution, night bazaars, and vibrant street cultures.

State authorities were so adamant about maintaining a clean and orderly image that in 1979 they barred Hollywood producer Peter Bogdanovich from reentering the country after he had shot a film called *Saint Jack,* which was about a hustler wrestling with his con-

science amidst rampant graft and treachery in the Singapore under-
world of the early 1970s. Based on a bestselling novel by Paul
Theroux (1973), the film aroused the wrath of state authorities. The
world of brothels, including Bugis Street, and political intrigue portrayed in the film jarred the nation-state image that the authorities
hoped to project to the international polity. Both the film and the
director were banned in Singapore. Subsequently, plans were announced to demolish Bugis Street (*Economist* 1985). Alcohol, the
sale of pirated cassettes, stalls selling pig-intestine stew or turtle
soup, and sexual proclivities were, in official eyes, "dirt" that could
be found in Bugis Street and that was to be cleansed by purification
rituals of urban renewal.

Today, the erotica and exotica of international transsexualism and
Bugis Street are a thing of the past. Sex-change operations are no
longer available. The original Bugis Street made way for the mass
transit subway. Nearby stands "Bugis Junction," an area filled with
shops and restaurants that bears no relation to the activities of Bugis
Street except for the name. Bugis Junction is not even a sanitized version of the past. Modeled after Easton Center, a huge, glassed-in mall
in Toronto, Canada, Bugis Junction resembles part of Yonge Street
transplanted to Singapore.

The Technocratic Spirit and the Erasure of History

The campaigns that led to the cleansing of cultural forms were
brooms that swept away history, tradition, and heritage. In the cultural ethos of Singapore, history is regarded as insignificant or irrelevant. Such collective amnesia is partly a result of legitimation crisis:
in order to build a new nation the new state elites must transfer the
loyalties of the population from the colonial past and toward the
new regime. Nation-building thus entails forgetting some of the past.
A history that involved colonization by the British and expulsion by
the Malaysian Federation of States is, in the eyes of the new state
elites, not worthy of collective memory.

Collective amnesia stems also from a mentality of instrumental
reasoning (Marcuse 1968). In this mode of orientation, debates over
ends and goals are supplanted by an emphasis on means and technique. From the point of view of the state, debates about a good,
moral, or just society are endless and detract from the pressing need
to get on with the business of economic development. The focus thus
shifts to policy and planning. By actively orchestrating a symphony
of local corporate capitalism and multinational investments, state

elites in Singapore perceive themselves to be rational planners and social engineers (Wilson 1978).

While the dominant political party of elites is composed of financiers, economic entrepreneurs, and military men, a high premium is placed on system engineers to run the national economy and manage the everyday lives of the citizens (Sandhu and Wheatley 1989). The values of technocrats are marked by hardheaded pragmatism and instrumental rationality. Such values surface again and again in debates over history, restoration, and preservation.

In its purification rites of urban renewal, the state has erased large chunks of history as embodied in buildings and lifestyles. In 1982, plans were announced to demolish vast sections of Chinatown, Orchard Road, and other locations rich in architectural styles but located in choice areas with prime land values. The official justification for the demolition was that the buildings and houses were derelict and unsuitable for habitation. This proposal sparked a series of protest letters to the press. Preservation groups attempted to salvage the few visible embodiments of history that remained in Singapore— no easy task because in the eyes of state officials the past more often than not is construed as an enemy of modernity, obstructing the march of economic progress. Moreover, the ostensibly dispassionate approach of technocrats would dismiss all identification with the past as mere nostalgia, which had little place in the drive toward technological advance (Doggett 1983).

Accordingly, the preservation groups did not frame their arguments along lines of historical sentiment, but instead used the technocratic logic of instrumental reasoning and forward thinking. They argued that the low-rise and unique styles of housing in Chinatown and Emerald Hill were picturesque remnants that should be capitalized on by the tourist industry. As a compromise, large sections of Chinatown and Emerald Hill were demolished for the development of shopping complexes, office buildings, and hotels, while a few structures were preserved for tourism.

The demolition of parts of Chinatown is not merely a physical process of geographical transformation but also a sociopolitical act of state control. First, it represents the cleansing of deviant forms in the same manner in which Bugis Street was disinfected. Historically, Chinatown bustled with activities day and night centered around restaurants, theaters, singing halls, brothels, licensed opium dens (opium being a source of revenue in the colonial period), gambling houses, and Chinese secret societies. Through land clearance under the guise of urban renewal, the state effectively capped the activities of Chinese secret societies and seized a stronghold over gambling and prostitution.

Second, the demolition of parts of Chinatown represents an overall pattern of social engineering of the Chinese population. In 1979, the state instituted a nationwide Speak Mandarin Campaign in which the Chinese were encouraged to abandon their diverse dialects for a common language, Mandarin. Chinatown has always been a seedbed of Hokkien, Teochew, Cantonese, Hakka, and Hainanese dialects. Since the colonial period, dialect groups specialized in certain trades, occupations, and shops (DeGlopper 1991, 95). Organized as kinship units, these dialect or ethnic enterprises maintained their longevity through the intergenerational transfer of business and trade. The bulldozing of these shops in Chinatown destroyed these linkages and dispersed the linguistic enclaves. Groups were resettled in public housing.

Third, the demolition of segments of Chinatown reflects not just the primacy of the present over the past but also the neglect of the weak and the minority. One of the most colorful parts of Chinatown that has now disappeared was Sago Lane, which the Chinese called "street of the dead." The lane contained a row of funeral parlors and shops making and selling coffins, incense, and paper effigies of cars and houses, which were burnt together with the deceased's personal clothing. Above the shops were "death houses," where the infirm and old would lie, waiting for their final days.

Most of the dying were single immigrants. One prominent group was the Samsui women, who came from three districts of Kwantung in China and were easily identified by their scarlet headdress and loose black *samfoos* (jacket and trousers). They lived frugally, were mostly vegetarians, and were known to have kind and cheerful dispositions. They were remarkably industrious workers, toiling in construction sites and hard manual labor. By 1941, there were several thousands of Samsui women. But since many did not marry, they were the last of their people.

Today, a residential block, food center, market, and pedestrian walkway exist in place of Sago Lane. The erasure of history and the dismissal of things associated with the past perhaps represent the refusal to acknowledge the role of Samsui women and other immigrants in the economic growth and building of Singapore. School textbooks in Singapore chart a history of leaders and statesmen, never a history of the laboring class. The disappearance of Sago Lane reinforces such collective amnesia.

The clearance of Orchard Road took on a different cast, motivated by economic concerns rather than by social engineering. The list of buildings, monuments, and landmarks razed on Orchard Road is endlessly long (Tyers 1993, Lee 1990). Because Orchard Road is prime land and a tourist belt, low-rise units have been replaced by towering buildings. Indeed, not one of the old buildings and two-storied shophouses remains.

In this setting, religious land-use appears incongruous or anachronistic. Thus, Sivan Temple, a Hindu place of worship that dated back to the 1820s, was demolished to make way for a rapid transit stop. The primacy of economics makes Orchard Road a predictable street of shopping centers, hotels, offices, fastfood chains, and cineplexes. Few people would have guessed that Orchard Road was once an orchard of nutmeg and fruit trees.

Even though the past is often dismissed as romantic humbug or as a stumbling block to future growth, it can be "put on parade for tourists" (Sharp 1987). There are a few sites that STPB would classify as heritage tourism: Clarke Quay, Emerald Hill, Empress Place, Telok Ayer Market, and Raffles Hotel. All of these are reconstructed beyond recognition from their original state, making them new places rather than old. Even tourists feel that most of these places are reminiscent of Disneyland with its smarmy sleekness (McKillop 1991, Schoenberger 1992).

Ronald Lewcock, a UNESCO consultant, contends that such heritage tourism is an "extreme of prostituting oneself and falsifying the natural environment" (quoted in Powell 1994, 27). He argues that alterations in the built environment prompted by tourism miss the point about conservation. Conservation is a spirit, a sense of collective memory stemming from and directed toward an indigenous culture. Heritage tourism is a misnomer, for when the built environment is altered for the sake of tourist dollars, it has little to do with cultural memory and identity.

Ethnic Tourism in Surprising Singapore

Geography and landscape are not selling points for tourism in Singapore. Priorities of industrial and urban development have left little picturesque scenery for the mass tourist. The small island of 225 square miles (584 square kilometers) is largely a built-up area of commercial buildings and multistoried apartments that are not unique in design because they are mass constructed by the state. There is no differentiating characteristic of the environment when compared with any other metropolitan city.

And given the historical amnesia or erasure of most of the history of the settlement through cleanliness campaigns and technocratic rejection of the past, heritage tourism is not something the STPB can boast about. In place of scenery and heritage, the tourist industry capitalizes on the country's multicultural traditions. The STPB has stressed the uniqueness or exoticness of Singapore by marketing the traditions of different ethnic groups. Images of ethnic traditions are emphasized repeatedly in tourist attractions such as shopping areas, places of worship, festivals and public holidays, food, and cultural performances.

The first few pages of a colorful and glossy tourist brochure (published in 1983 and circulated locally and internationally) introduce Singapore as a modern country with a rich diversity of ethnic traditions:

> Singapore today has been transformed from the entrepot of old as commerce and industry have grown in importance. Its sophisticated communications and transport networks, its remarkable cleanliness and modern facilities have produced an island that would surpass even Raffles' most ambitious dreams. One aspect of Singapore that Raffles would recognize is its multi-racial makeup: Singapore's population of 2.5 million is 76% Chinese, 15% Malay, 7% Indian and Pakistani and 2% Others. Mosques, temples and churches exist virtually side by side in Singapore, where there is complete freedom of worship. Constant contact with each other has led to a rare harmony and tolerance. This equality among races is present even when it comes to languages (*Surprising Singapore: A Magic Place of Many Worlds*, 1983, 4–5).

This message is repeated ten years later in another tourist brochure from the STPB:

> Singapore is a surprising contrast of racial and cultural roots. Immigrants came from China, Indonesia, India and the Middle East, joining the local Malay villagers and fisherman and seeking a better life for themselves and their families. Their belongings were few, their traditions, costumes, language, cuisines, festivals and religions were rich and varied. To help prevent conflict and misunderstanding, Raffles divided the town into separate Chinese, Malay and Indian enclaves. Although the communities today live harmoniously together, each racial group has retained its own cultural identity and visitors today can delight in the cultural variety that exists throughout the older parts of the city (*Surprising Singapore*, 1993, 4).

The brochure does include recreational sites, theme parks, and nightlife, but the introductory remarks on ethnic traditions in the first few pages set the tone and serve as the baseline for other forms of tourism. Thus, sections on shopping, festivals, and food refer back to ethnicity. While elsewhere ethnic tourism is a kind of "special interest tourism" catering to a particular kind of clientele (Harron and Weiler 1992), ethnic tourism in Singapore is general tourism: experiences of sights and taste are organized around the broad theme of ethnicity.

The Commodification of Ethnicity

When the tourist industry commodifies ethnicity, producing ethnic goods and behaviors for consumption of visitors (Swain 1990), certain transformations of ethnicity take place. Tourism is contextualized in an existing system of native ethnic relations (van den Berghe 1980), but the process of commodification reconstructs and changes these ethnic categories in subtle ways (MacCannell 1984, Cohen 1988).

In particular, commodification obscures the gap between living ethnic traditions and the official versions of those traditions. In the marketing of ethnicity in Singapore, the finer distinctions that exist in everyday life become blurred. Official brochures and handbooks give the impression of four categories of ethnicity: Chinese, Malay, Indian, and Other. These categories are always spoken of and presented in that order: CMIO.

In reality, there are boundaries within a given Chinese group, where at least sixteen categories can be distinguished on the basis of dialect and province of origin in China, the most common being Hokkien, Teochew, Cantonese, Hainanese, and Khek. These various groups differ not only in terms of cuisine but also in regard to celebrations, customary practices, and, most importantly, language. A Cantonese and a Hokkien who speak their respective languages will not understand one another.

Within the category of Malay, there are more than seven groups defined in terms of locality of origin in different parts of the Malay Archipelago: Javanese, Bataks, Minangkabau, Bugis, Banjarese, and so on. And within the category of Indian, there are the Tamils, Hindus, Gujerati, Bengali, Punjabi, Malayalam, Sikhs, Sinhalese, Gurkhali, and many others distinguished by language, religion, caste, and region of origin.

As is true of the various Chinese groups, many of the languages spoken by these Indian groups are not necessarily mutually comprehensible. Finally, the "Other" classification is a residual category that covers a wide range of people from Australia to America and that often includes the offspring of interethnic unions, such as Eurasians.

The CMIO classification is, by and large, the product of colonial administration. The British played a large part in the immigration of peoples from China and India to secure a cheap source of labor for the colonial exploitation of resources. Given all the various groups, the colonial administrators found it expedient to classify immigrants according to the nation-state of origin (India, China, Malay Archipelago). For this reason, ethnic labels carried the pervasive ideology of the nation-state during that period of British imperialism and were essentially administrative categories that facilitated day-to-day governance by the British civil service.

The CMIO categories were convenient labels for bureaucratic functions of form-filling and rational administration, but the British recognized much finer distinctions in census surveys. In the census of 1881, forty-seven ethnic groups were named; these increased to fifty-six in the 1921 census (Purushotam 1995). The reduction of ethnicity to four categories and the use of these narrow classifications in official policy began when Singapore was granted sovereign and independent status on 9 August 1965.

The achievement of new nationhood forged new relations between the state and individuals through the concept of citizenship. Citizenship was proven by a personal identity card, which carried the name, date of birth, and ethnic origin of the individual. Commemorative stamps of that era depicted four different colored hands gripped in a rectangular formation to symbolize national unity of the four ethnic groups. School textbooks depicted ethnic groups in their respective ethnic costumes interacting in the playground, school, and neighborhood.

Following this CMIO logic, the STPB today produces ethnic goods in the form of shopping regions, places of worship, festivals, and food. Tourists in Singapore are encouraged to shop in ethnic enclaves like Chinatown, Arab Street (Muslims and Malays), and Little India (Serangoon Road). Religious shrines singled out as tourist spots correspond with the CMIO categorization: Thian Hock Keng temple ("Chinese," actually Hokkien), Sultan Mosque ("Malay," actually attended also by Indian Muslims), Sri Veerama Kaliaman Temple ("Indian," actually Hindu), and St. Andrew's Cathedral ("Other," actually attended by diverse ethnic groups).

In practice, the religious pluralism of Singapore is marked by varieties of Buddhism, Islam, Christianity, Taoism, Shintoism, Sikhism, Jainism, Judaism, Hinduism, and Zoroastrianism. These religions are drawn from various ethnic groups but are not necessarily coterminous with ethnicity (Clammer 1991).

In the calendar of events, the STPB promotes festivals and celebrations largely along ethnic lines. These festivals coincide with the CMIO distinctions: Lunar New Year, Chingay Festival, Festival of the Hungry Ghosts, and Mooncake Festival (Chinese), Hari Raya Puasa (Malay), Thaipusam and Deepavali (Indian), and National Day, which commemorates the nation's independence by a display of these cultural traditions coexisting harmoniously. Although these festivals only occur once a year and tourists seldom plan their arrival according to these dates, they are colorful events expected to draw many spectators. Thaipusam is a particularly exotic ritual festival in which Hindu devotees pierce their bodies with spikes, hooks, and skewers in a three-kilometer walk from one temple to another.

The STPB's marketing strategy amplifies these events by adding more spectacle and prolonging the period of celebration. It gets private sponsors and public funds to participate in so-called light-ups of representative ethnic enclaves for a period of about fifteen days during the festive season. Thus, Chinatown is flooded with lights, lanterns, and decorations during the Chinese New Year, as is the Geylang area for the Malays during the festival of Ramadan and Serangoon Road for Indians at Deepavali. The year ends with the "Other" ethnic category, represented by Christmas decorations on Orchard Road, where the STPB holds contests to urge shopping centers and hotels to indulge in spectacular displays.

Even though the four CMIO categories are represented in festival light-ups, not all of them command equal attention or degree of elaboration. "Christmas at the Equator" is the most spectacular, largely because of commercial sponsorship: 100,000 sparkling lights and giant displays grace Orchard Road. Reflecting the dominant demographics of the Chinese, Chingay Festival is the most elaborate, consisting of a carnival of floats, pugilistic displays, lion and dragon dances, stilt walking, Chinese acrobats and operas, and other things Chinese.

Food is also advertised as generic to the respective ethnic groups—noodles (Chinese), satay (Malay skewered meat, and Indonesian dishes lumped under Malay), and curry and murtabak (Indian pancakes). In practice, food in Singapore represents the crossbreeding of ethnic elements: there are Chinese versions of satay and fish-head curries; the Muslims have *halal,* Chinese noodles and dishes prepared in accordance with Islamic principles; and *rojak,* a salad of local vegetables and spices, is eaten by all ethnic groups.

The manufacture of exoticness includes the objectification of women in ethnic costumes, as shown by this excerpt from *The Singapore Visitor:* "Costumes like the Malay *sarong kebaya,* a form-fitting batik sarong worn with a lacy overblouse which some say is the sexiest outfit worn by women anywhere! Then there's the Chinese *cheongsam,* another figure-hugging creation, its tight Mandarin collar offset by thigh-high slits on either side of the skirt! And finally, there's the *sari,* the most alluring way of arranging six meters of fabric on the female form that woman has ever devised! Exotic, provocative, and eternally lovely, these age-old costumes are all part of daily life here, visible evidence of the cultural melting pot that is Singapore" (c. 1985, 39–40).

In the late 1970s and the 1980s, the Cultural Theatre on Grange Road gave tourists a package of cultures, wrapped up in forty-five minutes of staged spectacle, appropriately called "Instant Asia" (*Singapore Visitor* c. 1985, 98). These packages were displays of Chinese, Malay, and Indian "cultural traditions": a snippet of classical Chinese opera, a Chinese lion dance, a Malay "folk" dance, and an Indian "traditional" dance (with a snake charmer). Today, the Cultural Theatre has made way for a shopping complex, and Instant Asia performances resurface on National Day pageants.

While the commodification of ethnicity for tourism sanitizes and reduces ethnic diversity to the four groupings, such cultural abbreviation is also typical of media production. For example, advertisements and television news stories are limited to a time spot of fifteen to no more than ninety seconds. Since the message must be condensed, visual representation often relies on stereotypes for the audience to identify readily with characters and themes.

Similarly, touristic images in broadcast advertisement and print literature seek to capture the attention of viewers and readers. Complexities and subtleties of ethnicity are abridged to achieve economy of communication. Moreover, the need to make everything look exotic for the potential tourist results in visual representation that is spectacular, extraordinary, and even exaggerated. The more perceptive tourists will not be surprised to discover in "Surprising Singapore" that many native peoples do not dress in ethnic costumes and are not surrounded by ethnic objects as displayed in travel brochures.

The Peranakans, an Ethnic Anomaly

The commodification of ethnicity selectively highlights and dramatizes the exotica of ethnic cultures for tourism, but it omits other groups in this process. In Singapore, the Peranakans are variously termed "Straits Chinese" (by virtue of their historical sojourn in the Straits Settlement of Singapore, Malacca, and Penang), *babas* (males), or *nonyas* (females) (Clammer 1980). Their settlement history qualifies them to represent the real heritage of Singapore, since their immigration preceded that of most other groups. But for a long time, the Peranakan culture has been ignored in the marketed tourist package of ethnic imagery because it does not fit neatly into any of the CMIO pigeonholes. Racially, the Peranakans are Chinese and are indistinguishable from other Chinese in facial and physical appearance, but they have few ties with China and do not belong to traditional Chinese clan associations.

Whereas the later Chinese migrants (*hua chiao*, or overseas Chinese) were oriented to China through kinship ties and hoped to return to their homeland, the Peranakans were more settled and regarded Singapore as their homeland. Having moved up the social ladder in the colonial administration, many Peranakans associated their ancestral land with backwardness and instead aligned themselves with the Europeans, cultivating recreational pursuits like football, riding, swimming, and shooting. They were the first to take advantage of the colonial administration by sending their children to English schools.

The Peranakans were also influenced by inhabitants of the Malay Archipelago, adopting Malay language, costume, and cuisine but not assimilating the Islamic religion. The female attire—the *sarong* and *kebaya*—was an adaptation of the Malay *baju kurong,* but with more extensive use of lace and embroidery to signify the Peranakans' higher social position. Indeed, Peranakan culture was rich in display, replete with ornate jewelry, finely embroidered cloth, distinctive porcelain, unique household objects that have now become antiques, and decoratively tiled houses.

The Peranakans are officially labeled "Chinese" on identity cards, forms, and census classifications. They constitute an anomaly in the CMIO model principally in matters concerning language. In the CMIO model, English, Mandarin, Malay, and Tamil are constitutionally recognized as the four official languages. These languages are mislabeled in official discourse as "mother tongues," even though not all Chinese speak Mandarin at home and not all Indians are literate in Tamil. Schoolchildren are made to learn their respective mother tongue as a language second to English.

The Peranakans are caught in this cultural muddle. Their children are required to read Mandarin, which by official definition is the mother tongue of the Chinese, but in reality Malay is their home language. The Peranakans have been traditionally multilingual, speaking Hokkien, English, and Malay patois. Few Peranakans speak Mandarin, and even fewer can read or write Mandarin.

The logic of the CMIO categorization is based on a multicultural model that presupposes and reinforces the separateness and uniqueness of each different ethnic group. However, the Peranakan group defies this separateness because it is a hybrid culture of Malay, British, and Chinese elements. For example, *nonya* cuisine blends Chinese ingredients with Malay spices like *sambal blachan* (chili and shrimp paste). Their variety of desserts is rich in coconut molasses *(gula melaka)* and coconut flakes. And many Peranakans traditionally eat with their fingers like Malays and Indians.

Another example of the diverse culture of the Peranakans is the architectural style, a bricolage of the Chinese baroque, neoclassical European design that originated in Malacca. These houses are scattered throughout Singapore, but those located in the tourist belt are problematic. Their unique architecture should be a draw for tourism, but, given the technocratic ethos that disdains the past as irrelevant, sentimental, and antidevelopment, old buildings have to give way to the new.

In the clash between conservation groups, the state, and tourism, certain concessions have been made. Since Orchard Road is the tourist thoroughfare, buildings along this road must be put to uses that generate revenue. The row of Peranakan residential houses at Emerald Hill escaped demolition because Emerald Hill is a side street of Orchard. Thus, in 1981 Emerald Hill was slated for conservation. But different standards were applied according to the distance from Orchard Road. The uphill residential properties on the gently sloping Emerald Hill had to be upgraded at the owners' expense. Owners could reassemble existing components of the building and add new materials to restore the architectural style. Down the hill, at the junction of Orchard Road, the Urban Redevelopment Authority demolished the old buildings, rebuilt new ones modeled after the original, and later sold these units for commercial purposes—thus giving birth to "Peranakan Place."

Architects make a distinction between restoration and reconstruction (Powell 1994, 17). Restoration adds new materials and secondary structures to existing structures while retaining specific materials of a building fabric. Reconstruction starts anew but replicates the demolished building and is usually followed by "adaptive reuse," in which the reconstructed building is put to new uses. Peranakan Place is an example of reconstruction and adaptive reuse. There was total demolition of all the old shophouses, and new ones have been built based on the design of the old. They are clearly oriented toward tourism, particularly shopping.

The reconstruction of Peranakan Place for tourism does not imply an official valorization of the Peranakan culture. Reconstruction and adaptive reuse imbue Peranakan Place with a spirit of shopping, not ethnicity, a sense of modernity, not heritage. It is not a specialized market; the sundry goods and various foods sold here can be bought from any shop in Singapore. The aura of heritage is subdued by new interiors and pastel paint. The new exists in the guise of a reconstructed past.

In recent years, official tourist guidebooks refer to Peranakan culture, particularly the *nonya* cuisine, which is not found in many other parts of Asia. But such a brief mention does not bestow on Peranakans the same degree of attention accorded to the Chinese, Malays, and Indians. Officially, the Peranakans are conceived as a mere subset of the Chinese category and not as a distinctive cultural group. The CMIO model for commodifying ethnicity thus poses categorical limits on the state endorsement of the Peranakans.

More important, the logic of commodifying ethnicity for tourism is marketability. *Nonya* cuisine, no matter how unique and indigenous it may be, does not always suit the palates of tourists. The spicy sting of chilies, the pungent odor of fermented prawn paste, and the decadent richness of coconut molasses are all acquired tastes. Tourists who on average stay no more than three days in Singapore seldom become *nonya* fans.

Outside the realm of state tourism, however, Peranakan culture finds sustenance in the local population and private sponsorship. *Nonya* cuisine is an elaborate art that involves gastronomic skills and lengthy preparation, which have traditionally confined it to domestic consumption, being less than economical for restaurant production. But local demand for the food has increased geometrically over the last decade, stimulated principally by changes in labor conditions.

Since most Singaporeans work until seven or later in the evening, eating out is a convenient alternative to home cooking. Eating out is also part of the consumerist revolution sparked by an emerging middle class and general affluence. *Nonya* food has always been available in local hawker kiosks as side dishes to the Chinese menu. In recent years, specialist *nonya* restaurants have sprouted and *nonya* recipes have been codified in popular cookbooks. Automation has reduced the labor-intensive production of *nonya* cakes, snacks, and tidbits, which are now ubiquitous.

While Peranakan food has become part of popular consumption, Peranakan theater has emerged as a sign of ethnic renaissance. Peranakan theater centers on domestic life and wedding pageants, which display their intricate costumes. While theater in general is limited to an elite audience, Peranakan theater has even a smaller audience because of its use of Baba Malay patois, which is not popularly understood and is definitely beyond the comprehension of tourists. Nevertheless, there is a clear burgeoning of Peranakan theater (Chia 1994, 187), sustained by corporate sponsors and Peranakan audiences. The revitalization of the arts in Singapore provides a space for Peranakan theater to grow.

Despite these two trends, Felix Chia (1994), an expert on Peranakan culture, predicts its demise in generations to come. Interethnic marriage dwindles the population of the Peranakan group and dilutes the influence that Peranakan grandparents have over the socialization of children. Compulsory bilingualism in school forces Peranakan children to master English and Mandarin to the neglect of Baba Malay. The breed of *nonya* artisans who painstakingly embroidered beads and silk onto purses, shoes, collars, and kneecaps has already vanished (Chia 1983).

Tourism, the State, and Ethnicity

Ethnic classifications, ethnic boundaries, and ethnic relations do not simply arise from ecological conditions or group dynamics. Such manifestations of ethnicity are to a great extent shaped by the state (Brass 1985, Eriksen 1993, Brown 1994), which plays a major role in defining the terms of ethnic relations, in mediating or escalating ethnic conflicts, and in managing ethnicities.

In Singapore, the state manages cultural diversity in reductionist terms. The CMIO model cognitively streamlines society into four ethnic groups (or "races" in official discourse and public consciousness). The conceptual map of ethnicity is simplified as finer distinctions of cultural groups are collapsed into these four categories. In addition to the cognitive economy of categorization, the CMIO eases the administrative tasks of the state—filling out forms is easier when there are only four races rather than fifty-four groups. Bureaucratic officials tend to deal with clients not as unique individuals but in terms of typecast roles.

When tourism in Singapore mines, manufactures, and markets ethnicity as commodities, it operationalizes the preexisting CMIO model. Reducing Singapore society into four groups makes communication in mass advertising and mass tourism much easier and more economical. Mass tourists are not anthropologists who seek a textured understanding of another culture; rather, they often want a formula of an abbreviated culture.

While the CMIO model is in tune with the demands of mass society and global consumerism, it influences ethnic stereotyping in Singapore. On the one hand, most Singaporeans are aware that folk dances and exotic customs are no more than performances presented for the sake of tourist dollars and no more than extraordinary events represented in visual layouts. And Chinese who interact within their own ethnic group are not blind to the reality of finer distinctions among the Hokkien, the Teochew, or the Cantonese, despite the official tendency to lump these groups into one category.

However, *interethnic* perceptions are less sophisticated and tend to follow official CMIO labels (Purushotam 1995). Thus, a Hokkien tends to perceive the Malays as a uniform group ("they all look alike"), and all Indians are thought to be one and the same (Wu 1982, 13). In addition, tourists who are unaware of the wide diversity interact with Singaporeans according to the official stereotypes presented in tourist imagery. The locals would thus find it difficult to escape the typecast of those packaged images.

To the extent that the CMIO model is continuously propagated by the state, the state in Singapore has made ethnicity a salient factor in social interaction. Generally, ethnicity, not social class, is the key marker of social differentiation in Singapore: "The first thing that one Singaporean normally wishes to know about another is whether he or she is Chinese, an Indian or a Malay: other possible criteria such as class, age or degree of educational attainment are of secondary importance in placing someone in the scheme of things" (Benjamin 1976, 120).

Ethnic tourism by itself does not forge such links between ethnicity and the state. Tourism represents one instance of operationalization of the CMIO model. Policies on language, education, social welfare, and national celebrations also operate on that model. Identity cards, bureaucratic forms, and official statistics constantly remind Singaporeans of their assigned race.

The CMIO model presumes the uniqueness and separateness of respective ethnic groups. This separateness does not foster or permit crossovers and hybridization: so the Peranakan case constitutes an anomaly. The presumption of separateness has the effect of cultural involution as individuals are pressured to identify with one ethnic group, to search for their respective ethnic roots, and to act according to the official stereotypes of their cultural traditions. Cultural involution is the return to ethnic origins to define oneself, and this return assumes that ethnicity is a primeval and immutable essence.

For example, in mandatory bilingual education, all racial Chinese must learn Mandarin, even if it is not their home language, and all Indians must read Tamil, even if it is not the language of the diverse Indian communities. It is extremely difficult for a Punjabi child to read Mandarin as a second language in school since Tamil has already been thrust upon him or her. "Singapore's multiracialism puts Chinese people under pressure to become more Chinese, Indians more Indian, and Malays more Malay in their behaviour. . . . It is bringing about a marked degree of cultural involution in Singapore, in which each 'culture' turns in on itself in a cannibalistic manner, struggling to bring forth further manifestations of its distinctiveness" (Benjamin 1976, 122–124).

In moral education classes, pupils are expected to study the religion of their designated tradition: Confucian ethics for the Chinese, Islamic studies for the Malays, Hindu or Sikh studies for the Indians, and Buddhism or Christianity as options open to all. Pupils are not encouraged to learn about ethics and religion other than their own.

In social welfare, cultural involution returns individuals to their respective ethnic groups for support. The Chinese have the Chinese Development Assistance Council (CDAC), the Malays have the Council for the Development of the Singapore Muslim Community (MENDAKI), the Indians have the Singapore Indian Development Association (SINDA), and the Eurasians have the Eurasian Association Endowment Fund (EAEF). Each of these ethnic self-help groups provides financial support for educational advancement, tuition classes for underachievers, and welfare assistance for the needy.

The funds for such activities are obtained from a voluntary

monthly deduction from the paycheck of an ethnic member. Thus, a monthly one dollar debit from the salary of a Malay worker will automatically go to MENDAKI while one dollar of an Indian worker goes to SINDA. In effect, the state transforms social welfare into ethnic welfare: individuals provide support for, or seek assistance from, their own ethnic group and not society as a whole. Cultural involution in this sense potentially breeds communalism.

State officials (including tourist brochures) boast of the ethnic harmony in Singapore, as indicated by the absence of ethnic riots. However, open conflict is not a good gauge of ethnic relations, especially as tensions are always submerged and are in danger of surfacing and escalating in certain social contexts. Singapore is fortunate in registering high economic growth rates that trickle down to the general population. Should the economy plunge, social groups would have to compete for scarce resources and, given the salience of ethnicity, would rally along communal lines.

If interethnic marriage were an index of ethnic harmony, Singapore scores low. Between 1954 and 1984, marriages across ethnic lines remained at a stable 5 to 6 percent of all marriages (DeGlopper 1991, 102). Interethnic marriages comprised mostly divorced or widowed individuals. A 1990 survey of 706 Singaporeans found that the Chinese were the least receptive to marriage outside their group (*Straits Times,* 23 September 1990, 18).

Scholars like Brown (1993), Purushotam (1989), and Benjamin (1976) have noted that ethnic relations in Singapore are strained by official policies that purport to unite and incorporate various groups. If this analysis is true, ethnicity will always occupy a prominent place in social life, continuing to be a resource for the tourist industry for a long time to come.

References

Adatto, Kiku
  1993 *Picture Perfect: The Art and Artifice of Public Image Making.* New York: Basic Books.
Benjamin, Geoffrey
  1976 The Cultural Logic of Singapore's Multiracialism. In *Singapore: Society in Transition,* ed. Riaz Hassan, 115–133. Kuala Lumpur: Oxford University Press.
Brass, Paul, ed.
  1985 *Ethnic Groups and the State.* London: Croom-Helm.

Brown, David
  1993 The Corporatist Management of Ethnicity in Contemporary Singapore. In *Singapore Changes Guard,* ed. Garry Rodan, 16–33. New York: St. Martin's Press.
  1994 *The State and Ethnic Politics in South-East Asia.* London: Routledge.
Chia, Felix
  1983 *Ala Sayang!* Singapore: Eastern Universities Press.
  1994 *The Babas Revisited.* Singapore: Heinemann Asia.
Clammer, John
  1980 *Straits Chinese Society.* Singapore: Singapore University Press.
  1991 *The Sociology of Singapore Religion.* Singapore: Chopmen.
Cohen, Erik
  1988 Authenticity and Commoditization in Tourism. *Annals of Tourism Research* 15:371–386.
DeGlopper, Donald R.
  1991 The Society and Its Environment. In *Singapore: A Country Study,* ed. Barbara Leitch LePoer, 65–117. Washington, D.C.: Library of Congress.
Doggett, Marjorie
  1983 *Characters of Light: Early Buildings of Singapore.* Singapore: Times.
Douglas, Mary
  1966 *Purity and Danger.* London: Routledge.
The Economist
  1985 Singapore without Sin. *Economist,* 5 October, 42.
Elias, Norbert
  1978 *The Civilizing Process.* Vol. 1. New York: Pantheon.
Eriksen, Thomas Hylland
  1993 *Ethnicity and Nationalism.* London: Pluto.
Furnivall, J. S.
  1948 *Colonial Policy and Practice.* Cambridge: Cambridge University Press.
Gamer, Robert E.
  1972 *The Politics of Urban Development in Singapore.* Ithaca, N.Y.: Cornell University Press.
Goffman, Erving
  1959 *The Presentation of Self in Everyday Life.* New York: Doubleday.
Hachten, William
  1993 *The Growth of Media in the Third World.* Ames: Iowa State University Press.
Harron, Sylvia, and Betty Weiler
  1992 Ethnic Tourism. In *Special Interest Tourism,* ed. Betty Weiler and Colin Michael Hall, 82–94. New York: Halstead Press.

Hodder, B. W.
  1953   Racial Groupings in Singapore. *Journal of Tropical Geography* 1(October):25–36.

Lent, John
  1984   Restructuring of Mass Media in Malaysia and Singapore. *Bulletin of the Concerned Asian Scholars* 16(4):26–35.

Lee, Edwin
  1990   *Historic Buildings of Singapore*. Singapore: Preservation of Monuments Board.

MacCannell, Dean
  1984   Reconstructed Ethnicity: Tourism and Cultural Identity in Third World Communities. *Annals of Tourism Research* 11:375–392.
  1989   *The Tourist*. New York: Schocken.

Marcuse, Herbert
  1968   *One-Dimensional Man*. Boston: Beacon.

McGee, T. G .
  1967   *The Southeast Asian City*. New York: Praeger.

McKillop, Peter
  1991   Five Stars but No Soul: Raffles Hotel. *Newsweek,* 14 October, 25.

MITA (Ministry of Information and the Arts)
  1993   *Singapore 1993*. Publicity Division: Singapore Government Publication.

Parker, Elliott
  1988   Press Control in Singapore. *Australian Journalism Review* 10: 78–84.

Powell, Robert
  1994   *Living Legacy: Singapore's Architectural Heritage Renewed*. Singapore: Select Books.

Purushotam, Nirmala
  1989   Language and Linguistic Policies. In *Management of Success: The Moulding of Modern Singapore,* ed. Kernial Singh Sandhu and Paul Wheatley, 503–522. Singapore: Institute of Southeast Asian Studies.
  1995   *Disciplining Differences: "Race in Singapore."* National University of Singapore: Department of Sociology Working Papers, no. 126.

Ratnam, S. S., Victor Goh, and W. F. Tsoi
  1991   *Cries from Within: Transsexualism, Gender Confusion and Sex Change*. Singapore: Longman.

Sandhu, Kernial Singh, and Paul Wheatley, eds.
  1989   *Management of Success: The Moulding of Modern Singapore*. Singapore: Institute of Southeast Asian Studies.

Schoenberger, Karl
  1992   Face Lift Leaves Clubby Old Raffles a Bit Tight. *Los Angeles Times,* 22 March, L–3.

Sharp, Ilsa

1987   The Past Put on Parade for Tourists in Singapore. *Far Eastern Economic Review,* 5 March, 47–49.

Singapore Tourist Association

1966/1967 1968/1969   *The Annual Report.* Singapore.

Singapore Visitor

c.1985 *The Singapore Visitor.* Singapore: Creations and Communications.

Sullivan, Margaret

1991   The Economy. In *Singapore: A Country Study,* ed. Barbara Leitch LePoer, 119–174. Washington, D. C.: Library of Congress.

Swain, Margaret Byrne

1990   Commoditizing Ethnicity in Southwest China. *Cultural Survival Quarterly* 14(1):26–30.

Theroux, Paul

1973   *Saint Jack.* London: Bodley Head.

Tyers, Ray

1993   *Singapore Then and Now.* Singapore: Landmark Books.

van den Berghe, Pierre

1980   Tourism as Ethnic Relations: A Case Study of Cuzco, Peru. *Ethnic and Racial Studies* 3:375–392.

1992   Tourism and the Ethnic Division of Labor. *Annals of Tourism Research* 19:234–249.

Wilkie, Jacqueline S.

1994   Cleanliness. In *Encyclopedia of Social History,* ed. Peter Stearns, 144–145. New York: Garland.

Wilson, H. E.

1978   *Social Engineering in Singapore.* Singapore: Singapore University Press.

Wood, Robert E.

1984   Ethnic Tourism, the State and Cultural Change in Southeast Asia. *Annals of Tourism Research* 11:353–374.

1994   Cultural Tourism: Ethnic Options and Constructed Otherness. Manuscript presented at International Sociological Association Meeting, Bielefeld, Germany.

Wu, David Y. H.

1982   Ethnic Relations and Ethnicity in a City-State Singapore. In *Ethnicity and Interpersonal Interaction,* ed. David Y. H. Wu, 13–36. Singapore: Maruzen Asia.

➤ 4

Culturalizing Malaysia: Globalism, Tourism, Heritage, and the City in Georgetown

In February 1993, Kee Phaik Cheen, the chairperson of the tourism committee in the Malaysian state of Penang, announced that $400,000 (Malaysian *ringgit*) would be allocated from the state budget for restoration work on the "historic" Syed Alatas mansion in Lebuh Armenian (Armenian Street) in downtown Georgetown. It was also revealed that this sum would be augmented by several agencies: the federal government, which allocated a grant of $600,000 under the Sixth Malaysia Plan; the Penang Municipal Council, which set aside $200,000; and the German and French governments, which provided technical assistance for the restoration works. The main reason given by various officials for supporting the project was that it would contribute to the development of Malaysia's, and particularly Penang's, tourist industry.[1] To quote Kee on such projects:

> With the present emphasis, the city's colonial past, living traditions, architectural richness and multi-cultural heritage can be thematically re-created as "historical precincts," "ethnic enclaves," "zones of adaptive reuse," and "ensembles of aesthetic buildings." These, together with Penang's food and handicrafts, are cultural and heritage attractions which can be re-packaged in the form of informative "guided tours" that may even encourage "tourist participation" in the living

culture of Penang's people. Furthermore such products are readily marketable to incentive groups which are invariably here for a "cultural experience" (Kee 1994, 5).

While perhaps not so important a relative generator of national income as in other countries of the Asia-Pacific region and while its impact through direct interaction between tourists and locals is less intensive than in better-known regional tourist destinations such as Bali,[2] tourism in Malaysia is nonetheless of growing significance. In 1963, for example, Malaysia had only about 27,000 tourists. The number of tourist arrivals increased to 76,000 in 1970, 1.2 million in 1976, 2.25 million in 1980, 2.7 million in 1985, 3.67 million in 1989, and, during Visit Malaysia year in 1990, the number rose to 7.4 million, exceeding all expectations.[3] Significantly, the major proportion of Malaysia's tourist arrivals are not from the West, but from neighboring countries. In 1990, for example, 73.8 percent came from the ASEAN countries (mostly from Singapore), 6.8 percent from Japan, 2.6 percent from Taiwan, 2.6 percent from the United Kingdom, 2.0 percent from Australia, 2.0 percent from the United States, and the rest mainly from India, Hong Kong, Germany, Korea, and France.[4]

Given this expansion of tourism and the various attempts by the Malaysian government to promote its future growth, it is not surprising that the familiar debate between those who argue that tourism is harmful and those who argue that it is beneficial to the economic, social, and cultural life of the nation has been raised in the Malaysian context.[5] And yet despite the call—by the editors of this volume among others—for a more nuanced analysis of the relationship between tourism, the state, and culture, the growing literature on tourism and its impact on Malaysia still lacks detailed attention to particular cases of tourist-related development. Hence, this chapter explores a number of issues related to the very concrete example of "tourist development" in Georgetown.

Specifically I will use this example to raise two related issues. First, in discussing the particular case of urban renovation in the Lebuh Acheen–Lebuh Armenian district of Georgetown, I want to uncouple its apparently intimate relationship from the policy of tourist promotion. Along with other contributors to this volume, I shall argue that tourism constitutes only a part of what is actually going on here. Instead, the more closely one looks at the drive to renovate the Syed Alatas mansion, the more it appears to be embedded in more general cultural processes taking place in contemporary Malaysia. To grasp the significance of this particular case, therefore, requires us not so much to focus on the tourist industry, but, to borrow a term favored by Roland Robertson, to thematize the more general process of culturalization in Malaysia.

Second, I shall suggest that thematizing Malaysian culturalization takes us in two quite different directions, one local and one global. On the one hand, it leads us to examine closely the local factors that have given rise to projects such as the Lebuh Acheen–Lebuh Armenian restoration. In other words, the examination of a specific case leads us even further away from the problematic of tourism as a particular kind of interaction between West and East and toward a consideration of the local political and cultural forces that shape such developments.

The more we seek to understand the particular interests of the producers and consumers of "historic Georgetown" and the sorts of images that circulate among them, the more we realize that they are not generated simply by marketing exercises aimed at promoting Malaysia to foreign tourists. Instead, what becomes increasingly clear is that the forces behind the Georgetown urban conservation scheme stem from a much broader range of peculiarly local political and cultural circumstances. In this case, we should note especially the current drive by the Malaysian state to represent indigenous culture and spatiality in new ways to both outsiders and insiders. In addition, we should also consider how several nongovernmental local groups and institutions with different kinds of economic, political, cultural, aesthetic, and moral concerns are today assuming a highly involved and influential presence on the Penang urban scene.

On the other hand, it is evident that the process of culturalization is a global one and that thematizing Malaysian culturalization can only take place by understanding its relationship to an apparently global pattern. Thus, in examining a national pattern of culturalization, we are led back to cultural globalization and to one dimension of the tourism problematic, namely the so-called global/local and East/West dichotomies that are, paradoxically, themselves central to contemporary global culture.

Lebuh Acheen–Lebuh Armenian as Historical and Cultural Enclave

At least for many Western visitors to Penang, the streetscapes of downtown Georgetown constitute an eminently desirable object of what John Urry has called the "tourist gaze".[6] Like other such "sights" they are gazed upon for purposes not directly connected with paid work. Indeed, they provide a sharp contrast with the work environment. In Georgetown the gaze is directed to features of landscape and townscape that are not only geographically but also culturally separate from the daily experiences of tourists. Moreover, the gaze is increasingly being constructed through signs by a corps of tourist professionals and historical, technical, cultural, and architectural experts whose participation in the process of constructing these signs of old Georgetown helps to validate them as authentic (see Urry 1990, 93). A case in point is the "rehabilitation" and "revitalization" of the Lebuh Acheen–Lebuh Armenian district as a prime area for the tourist gaze.

After being declared a historical and cultural enclave in the structure plan prepared by the Penang Municipal Council, the Lebuh Acheen–Lebuh Armenian district then became an object for tourism development. In 1991, planners from the Universiti Sains Malaysia prepared a detailed description of the social, cultural, and architectural features of the area (Tan et al. 1991) and entered into discussions with community groups and the municipal council to push for restoration work, to provide amenities and improvements to benefit residents (particularly property owners), and to promote the area as a tourist destination. In addition, a local nongovernmental organization, the Penang Heritage Trust, was also pressing for the development of the district as a tourist precinct. These efforts had their first major reward early in 1993 when money was allocated for the restoration of the Syed Alatas mansion. Let us look at how these particular groups and individuals—governmental and nongovernmental—are seeking to construct the tourist gaze.

The overwhelming focus of attention in the district has been on a particular sign, or symbol, namely the built environment of Acheen and Armenian Streets, consisting of a number of "historic" buildings. A mosque, originally constructed in 1808 and said to be the oldest existing one in Penang, provides the focus for the enclave. Its distinctive octagonal minaret is of the early Mughal style, which spread to the region in the sixteenth century; its swallowtailed roof reflects the influence of Chinese Muslim settlers, and it features certain Anglo-Indian details such as wooden transoms, stucco work, and round brick columns in its outer aisle (Khoo 1990, 27). Other buildings the tourist is invited to gaze upon include a warehouse, the Gudang Acheh, or "Rumah Tinggi" that fronts on Beach Street and that was the first four-story building in Penang; textile shops; a 1940 Art Deco shophouse that functions as a bookshop; Acheen Street buildings that housed the Arab-run pilgrim agencies that flourished in the 1950s; and a bungalow at 128 Armenian Street built between 1860 and 1875 by Syed Mohamed Alatas, a trader, leader of the Red Flag Secret Society, and prominent Georgetown citizen in the late nineteenth century. This last building, acquired by the municipal council some years ago, is the focus of restoration efforts.[7]

It is planned that visitors to this cultural enclave will do more than gaze at buildings. An important feature of the plans is that the area will become a precinct in which tourists will interact more closely with, even directly consume, the objects of their gaze. One such proposal is for the provision of museums. For example, the chairman of the Mosque Heritage Committee has proposed that a former Quranic school (the former residence of Penang's first mufti) and the former office of the Jeddah Pilgrims ticketing agency be turned into a minimuseum/resource center and a Pilgrims Museum respectively at a cost of some $1.5 million to the federal government.[8] The Syed Alatas mansion is also slated to contain exhibits and a research and documentation center. Tourists will be encouraged to spend their money in proposed handicraft shops, restaurants, and hotels. In 1993, Penang's chief minister announced:

> Following Penang's high level of economic growth, it is now timely to develop upmarket restaurants, heritage hotels, cultural venues, elegant business premises and conference venues which make the most of our heritage buildings.

He proclaimed that the deputy general manager of the Penang Development Corporation, Tungku Idaura Askandar, would be given the task of coordinating heritage projects undertaken by the government and the private sector in order to make heritage development an integral part of Penang's "tourism products" (*New Straits Times,* 10 June 1993).

If the buildings of Acheen and Armenian Streets are signs or symbols that will serve to focus the tourist gaze, then what do they signify? This question is difficult to answer as the construction of the gaze is at an early stage and as there are few accounts by the prospective consumers of these images. But in a British guidebook, several key phrases from the description of a walk—or trishaw ride—through downtown Georgetown indicate how some Western tourists are likely to read their experiences. The book mentions Georgetown's

British heritage (many streets still carry British names); its unique, lively, and interesting street life; the numerous buildings that lend the town its historic atmosphere; and the wealth of architectural detail, riot of colors, statuary, and carvings.[9] This particular guidebook draws attention to the threat posed by urban redevelopment to these virtues of historic Georgetown, and it reflects the general focus found in most travel writing on Malaysia—whether promotional material emanating from Malaysia or by outsiders—on cultural diversity and multiculturalism.

There are several key points here. First, the general impression is that most tourists have visited Penang not for cultural or heritage tourism but largely for sun, sand, and sea in an exotic tropical locale, the "Pearl of the Orient." This exotic natural experience is provided not in Georgetown but in the various beach resorts to the north, notably Batu Ferringhi. Georgetown is a destination only for the more adventurous tourists and low-budget backpackers, some of whom are more interested in the street life and the lower priced accommodation located in the city center. In this case, however, it is not the "natural" attraction of the beach, but the cultural and historical attractions of a city that are on show in Georgetown itself.

Second, and following from Urry's comments, Georgetown is being read here for its presumed "otherness" to the everyday experience of the tourist—its other cultures and cuisines (Chinese, Indian, Malay), its teeming street life, its wealth of historically distinctive buildings, its particular history, its color. In particular, Acheen and Armenian Streets are being constructed as the urban space of a particular cultural group, the Malays—hence the area is a piece of that mosaic of Malaysian cultures represented in Georgetown.[10]

Third, however, Georgetown is not just being "othered" here, for two main reasons. First, part of its appeal is its Britishness, a legacy of its colonial ties with Britain. Second, like the landscape upon which they gaze, most Western tourists in Georgetown will have come from urban centers, and it is precisely urbanism that is being sold here. This contrasts not only with the natural delights of the beach holiday but also with the pastoral that is a feature of other tourism projects in Malaysia (see, for example, Kahn 1992).[11]

Fourth, there is an aspect of the imagery being employed here that is both significant and overlooked in the literature that focuses solely on the exotic features of objects of the tourist gaze in places like Malaysia. This aspect concerns the fact that the attention of the tourist is very often drawn, as here, to the ever present "threat" to the symbols of the tourist gaze. The guidebook cited above is no exception. The reader, and those who gaze on the historic buildings of Georgetown, are invited to worry about the fragility of the objects of the tourist gaze (comparisons with Singapore, invariably unflattering for the latter, are almost always implicit here). This sense of fragility constitutes an important dimension of the pleasure that tourists experience in much the same way that a significant dimension of ecotourism lies in the experience of danger to the environment, or of cultural tourism in "tribal" regions, in the possibility that they are watching a "disappearing world." This theme is directly incorporated into the representation of Acheen Street as a place where the tourist may admire the efforts being made to preserve the symbols of Georgetown's unique cultural history.

The fact that Georgetown is being read as both unique (and hence out of the ordinary, or other) and the same is especially significant. For this duality speaks to an emerging sensibility, at least on the part of consumers, of images of place in the contemporary world, a sensibility by no means restricted to tourists. This involves a sense that, while at one level, the world is becoming increasingly homogenized by global cultural flows (e.g., of commodities, images, information, money, technology, ideologies, and so on), at another level, the uniqueness and specificities of place (and culture) are on the rise. In the representations of cities, we increasingly encounter images not of cities in general but of particular cities; not of urbanism as a (general, universal) way of life, but of particular urbanisms, to quote Wirth. The invitation to the tourist from a city in Europe to experience and gaze upon a city in Southeast Asia constituted by the redevelopment of Acheen and Armenian Streets is, therefore, something quite different than an invitation to experience life as it is back home. But it also differs considerably from the invitation to witness another culture in the classic anthropological sense, for here the consumer is specifically invited to bear in mind both the global and the local, both the East and the West, both the particular and the universal at the same time.

Tourism or General Cultural Process?

Recalling the words of Kee Phaik Cheen, the head of the tourism committee of Penang State, we can read the various efforts to "revitalize" Acheen and Armenian Streets as an instrumental attempt to increase the flow of tourist dollars into Penang. Kee maintained that "the city's colonial past, living traditions, architectural richness and multi-cultural heritage can be thematically re-created as 'historical precincts,' 'ethnic enclaves,' 'zones of adaptive reuse,' and 'ensembles of aesthetic buildings.' These, together with Penang's food and handicrafts, are cultural and heritage attractions which can be re-packaged [to promote increased tourism]" (Kee 1994, 5). Some years earlier, the head of Malaysia's Tourist Development Corporation addressed the need to provide Malaysia with a particular profile in order to attract tourists and noted that, while places like Hong Kong and Singapore could promote themselves as the sites of exciting night life, Malaysia's comparative advantage lay with its natural and cultural attractions. The Acheen Street project can be seen as a typical example of just such a profiling exercise, a more or less instrumental exercise in maximizing revenues drawn from the tourist industry.[12]

While it cannot be denied that cashing in on Malaysia's culture(s) is an important part of the current cultural developments that are going on here, it is still only a part of it. In this regard, let me briefly outline two of the reasons that have led me to this conclusion.

First, the forces that are driving the project of urban renovation and restoration in Georgetown clearly amount to much more than the imperatives of the tourist industry alone. Since a full explanation of this is beyond the scope of this chapter, let me simply mention two among the many forces or groups, apart from "tourist promotion," with a strong interest in the preservation of the prewar built environment of downtown Georgetown—a movement that has gathered momentum in the early 1990s. To begin with, there are the economic planners, who are seeking to promote Penang as a high-tech environment; then there are, quite significantly, the members of Penang's growing and changing middle classes, who are seeking to create an urban environment appropriate to their aspirations, desires, and tastes.

For some time, critics of the development policies of developing nations such as Malaysia have argued that the drive to promote export-oriented industrialization through large amounts of direct foreign investment was leading to a new international division of labor between the rich, industrialized countries of the North, and the poor countries of the South. It was argued that centers like Penang, which sought to attract foreign transnational investment through tax breaks, a relaxation of restrictions on profit repatriation, and so on, would receive few long-term benefits from the presence of transnational corporations because of an anticipated absence of linkages to the local economy and the low levels of technology transfer. Moreover, the major attractions for transnational corporations were the

low wages and the labor force discipline imposed by host governments in order to attract the investment in the first place. Given that
these corporations were regarded as "footloose," world recession
and the opening of new areas with even lower wages and greater
political controls on workers would lead to the loss of even those
minimal benefits brought by foreign firms as they withdrew capital
from the host country. Indeed, the world recession of the early 1980s
and the recent flow of capital into countries such as Vietnam and
China seem to have confirmed these fears.[13]

These fears were shared by policymakers in Malaysia and, more
especially, Singapore. They proposed various measures to prevent the
flight of foreign capital and to promote what, at least in Singapore,
has come to be called a second industrial revolution, whereby host
countries would attempt to "lever" themselves up the technological
ladder and offer advantages to the transnational firms that they
could not obtain in either the cheap labor economies of the South or
the labor markets of the North. Among the many measures taken
were those directed at promoting and upgrading local "human
resources" through educational and training programs—in short, to
increase the pool of skilled technical workers, professionals, and service workers on which the world electronics industry was coming to
depend. And, to cut a long story short, this project included not only
training but also providing an attractive environment in order to prevent members of this new generation of skilled workers from emi-
grating elsewhere.

In this sense it can be argued that influential planning bodies in
Malaysia, such as the Penang Development Corporation and the
Institute for Strategic and International Studies, are firmly behind
both educational, high-tech ventures and projects that emphasize the
creation of an attractive natural, cultural, and social environment. They see this environment as part of a strategy to retain their
own skilled workers and to attract skilled workers, professionals,
and executive and managerial personnel from elsewhere. Promoting
Penang as a "civilized" urban center will, they hope, persuade existing transnational corporations to stay and convince new companies
to establish regional headquarters or branch offices.

This strategy and the way it is related to projects such as the one
described above are nicely illustrated by a glossy brochure produced
in the early 1990s by the Human Resource Development Council
of the Penang state government, with assistance from the Penang
Development Corporation, entitled "High Tech Career in a Resource

Environment." The section entitled "Life in Penang" stresses both the facilities and the resort environment, and one can well imagine that in the future such a brochure will include a section on a beautifully restored, postmodern heritage environment in downtown Georgetown, with a plethora of elegant (but still heritage) shops, restaurants, conference centers, and the like. The desire to attract transnational corporations, and to retain local professional and skilled workers, more than the desire to increase the number of Western tourists, explains why government agencies have been so willing to provide funding for projects like the restoration of the Alatas mansion in Armenian Street.

But the impetus behind urban restoration does not come solely from economic planners. It also comes from the new middle classes in places like Penang, an important group of consumers all too often overlooked in the tourism literature. As previously noted, the vast majority of foreign visitors to Penang are from neighboring countries, notably Singapore. In addition, domestic tourists in Penang have been rapidly increasing in number since the completion of the north–south highway, as, presumably, have local and regional tourists and day trippers. But the majority of the people who visit the sights of Georgetown are middle-class residents of Penang itself. These people—professionals, the educated, the more affluent Penangites—are, after all, the main movers in organizations such as the Penang Heritage Trust (together with the property developers, who have their own agendas). These residents are genuinely committed to improving their city's social, cultural, and natural environment. While they are unlikely to live in the inner city, they certainly go there and would presumably do so even more so if there were more attractive shops, museums, and restaurants. Perhaps downtown Georgetown will even begin to attract the local, middle-class gentrifiers found in many European and American cities. That certainly is one of the main aims of the restorers of the Alatas mansion, since they are introducing classes and an information center for would-be renovators of inner-city shophouses.

The role played by Penang's middle classes in the preservation of a desirable environment has already been seen in the battle to save Penang Hill from the developers. Penang Hill is a complex of hills in the north-central uplands of the island and includes Western Hill, which, at 830 meters above sea level, is the highest point on the island. Much of the area is owned by the state government, the Penang Municipal Council, and the Penang Water Authority, and it is protected from major development by various statutes. Since the colonial period, Penang Hill—reached either by road or by funicular railway—has been a place to escape the heat and noise of George-town, to hike, or take tea at one of the colonial hotels. It is also the site of a number of bungalows where those with the proper connec-tions can stay the night.

In 1990 the state government signed a memorandum of under-standing with a private developer, Bukit Pinang Sdn. Bhd., under which the company was to produce a detailed plan for the develop-ment of Penang Hill. The envisaged development included a water-world complex, a cable car, "two large hotels, a condominium, an 'Acropolis' complex on the summit (with a dome, planetarium, the-atre, shopping and sports centre, cinemas and night clubs); a forest lodge and over 300 units of houses and chalets; artificial gardens and aviary; and a Tiger Hill Adventure Park with a golf course and fea-tures such as a moon walk, space shuttle, shipwreck and 'haunted mansion' with social [sic] effects" (Friends of Penang Hill, 1991, 17).

As news of these plans spread, Friends of Penang Hill was orga-nized to oppose the development, partly under the auspices of the Consumers' Association. Drawing on a surprisingly wide range of predominantly middle-class and professional Penangites, the opposi-tion appealed to the government, made detailed and expert submis-sions to the inquiry, and publicized their objections throughout Malaysia and overseas. Despite the backing of many government agencies and powerful business interests linked to the government, the plan seems to have been defeated, although a final ruling has yet to be made. This community response is quite remarkable in a coun-try that increasingly brooks little opposition from its citizens.

Perhaps most interesting about this movement is the way in which a particular urban imaginary, this time oppositional (although by no means radical), is shaping the pattern of development in modern Penang. The sentiments expressed by one supporter of the Friends of Penang Hill reflect the feelings of many of the middle-class Penang residents who opposed the development:

> I am aghast at the proposed "development" of Penang Hill. Such a project would be a travesty of the hill and the island's heritage. As a Penangite, the hill to me is not only part of the land but more a part of my being. One does not go up the hill to visit a "pleasure dome" but to retreat from the hustle and bustle of city life. It is a place to commune with nature. . . . Sacrificing the rich and variant life forms

for neon-lit concrete structures that would be no different from the many others already in existence in all corners of the world, is tantamount to insanity! (Friends 1991, 42).

While not nearly so large or influential, the movement to preserve downtown Georgetown is of similar social composition to the Friends of Penang Hill, and is similarly motivated, although in this case by a desire to preserve a historical and cultural, rather than a natural, heritage.

The economic planners and part of Penang's growing middle-class population are two groups interested in urban restoration, although for reasons different than those of the promoters of overseas tourism. This broader involvement suggests that such projects cannot be explained by reference to tourism alone. Instead the touristic is embedded in something much more encompassing.

This leads to a second reason to suggest that there is more to tourism than meets the eye, a reason that draws on the history of the region. In his work on Bali, Michel Picard shows how the development of Balinese "culture" was closely related to the interaction between Western tourists and the Balinese beginning in the colonial period. It was not so much a case of an encounter between Westerners and a preexisting Balinese culture, but of a dynamic process out of which Balinese culture was itself constructed.[14] While the intense touristic encounter between Bali and the West in the 1920s and 1930s makes the processes involved in the creation of the modern discourse about Balinese culture unique, it is interesting to note that very similar processes were at work at much the same time elsewhere in the Netherlands Indies, in places where tourism was of negligible significance. Elsewhere (Kahn 1993a) I have documented one such case of the "constitution" of Minangkabau as a discrete and unique "culture."

The Minangkabau peoples who inhabit the central western region of the island of Sumatra are said, by Minangkabau and non-Minangkabau alike, to constitute a distinctive cultural group with customs and worldviews (such as the practice of matrilineal inheritance and kin group control of land) that mark them off from Indonesia's many other ethnic groups. The notion of Minangkabau cultural distinctiveness and the ideas pertaining to the contents characteristic of this unique culture were developed, as I have argued, in the context of an often highly critical encounter with Dutch liberalism and Islamic modernism, an encounter that was carried out and negotiated at a discursive level by intellectuals and colonial government officials (both Minangkabau and Dutch) at this time. This discursive constitution of the Minangkabau was, therefore, a part of the profound transformations wrought by the colonial encounter during the early decades of this century, and had little to do with the marketing of Minangkabau uniqueness or localism to Western tourists.

It seems significant that both Balinese and Minangkabau culture and cultural understandings were being reworked at much the same time and under similar conditions. This suggests strongly, as Picard himself implies, that at the very least tourism and local culture are only two of the factors embedded in a complex set of historical relationships (and the element of tourism may in fact be relatively insignificant) that need to be analyzed as a whole. In the case of urban restoration in Penang, it may be that tourist promotion is being used as a cover or a rationalization (perhaps in order to attract financial support from bodies involved in tourist promotion) for a more general project of culture-building that in origin has very little to do with the tourist industry.

Reworking Malayness in Acheen Street

To argue, as I have, that the project to restore and revitalize the Lebuh Acheen–Lebuh Armenian "cultural enclave" arises mainly out of a perceived need on the part of development planners and middle-class activists is still not sufficient fully to appreciate and grasp the distinctive features of this development. To see that this is so, we merely need to point to the fact that the discursive procedures through which this specific cultural enclave is being constituted appear thoroughly arbitrary. To put it another way, it should be carefully understood that the constitution of this cultural enclave, whereby particular built structures (e.g., the mosque, the Syed Alatas mansion, the shophouses in Acheen Street, and so on) are made to signify a unique cultural neighborhood and to conjure up images of a particular urban "community" of "Penang Malays," involves a concerted effort to draw cultural boundaries, to construct relations across those boundaries, and to characterize the cultural traits contained within each of them. Why should the resultant image of a vibrant, commercial, cosmopolitan, Islamic, but also tolerant "Penang Malay community" acquire particular saliency for the planning arms of both federal and state governments and for particular middle class Penangites? The reasons are deducible neither from the logic of the tourist industry nor from the demands of urban planners. Instead they are distinctive to the contemporary cultural landscape of Malaysia in general and of Penang in particular.

The image of an urban Malay community constituted out of the project to restore Lebuh Acheen–Lebuh Armenian district is particularly interesting because it contrasts so markedly not only to the existing pastoral images of Malayness promoted by the tourist industry but also to the writings of Malay intellectuals, politicians, journalists, advertising executives, and prominent figures on the Malay left. The former is clearly captured in the following, taken from a series of articles that appeared in the *Pulau Pinang Magazine,* a glossy periodical that styles itself as "a guide to the local way of life and culture of Penang" and that first appeared in 1989. Several articles published in the January 1990 issue and written by Khoo Su Nin, currently the secretary of the Penang Heritage Trust, trace the history of the neighborhood founded by Syed Sheriff Tengku Syed Hussain Al-Aidi—"an Achehnese tycoon of Arab descent" and a member of the royal house of Acheh. Syed Hussain settled in Georgetown in 1792 and quickly acquired large landholdings, having negotiated a position of authority with Francis Light, who was eager to woo investors and traders to the new settlement. The community that emerged is described in the following terms:

> With the leadership and patronage of Tengku Syed Hussain, traders from all parts of the Malay archipelago converged on Acheen Street, forming the first predominantly Malay entrepreneurial community on the island. The Achehnese, Bugis, Dayaks, Javanese, Arabs, and Chuliers fostered an urban society probably as diverse as that found in Acheh's old capital, and similarly bound together in the spirit of Islam (Khoo 1990, 17).

The articles describe Lebuh Acheen–Lebuh Armenian as a center of both Islam and commerce and establish its cosmopolitan nature: cosmopolitan because its membership was drawn throughout the Malay-Indonesian archipelago and because it interacted closely with other ethnic groups in Penang. For example, the leader of the community in the late nineteenth century, Syed Alatas, was the head of the so-called Red Flag Secret Society, an organization that allied itself with the Hokkien-dominated Khian Teik (secret society). Their rivals were the Cantonese-dominated Ghee Hin Secret Society and the Malay White Flag Society. Khoo also writes about the performance tradition of *bangsawan* that developed among the Penang Malays, a tradition that drew its musical and dramatic inspiration from all of

Penang's different cultural influences.[15] This image of a dynamic, commercial, worldly urban community differs significantly from the more general discourse about Malayness as having its roots in dignified, subsistence oriented, communal, culturally homogeneous villages—the very antithesis of life in the modern city.[16] Why should images of the essence of Malayness be so important in the Malaysian context?

Since independence in 1957, the incorporation of parts of North Borneo, and the separation of Singapore in 1965, the Federation of Malaysia has been comprised of the ten peninsular states and Sabah and Sarawak, the two states of East Malaysia. Peninsular Malaysia has been populated since the colonial period by a number of different ethnic groups (Malaysians tend to speak of races), the predominant ones being the Chinese (descendants of migrants from southern China who came mostly as workers in the tin mines), the Indians (mainly descendants of contract laborers on the rubber plantations), and the so-called indigenous Malays (overwhelmingly Muslims, who are generally referred to as *bumiputera* or "sons of the soil"). In general, a rough cultural division of labor developed and crystallized during the colonial period when the Indians worked as agricultural laborers (although many, especially migrants from the northern subcontinent, worked as merchants or in government service), the Chinese worked in business (although many remained as laborers), and the Malays were peasant villagers. At the same time, the descendants of the traditional Malay aristocracy—the sultans and their families who had entered into agreements and signed various treaties with the British—were rewarded with some role in the emerging colonial state, either as traditional rulers (like the current rulers of the states) or as civil servants. Despite significant patterns of differentiation *within* these various groups (different language groups, differences between English- and vernacular-educated groups, even differences of religion) and the fact that the general categories excluded many others (notably aboriginal groups on the peninsula and indigenous, non-Muslim groups in Borneo), it was generally perceived that Malaysia was inhabited by three main races or ethnic groups.

For a number of historical and cultural reasons, the Malays, defined as the indigenous peoples, were considered to have a special status, and when independence was negotiated with the British that status was ensured. Although Malaysian independence was achieved without a nationalist revolution as in neighboring Indonesia, the years leading up to independence were marked by two struggles that have left their imprint on modern Malaysia. First, there was the armed struggle against colonialism by the, allegedly largely Chinese, Malaysian Communist Party (MCP), which resulted in the so-called Emergency—a struggle quelled by the British with help from the Malay political elite. Second, there was the nonviolent confrontation between the British forces, who wished to cede Malaysia to a multi-racial coalition under the provisions of the Malayan Union, and the Malay nationalist movement, whose separate groups formed the United Malay Nationalist Organization (or UMNO), which has since independence been the dominant political party in all ruling coali-tions. The British ultimately accepted the claims made by the UMNO leadership to represent the indigenous Malays, partly in return for UMNO's cooperation in the conflict with the MCP and partly because UMNO had already formed a "multiracial" alliance with the Malaysian Chinese Association (MCA). All this set the framework for Malaysian politics, which has since been characterized by ethni-cally based parties (the few attempts to set up nonethnic parties have largely been unsuccessful) and by a general acceptance of the "special privileges" of the Malays.

In the early years of independence little changed to alter this discourse of race and the division of labor. But among the Malays, or at least among the Malay middle classes (including government em-ployees, a small number of Malay businessmen, and low-ranking UMNO party officials), a nationalist sensitivity developed based on the view that independence had not delivered much to them and that conditions still favored Chinese entrepreneurs and the Malay aristocracy. One consequence was the organization of two national "Bumiputera Congresses" in 1965 and 1967, during which Malay nationalists called for greater benefits for Malays through quotas, preferential licensing arrangements, and the like. It was this Malay nationalist pressure, probably more than anything else, that explains the social goals that were incorporated into Malaysian development plans in the years after 1970.

For more than two decades since that time, state planners have set Malaysia on a two-pronged developmental trajectory. On the one hand, this trajectory is characterized by strong economic imperatives —to increase income levels and national wealth by promoting rapid public and private sector industrialization, the latter in particular involving high levels of direct foreign investment. More recently, the prime minister, Dr. Mahathir, has rededicated his government to the task of industrialization, pledging to turn Malaysia into a "developed" country by the year 2020.[17] On the other hand, government planning during this period has also had a largely social goal, namely to achieve what in Malaysia is usually called economic restructuring, which basically entails an attempt to uncouple the connection between economic function and ethnicity that emerged in the colonial period.[18] This restructuring aim of the New Economic Policy (NEP), while often thought to have arisen from the so-called race riots of 1969, has in fact been the legacy of Malay nationalism itself.

Given this history, it is evident why the definition of the nature and boundaries of the cultural category "Malay," and the particular contestations over that category, are so important for all Malaysians. If nothing else, those who are classified or can classify themselves as Malay have always been able to claim privileges under the regime of "special position." But there is more to it than this, for it is the discourse of Malayness that seems to be driving the political and economic machines as much as it is merely reflecting political and economic "realities." While a number of commentators have noted the significance of this post-independence nationalist project in the shaping of the NEP (see Shamsul 1988, Khoo Kay Jin 1992, and Jomo 1990), fewer have noted the extent to which the NEP was the outcome of a gradual shift in the idea of Malayness that began to emerge in the years after 1957.

Students of the colonial period are fortunate to have William Roff's now classic *Origins of Malay Nationalism* (1967) to help elucidate the course of Malay cultural politics in the prewar period. Unfortunately, there is no study of comparable scope for the years since independence in 1957. But the evidence suggests that a new Malay imaginary, one that differed significantly from the identities crafted in the colonial period, began to take root after independence.

The shift has been documented in the changing images of the Malays that began to appear in Malay fiction around the mid-1960s and that are found in the work of writers such as Usman Awang and Shahnon Ahmad. For example, Shahnon's vision of Malayness, in particular the way he links Malay, and hence his own, identity to Malay culture as a distinctively nonurban, subaltern culture (see Kahn 1993b) should be read as part of the more general "discovery" of a rich and desirable cultural tradition in the world of the Malay village. Shahnon was part of a movement among Malay writers that not only constructed a particular vision of Malay village culture but also positively identified the Malay intelligentsia with that culture. Discussing significant differences between Malay novels of the pre-

and immediate post-independence period, David Banks has argued that there has been a shift toward a much more favorable regard for Malay villages and a greater appreciation of the positive features of Malay culture properly located there (see Banks 1987). In other words, the normatively valued concept of "Malay culture" with its rural location is a relative newcomer on the Malaysian intellectual scene, replacing an earlier construction that characterized Malay village culture as backward, primitive, and in need of modernization. In this earlier literature, Malay writers sought to distance themselves from rural Malays, seeing themselves as the educators and modernizers of the Malay peasantry. In the later period, writers like Shahnon became spokespersons for those same peasants and defenders of those subalterns whose culture they shared. At least in Malay literature, therefore, the concept of subalternity and the corresponding positive evaluation of Malay village culture by members of the Malay middle-class intelligentsia became integrated in the project of constructing an ethnic identity for Malays.

It might be assumed that the strongly rural flavor of this particular modern Malay imaginary means that it will play no part in influencing the pattern of urbanization in a place like Penang. This assumption would be misleading for a number of reasons. First, the purveyors of these new images of Malayness, while they may be preserving links with their villages of origin, are almost always urban dwellers. Second, this rural imagery is taking hold, paradoxically, precisely in the context of a large decline in the rural peasant economy. Finally, the traditional spatial dimension of Malaysian ethnicity has been and continues to be eroded, such that, statistically, the Malays will soon be as much an urban as a rural people. Table 4.1, for example, shows the changing ethnic composition of Malaysian cities, with the total urban population classified as Malays rising from 19 percent in 1947 to almost 38 percent in 1980.

Whatever their content, then, these images of Malayness are firmly rooted in the urban experience. But as such they represent more than the nostalgic reflections of a generation of urban Malays uncomfortable with city life, although in an important sense they do represent an attempt by the new Malay middle classes to come to terms with what they take to be the alien and anomic pattern of life on the new housing estates that they inhabit. These images, and others like them, are actually helping to reconstitute the colonial cities of the Malay Peninsula that had changed only gradually in the first decade after independence. And there is every sign that patterns

Table 4.1 Percentage Distribution of Urban
Population by Ethnic Group

Ethnic Group	1947	1957	1970	1980
Malays	19.0	21.0	27.6	37.9
Chinese	63.1	62.6	58.5	50.3
Indians	14.7	12.8	12.8	11.0
Others	3.2	3.6	1.1	0.7

Source: Saw 1988, 66.

of urbanization in places like Penang will increasingly be shaped by similar urban imaginaries.

While, for example, Shahnon Ahmad's construction of the spatiality of Malay life cannot be directly translated into an urban setting, it has been argued that such "traditional" Malay spatial forms can find a place in a city like Georgetown. In late 1991, the Penang edition of the *New Straits Times* reported on the opening ceremony for a new housing scheme in the densely populated area of Kampung Nyak Putih near Jalan Patani. With the backing of the state and federal governments, a private company, Duniaga Sdn. Bhd., was permitted to raze a block of land previously occupied by long-time urban residents who lacked full legal title to the land, and to replace their wooden houses with a large housing complex. The new complex consisted of three buildings of seven, twelve, and sixteen floors respectively, containing 410 low- and medium-cost flats and a commercial complex. While in no sense a direct imitation of Malay village housing, this commercial development (like many others these days) does borrow motifs and forms from village architecture. At the ground-breaking ceremony, the then Malaysian finance minister, now deputy prime minister, Datuk Seri Anwar Ibrahim (who originates from Penang), claimed that

it was imperative to maintain traditional Malay villages in urban areas in the State's efforts to achieve development. He said that development would be meaningless if people within these areas were neglected. It was also important to have comprehensive planning to maintain the identity of these villages. Datuk Seri Anwar noted that there were few traditional Malay villages left in Georgetown and it was therefore important for Penang Malays to face the rapid changes taking place around them.[19]

While in this situation the interests of property developers, the state, and advocates of a particular Malay urban imaginary might appear to coincide, that is not always the case, since the proposed benefits are not solely financial. By bringing "traditional" Malay housing to the city, planners can at the same time recreate traditional Malay social and cultural forms, hence offsetting the undesirable aspects of modern urban life. To quote Lim Jee Yuan, who, with his organization, the Consumers' Association of Penang, is a strong advocate of low-cost housing schemes that incorporate Malaysia's indigenous shelter system:

> The traditional Malay house was a major focal point of traditional Malay village society, incorporating so many of the positive aspects of life now being rapidly eroded by the processes described above. The Malay house provided the basic need of shelter to the villagers. It was designed and built by the villagers themselves, and thus is a manifestation of the creative and aesthetic skills of the community. It successfully and scientifically accommodated the needs of those staying in it with regard to control of weather, ventilation, shade and the optimal use of space. It blended perfectly with the natural environment and was also a natural expression of the social and cultural ways of life of the family unit and the community.... This book hopes to "capture" the spirit and form of the traditional Malay house not only because it is one of the richest components of Malaysia's cultural heritage but more importantly to show that the humble, simple and neglected Malay house has a vital and essential role to play in fulfilling the present and future housing needs of ordinary Malaysians (Lim 1987, 11).

As these examples show, the development of new kinds of urban space in Penang may be closely intertwined with changing notions of culture and identity. That housing development in particular should reflect concerns about Malay cultural uniqueness is not all that surprising as this is an area in which the Malaysian state, with its commitment to Malay rights, is particularly influential either directly (through the provision of public housing) or indirectly (through its support for both *bumiputera* finance and *bumiputera* building contractors). Moreover the demand for new housing is particularly strong among the new middle classes, a large proportion of whom are also in the *bumiputera* category.

The connection between urban space, culture, and identity brings us back to the particular project proposed for Lebuh Acheen–Lebuh Armenian. For what is striking about the planned image of Malayness is the way it contrasts strongly with the pastoralism of that image of homogeneous, nonmodern Malay communities constructed in the writings of Malay novelists and in the post-independence discourse of Malay nationalists seeking special privileges for Malays under the New Economic Policy. Indeed the language of the "Acheen Street Malay," unlike that of Shahnon, Lim, or Anwar in the extract quoted above, is neither anti- nor postmodern, but instead represents a rededication of the process of Malay culture-building to the modernist project. In so doing, and unlike the more pastoralist language of a Shahnon Ahmad, the language of the Penang Malay avoids a central contradiction in Malay existence that no amount of appealing to an idealized and romanticized Malay *kampong* (village) can avoid —namely, how to relocate "traditional" Malays within the modern, urban settings within which they increasingly find themselves. It does so, moreover, without recourse to the negative, colonial stereotypes that characterized the language of an earlier generation of Malay modernists, forced, like one former prime minister, to call for a "mental revolution" (or, like the current prime minister, who wants to call forth a New Malay) in order for (middle-class and wealthy) Malays to assume the economic and political role that is increasingly falling to them after more than two decades of economic growth and restructuring. Additionally, it represents an alternative to the more or less total rejection of modernity as "Western" that so characterizes the discourse of the contemporary Islamic revival in Malaysia. Finally, it envisages a multicultural rather than a monocultural future for modern Malays, a particularly apt discourse in the context of modern Georgetown. Yet for all that, this neomodern discourse on culture and urban space is no popular or vernacular one. Its authenticity must be continually guaranteed by "experts" and planners—significantly members of the Penang Heritage Trust who appear to be just as hostile to the popular forms of urban renovation and restoration as they are to those redevelopment schemes that seek to destroy the prewar fabric of Georgetown and replace it with international-style (including postmodern) built forms.

In sum, a fuller appreciation of the plan to revitalize and restore

Acheen and Armenian Streets cannot be derived from looking at it as just another attempt to lure foreign tourists or as a further example of urban planning. Instead, the processes of signification that are shaping it must be firmly located within the developing Malaysian cultural landscape.

Culturalization and Globalization

Having argued that a particular project aimed at tourism development in Georgetown must be understood less in the context of tourism, or as a particular encounter between West and East, and more in the context of specific economic, political, and cultural developments in Malaysia, I want to return to the global encounter and use this example to thematize processes of what has been called the globalization of culture. For while clearly in one sense the plan to redevelop Acheen and Armenian Streets is shaped by significant local forces, we cannot avoid the strong parallels between this project and similar urban developments elsewhere in the world. To what extent is this particular project also shaped by global forces?

At least on a superficial level, events in Georgetown are quite clearly related to a worldwide process that some have termed the "culturalization" of social life. Jean Baudrillard, for example, has maintained that we have entered a new phase of postmodernity in which there is "an endless reduplication of signs, images and simulations through the media which effaces the distinction between the image and reality. Hence the [postmodern] consumer society becomes essentially cultural as social life becomes deregulated and social relationships become more variable and less structured by stable norms. The overproduction of signs and reproduction of images and simulations leads to a loss of stable meaning, and an aestheticization of reality in which the masses become fascinated by the endless flow of bizarre juxtapositions which take the viewer beyond stable sense" (summary in Featherstone 1991, 15).

In a similar vein Frederic Jameson has argued that contemporary postmodern culture is the culture of the late or consumerist phase of capitalism, where "culture is given a new significance through the saturation of signs and messages to the extent that 'everything in social life can be said to have become cultural' " (in Featherstone 1991, 15). For Baudrillard and Jameson, the contemporary world has become culturalized. Our world is then characterized by depthlessness, pastiche, and self-conscious enjoyment of inauthenticity, a consequence of the fact that we no longer live in reality but, to use

Baudrillard's term, in hyperreality, a space in which image replaces reality, signifier replaces signified. And while these theorists of postmodernity have largely confined their remarks to discussions of the West and to the United States in particular, others, such as Featherstone and Robertson, push the analysis further, showing how, particularly as a consequence of the revolution in communications technology, the process of culturalization has spread throughout the globe (see, for example, Robertson 1990, 1992, Featherstone 1993).

In a very obvious sense Lebuh Acheen–Lebuh Armenian is just the sort of phenomenon that Baudrillard seeks to describe by the term "simulacrum," a signifier with a life of its own, unwilling to be anchored in any real community—either contemporary or historical—that it is supposed to represent. We should not be surprised to find such parallels with urban planning elsewhere in the world, for this cultural enclave is being designed by individuals whose careers are themselves global not only because they are geographically mobile but also because they share an arena of discourse about modern architecture, postmodernism, and heritage that has no national boundaries.

And yet, as we have already seen, if anything characterizes developments such as those discussed above, it is their particularism. Like other such projects, the one in Acheen and Armenian Streets represents precisely a rejection of an international style of urban space and is explicitly cast in terms of a distinctive, localized vernacular. Is calling this global, therefore, a contradiction in terms?

It would be a mistake to read this particular case as an example of global cultural heterogeneity, as representing some more authentic cultural voice that has its roots somewhere *outside* global culture. A number of theorists of the global condition are eager to point out that the current phase of cultural globalization neither implies that we are merely witnessing a new kind of cultural imperialism nor means that world culture is becoming more homogeneous. If anything, the current phase of globalization is characterized as much by cultural differentiation as it is by homogenizing processes.[20] That may well be true. But the eagerness of some to seize on all instances of difference as though these represented a successful escape from the homogenizing and imperializing tendencies of world culture often causes them to overlook an important dimension of contemporary world culture and their own discourse about it, namely that it is *simultaneously* universal and particular, Eastern and Western. In other words, the local:global tension manifested in the plans for

Acheen and Armenian Streets is itself part of global culture. This is not necessarily to resurrect older ideas about cultural imperialism. Clearly Arjun Appadurai is correct to speak of a "disjuncture" in global cultural flows that confuses any simple attempt, for example, to speak of the imposition of Western culture in the East. As places like Malaysia increasingly challenge the kinds of world political and cultural orders that the West currently attempts to impose on them, the disjunctural nature of such cultural flows will only increase. In any case, strong and "successful" states such as Malaysia are already significantly able to control the ways in which global culture is consumed at home. The strongly neomodernist character of the image of urban Malays in the plans for Acheen and Armenian Streets is an interesting case in point and owes a good deal to what some Asian scholars at least have termed the discourse of "westoxification," wherein local culture is constructed precisely in opposition to the "decadent"—for which one might read "postmodern"—cultures of the West. But a process of culture-building that rests on the rejection of globalism is as much a global discourse as one that seeks slavishly to follow it. The campaign to restore Acheen and Armenian Streets therefore is once again located within an encounter between West and East, although not necessarily, as its proponents claim, a touristic encounter, but rather a conceptual clash that occurs in the hyperspace of global culture.

Notes

1. See articles in the *New Straits Times,* 17 February 1993, Penang City Extra section, and 6 October 1993.

2. Victor King (1993) has cited the relatively small size of the tourist sector, the fact that tourists come overwhelmingly not from the West but from other Asian countries, and the substantial confinement of tourists to limited areas in Peninsular Malaysia to take issue with the more apocalyptic fears about the destructive effects of Malaysian tourism.

3. Tourist Development Corporation of Malaysia figures cited in King (1993, 105).

4. Figures cited in Hall (1994, 83).

5. For an example of the latter see Evelyne Hong (1985). A more positive stance is taken by Hall (1994). The now widely accepted revisionist/compromise position—that the existing terms of the debate are highly problematic and that the relationship between tourism and culture is complex and needs to be examined in particular instances—is taken by anthropologist Victor

King in his 1993 article. And yet King does not provide any detailed case studies.

6. Roughly, what John Urry (1990) refers to by the idea of the "tourist gaze" is the way the unique and "out of the ordinary" cultural characteristics of landscapes, townscapes, and other spatial settings come to be "seen" as such by tourists not through some kind of natural, unstructured process simply reflecting preexisting situations out there in the real world, but through particular kinds of socially organized and systematized practices, constructions, and collections of images. According to Urry, the emergence of modern and postmodern tourism is linked to the development of socially specific regimes of "signs" and "signposts," which, in their turn, shape what have become the typical modalities of perceiving, consuming, absorbing, and even seeking out certain scenes as a tourist. Moreover, it should be noted that, even though Urry remains tied to a realist-based sociology, as he more or less admits himself, his work on these "gazing" frameworks and their operationalization is extremely useful because it draws our attention to the discursive dimension and constitution of the social world—that is to say to the manner in which the social world is a product of countless ideological, linguistic, textual, figural, and conceptual formulations, and not simply a preexiting reality isomorphically mirrored in our representational apparatuses.

7. Currently the tourist is directed to the area and to these particular buildings by a guidebook (Khoo 1993) and by various attractively produced brochures such as "Acheen St. and Armenian St.: Penang's Historic Melting Pot," published by the Technical Committee for the Conservation and Development of the Acheen Street–Armenian Street Area in association with the Penang Heritage Trust. Most recently American Express and the Penang Heritage Trust have published a brochure entitled "Penang Heritage Trail" (Jejak Warisan Penang), which gives particular prominence to the mosque and the Syed Alatas mansion. *The Penang Guide,* written by the historian Paul Kratoska (1988), directs the reader to the "Malay mosque" in Acheen Street, but the small space devoted to it and the omission of other sights reflects the fact that the book was written before the whole area was declared a cultural enclave.

8. See report in the *Star,* 5 December 1993.

9. See Hatchell (1990).

10. Cities in Malaysia have traditionally been more Chinese than Malay, although the proportions are changing under the impact of the New Economic Policy, which took as its central aim ethnic restructuring. But Penang continues to be seen as an overwhelmingly Chinese city. In 1980, 50.3 percent of urban dwellers in Malaysia were classified as Chinese, 37.9 percent as Malay, and 11.0 percent as Indian; in the same year 66.6 percent of urban residents in Penang were Chinese, 18.7 percent Malay, and 13.1 percent Indian.

11. The term imaginary is here used quite impressionistically to refer to certain stocks of images and ideas pertaining to some cultural and spatial setting or to some aspect of social life. In the work of, among others, Cornelius Castoriadis and Jacques Lacan, this term refers to complexes of both conscious and unconscious images, meanings, and fantasies that are usually conceived as escaping all forms of determination. In my discussion, in contrast, I am interested precisely in considering and outlining how the bases of these imagistic complexes lie in specific processual and discursive links that tie together power, knowledge, and social context.

12. These comments are cited in Hall (1994).

13. In the mid-1980s several studies argued that this is precisely what was happening in the Southeast Asian NICs; see, for example, Kunio (1988) and Bello and Rosenfeld (1990).

14. See Picard (1990, 1993); see also Vickers (1989) and Warren (1990).

15. For a very interesting history of *bangsawan* that also draws attention to its "multicultural" roots, see Tan Sooi Beng (1993).

16. For a discussion of such pastoralist imagery, see Kahn (1992, 1993b).

17. See Jomo (1994, chap. 3).

18. In fact the so-called New Economic Policy had two basic social goals: restructuring and the elimination of poverty. However, it has long been clear that the former was the main goal; the latter, it has been generally assumed, would follow on from economic growth (see Jomo 1994).

19. *New Straits Times*, Penang City Extra section, 2 November 1991, 1.

20. See, for example, contributions by Friedman, Appadurai, and Hannerz in Featherstone (1990).

References

Banks, David J.
1987   *From Class to Culture: Social Conscience in Malay Novels Since Independence.* Monograph no. 29. New Haven: Yale University Southeast Asia Studies.

Bello, W., and S. Rosenfeld
1990   *Dragons in Distress: Asia's Miracle Economies in Crisis.* San Francisco: Institute for Food and Development Policy.

Featherstone, Mike
1990   *Global Culture: Nationalism, Globalization and Modernity.* London: Sage.
1991   *Consumer Culture and Postmodernism.* London: Sage.
1993   Global and Local Cultures. In *Mapping the Futures: Local Cultures, Global Change,* ed. J. Bird et al. London and New York: Routledge.

Friends of Penang Hill
1991   *Penang Hill: The Need to Save Our Natural Heritage*. Penang: Consumers' Association.

Hall, Colin Michael
1994   *Tourism in the Pacific Rim*. Melbourne:Longman Cheshire.

Hatchell, Emily
1990   *Travellers' Survival Kit to the East*. Oxford: Vacation Work.

Hong, Evelyne
1985   *See the Third World While It Lasts: The Social and Environmental Impact of Tourism, with Particular Reference to Malaysia*. Penang: Consumers' Association.

Jomo, K. S.
1990   Beyond the New Economic Policy? Malaysia in the Nineties. Sixth James C. Jackson Memorial Lecture. Brisbane: Griffith University and Malaysia Society of the Asian Studies Association of Australia.
1994   *U-Turn? Malaysian Economic Development Policies after 1990*. Townsville: James Cook University of North Queensland, Centre for East and Southeast Asian Studies.

Kahn, Joel S.
1992   Class, Ethnicity and Diversity: Some Remarks on Malay Culture in Malaysia. In *Fragmented Vision: Culture and Politics in Contemporary Malaysia*, ed. Joel S. Kahn and Francis Loh Kok Wah, 158–178. Sydney: Allen and Unwin.
1993a *Constituting the Minangkabau: Peasants, Culture and Modernity in Colonial Indonesia*. Oxford and Providence: Berg.
1993b Subalternity and the Construction of Malay Identity. In *Modernity and Identity: Asian Illustrations,* ed. Alberto Gomes, 23–41. Bundoora: La Trobe University Press.

Kee Phaik Cheen
1994   Tourism and Leisure Industries in Penang—Challenges, Response and Opportunities for Growth and Development. Unpublished paper.

Khoo Kay Jin
1992   The Grand Vision: Mahathir and Modernisation. In *Fragmented Vision: Culture and Politics in Contemporary Malaysia*, ed. Joel S. Kahn and Francis Loh Kok Wah, 44–76. Sydney: Allen and Unwin.

Khoo Su Nin
1990   The Legacy of Tengku Syed Hussain. The Acheen Street Community: A Melting Pot of the Malay World. The Acheen Street Mosque. *Pulau Pinang Magazine* 87 (January 1990):12–29.
1993   *Streets of George Town, Penang*. Penang: Janus Print and Resources.

King, Victor T.
  1993   Tourism and Culture in Malaysia. In *Tourism in South-East Asia,* ed. Michael Hitchcock et al., 99–116. London and New York: Routledge.
Kratoska, Paul
  1988   *The Penang Guide.* Singapore: Graham Brash.
Kunio, Y.
  1988   *The Rise of Ersatz Capitalism in South-East Asia.* Singapore: Oxford University Press.
Lim Jee Yuan
  1987   *The Malay House: Rediscovering Malaysia's Indigenous Shelter System.* Penang: Institut Masyarakat.
Picard, Michel
  1990   "Cultural Tourism" in Bali: Cultural Performance as Tourist Attraction. *Indonesia* 49:37–74.
  1993   Cultural Tourism in Bali: National Integration and Regional Differentiation. In *Tourism in South-East Asia,* ed. Michael Hitchcock et al., 71–98. London and New York: Routledge.
Robertson, Roland
  1990   After Nostalgia? Wilful Nostalgia and the Phases of Globalization. In *Theories of Modernity and Postmodernity,* ed. Brian Turner. London: Sage.
  1992   *Globalization: Social Theory and Global Culture.* London, Newbury Park, New Delhi: Sage.
Roff, William R.
  1967   *The Origins of Malay Nationalism.* New Haven: Yale University Press.
Shamsul A. B.
  1988   The "Battle Royal": The UMNO Elections of 1987. In *Southeast Asian Affairs, 1988,* 170–188. Singapore: Institute of Southeast Asian Studies.
Tan Sooi Beng
  1993   *Bangsawan: A Social and Stylistic History of Popular Malay Opera.* Singapore: Oxford University Press.
Tan Thean Siew, Mohd. Amiruddin Fawzi Bahaudin, and Ricardo Aranas
  1991   Lebuh Acheh–Lebuh Armenian Area: Planning for Conservation of Historical and Cultural Enclave. Report prepared for the Third International Training Workshop on Strategic Areal Development Approaches for Implementing Metropolitan Development and Conservation, organized by the United Nations Centre for Regional Development and Municipal Council of Penang Island. 11–16 September, Penang, Malaysia.
Urry, John
  1990   *The Tourist Gaze.* London and Newbury Park: SAGE Publications.

Vickers, Adrian
  1989 *Bali: A Paradise Created.* Harmondsworth: Penguin.
Warren, C.
  1990 *Adat and Dinas: Village and State in Contemporary Bali.* Ph.D.
         diss., University of Western Australia.

» 5

A Portrait of Cultural Resistance: The Confinement of Tourism in a Hmong Village in Thailand

Empirical research on the consequences of tourism-linked development in host societies in Thailand has not yet reached a stage of maturity. Despite the relative abundance of publications and articles attempting to apply general models to particular situations—often with the intention of confirming some theoretical model rather than genuinely accounting for a specific group or society (see, for example, Dearden and Harron 1994)—the hypothetico-deductive approach has yet to fullfil its promise. More open-ended and inductive approaches, based on intensive fieldwork over time, are needed. By presenting both original data and interpretations linked to the dynamics of the trekking tourist business in a single Hmong village of Thailand, this chapter attempts, in its own modest way, to fill in some of the gaps existing between Hmong, montagnard, and tourist studies in Northern Thailand.[1]

Thailand comprises several minorities from quite different ethnic origins. Keyes (1987, 14–16) states that although up to 97 percent of the population speak Thai (or one of the regional forms of the Tai language) and 95 percent declare Buddhism as their religion, the ethnic composition of the country is somewhat more complex. Keyes shows that 83 percent belong to the Tai-speaking group, 3 percent to the Malay group, 2.3 percent to the Austroasiatic-speaking group, and 10.8 percent to immigrant groups, of which the Chinese is the most important. A tiny 0.9 percent accounts for the so-called tribal groups, and this small proportion helps to explain why the Thai rulers have not been interested in, and often are not even aware of, the existence of these highland dwellers.

But however varied the country's ethnic composition may be, Thailand remains one of the most ethnically homogeneous countries of Southeast Asia, and national ethnic policies reflect this. The national identity is clearly defined according to the dominant Tai group (see Reynolds 1991). This official ethnic homogeneity has precluded the official promotion of any important cultural regionalism that could have been used to attract tourists in any particular area of the country. In fact, every foreign guidebook emphasizes that in northern Thailand there are several "tribes" culturally distinct from the bulk of the country's population that deserve visiting, and a high percentage of foreign tourists comply with this recommendation (Figure 5.1). This disjunction between the national (absence of) discourse on tourism in the highland minorities and the international tourist advertising indicates a denial of the very existence of these ethnically different montagnards as specific tourist attractions. Confirming the lack of political interest in regulating tourism among the hilltribes, Toyota notes that: "It is only since the Seventh National Economic and Social Development Plan (which came into operation last year) that the Tourism Authority of Thailand (TAT) has recognised the need to regulate trekking tours" (1993, 16). Trekking is the major method of visiting highland villages. In the *Manuel pour guides touristiques* (Bhangananda and Wiwatsorn 1989), a book translated from Thai and designed by Chulalongkorn University to prepare local guides to lead foreign tourist groups in Thailand, less than one page out of 250 acknowledges the existence of the montagnard minorities. This systematic avoidance is a symptom of the general policy of integration of the highland cultures into the national identity that precludes any official recognition of their distinctiveness, a common tendency in other countries of continental Southeast Asia with highland minorities.

Social change in highland societies in continental Southeast Asia is first determined by the states' authoritarian policies designed for controlling national minorities. In the particular case of highland minorities practicing rotational and shifting cultivation, examples of these policies are documented in North Vietnam (Do 1994), Laos (Stuart-Fox 1986), and Thailand (McKinnon and Bhruksasri 1983, McKin-

THAILAND
Main trekking zones

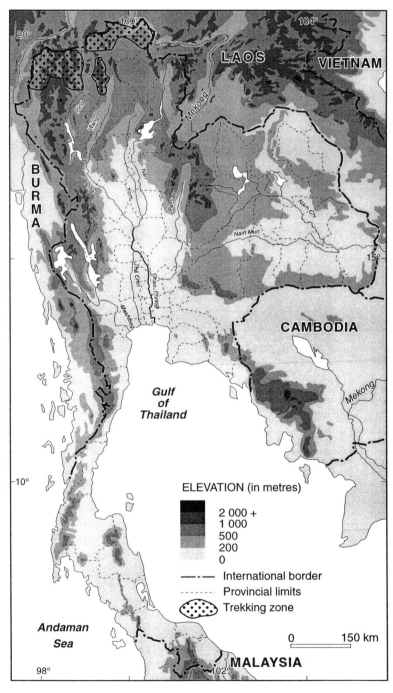

Figure 5.1. Northern Thailand. (Map by Jean Michaud)

non and Vienne 1989). Unlike highland minorities in insular Southeast Asia and those parts of the peninsula such as central Vietnam and continental Malaysia where ancient proto- and deutero-Malay migration waves have left remnant populations in isolated regions, highland minorities in the massif cannot be labeled indigenous as most of them are relatively recent migrants. The majority, principally from non-Han China, have been settled in the peninsula for less than three centuries (for the Hmong, see Lombard-Salmon 1972).

In the case of highland Thailand, and in contrast to neighboring countries that had been colonized by Europeans, the recognition of shifting cultivators from remote mountainous regions and the desire to incorporate them into the nation developed only recently and mainly under foreign pressure. As Huff (1967) showed, the new interest that the hilltribes generated in Bangkok during the late 1950s was linked to security issues related to the Indochina problem. Bhruksasri (1989) and Kesmanee (1989) demonstrated that control of highland minorities has remained a constant preoccupation of the Thai state ever since. As the security issue faded from daily preoccupations after 1982, environmental arguments were invoked to explain the state's strong will to intervene on the highland scene. Shifting cultivators were declared responsible for most of the forest degradation in the mountains (see Arbhabhirama et al. 1988), and the traditional economy of the hilltribes, based on rotational and pioneering swiddening, was severely constrained, particularly in cases where opium poppy cultivation was predominant.

Along with state intervention aimed at settling (Mongkhol 1981) and acculturating (Walker 1992) the non-Tai, nomadic or semi-nomadic, nonhierarchical, and animistic minorities to a national identity that is based on a shared Thai language, culture, Buddhism, and respect for the monarchy (Reynolds 1991), the provision of facilities for trekking tourism has become an additional factor of change in many highland villages. The state has taken very little specific action regarding mountain tourism, which has been left to entrepreneurs. It has been only when sporadic regional security problems have arisen that the authorities temporarily regulated the circulation of foreigners in particular areas. This laissez-faire attitude can be viewed as symptomatic of the low level of interest that highland minorities generate among Thai developers. But there may be other interpretations. Tourism in the mountains can also be considered a catalyst of social change that encourages and, in some cases, that even accelerates the pace of acculturation and incorporation into the national market (Forsyth 1992, Michaud 1993, 1995). With the help of a case study of a specific village, this chapter examines this process and poses specific questions: How does the trekking tourism business articulate with the processes of social change already taking place in that village? How similar or different are villager reactions to the tourist business and the transition to cash cropping and why? What can be expected in the long term?

The outcome is a dynamic portrait of a society in change. Quite unexpectedly, after twelve years of increasing tourist presence in the village, the economic attractiveness of the tourist business is astonishingly negligible. It is in fact limited to Hmong marginals to whom agricultural practices, the traditional activity, have become inaccessible, principally for reasons of opium addiction. Far from being considered backward by the villagers, traditional agriculture, either subsistence or cash-oriented, is still perceived by the majority as the most desirable and economically rewarding activity. The ease with which the Hmong villagers have adapted the traditional economy to modern market imperatives, and their general indifference toward tourists and tourist business, is atypical in tourist literature. Here, it has to be explained in relation to the resilient Hmong ethnic identity and social organization. Rooted in the household economy and an animistic understanding of the world, Hmong society has proven highly capable of adaptation without abandoning its central elements.

Ban Suay: Social Change in a Traditional Community

Like most of the highlanders of Thailand, the Hmong are traditionally animistic swiddeners and belong to a cultural group completely different from the ethnic Thai who compose the majority of Thailand's population (Moréchand 1968, Lemoine 1972, Chindarsi 1976). Since the early 1960s, the village of Ban Suay,[2] Chiang Mai province, has been subject to direct state intervention. The Thai state has incorporated the site into a *mooban*[3] along with two nearby Thai communities, has registered all residents, granting them land development certificates (see Ratanakhon 1978), and has tentatively begun to dispense occasional on-site health care and primary education, the latter without much success so far. This long-standing and unusually intensive state commitment is not unrelated to the importance of the traditional production of opium in the area.[4]

Apart from a Thai who runs a grocery store, all four hundred villagers in Ban Suay are Hmong, or have become so through marriage and adoption. All forty households are spatially grouped roughly along clan lines.[5] In former times, Ban Suay would have been abandoned by its inhabitants after some ten to fifteen years, as declining soil fertility pushed households to relocate to better land. However, after close to twenty years at their present location, most inhabitants of Ban Suay have stayed put. In present-day Thailand, where numerous policies have been adopted to protect forest resources and soil in the Chao Phraya watershed and its principal affluents, the Thai state officially forbids the clearing of forests in most of the mountainous parts of Northern Thailand (Arbhabhirama et al. 1988) (Figure 5.2). Most residents comply with the law, given that the prospect of pioneering new villages has, in any case, been foreclosed.

As is well documented (see Geertz 1963, Boulbet 1975, Kunstadter et al. 1978), the permanent settlement of shifting cultivators in one site sets in motion an important series of consequences. Among these, one in particular, the necessity of changing agricultural habits learned over centuries of migratory swiddening, is of utmost importance. Problems caused by the impossibility of clearing new patches in the forest are compounded by the difficulties swidden cultivators face in buying already cleared land, the most frequent being land scarcity, lack of citizenship, and, more likely still, lack of available capital. This uncomfortable situation is further compounded by a government policy of crop substitution under which highlanders are forbidden to grow the traditionally profitable, though illegal, opium poppy. Required instead to plant new, unknown crops for which it is theorized there will be a market demand, the residents of Ban Suay, like most highland villagers, have become vulnerable to both poor planning by outsiders and exterior market forces over which they have no control. Many among the economically least fortunate—those lacking in land, capital, or an effective labor force within their household—cannot resist this pressure and are obliged, albeit reluctantly, to leave the community periodically to look for wage work. Leaving the community to enter the Thai world is a stressful experience that, for most highland peoples, must be delayed as long as possible.

At the beginning of the 1980s, thanks to a reasonably usable dirt road, Ban Suay began receiving occasional visits from Thai guides accompanying a limited number of foreign travelers. A dramatic increase in numbers has occurred over the years and since 1987, an average (calculated annually) of ten tourists per day spend a night in the village during the course of a three- to four-day trek. Certain Hmong villagers seized upon the business opportunity the trekking

NORTHERN THAILAND

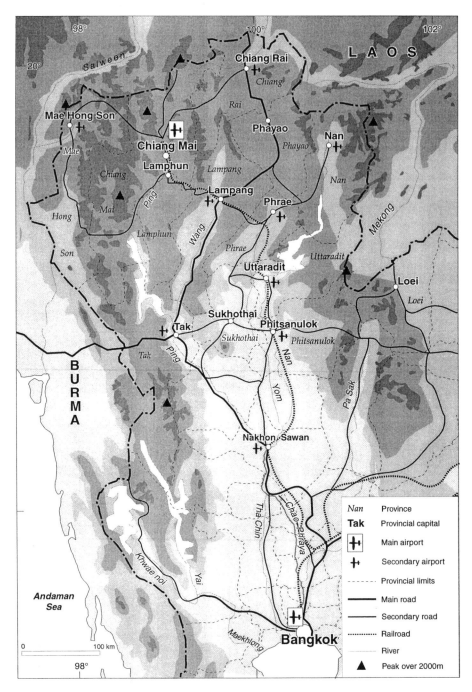

Figure 5.2. Thailand: topography and main trekking zones. (Map by Jean Michaud)

business offered and became involved with tourist agencies. However, early participants have dropped out over time as others have stepped in.

Trekking in the Ban Suay Area

According to a 1992 report by the Chiang Mai branch of the Tourism Authority of Thailand (TAT 1992), 62,210 foreign visitors went on a trek in Northern Thailand in 1990.[6] At that time, the total number of foreign visitors in the region was estimated at 562,000. If these figures are correct, trekkers would therefore constitute about 11 percent of all foreign visitors to the region. In Thailand's case, according to a classification proposed by Valene Smith (1989), we are dealing with ethnic tourism and its frequent partner, environmental tourism.[7]

The type of trek that passes through Ban Suay is fairly typical. Western tourists recruited primarily at cheap guesthouses in Chiang Mai are sold an equally economical trekking package by the owners or by representatives of a trekking agency authorized to recruit among guesthouse clientele.[8] Following a two- or three-night itinerary, groups of five to fifteen persons leave town in pickup trucks at 9 A.M. and are dropped off at a footpath a few kilometers from the village (Figure 5.3). Trucks then drive to the village site to deposit food and baggage. Drivers stay a while to eat, drink, and play cards for money in the Thai-owned grocery store and food stall (Figure 5.4). In the peak season, when there are five or six drivers in Ban Suay at the same time, they frequently remain in the village until after dark, often returning drunk to Chiang Mai. In the meantime, trekkers and two accompanying Thai guides reach Ban Suay after a two- to three-hour walk.[9] They eat and sleep in the village. Facilitating and controlling communications between villagers and visitors is the task of the guide-cum-interpreter (see Cohen 1982) (Figure 5.5). Thai guides generally do not speak any of the montagnard languages—but often pretend to in front of their customers. The translated commentary they provide the trekkers is from Thai or Northern Thai languages and is, in any case, presented from the Thai viewpoint.[10] The second day trekkers hike for another three hours toward another village that they will ultimately reach after a one- or two-hour elephant ride. After staying overnight in this second village, they spend the last day bamboo rafting (Figure 5.6). After floating downstream for a few hours, they lunch and then return by pickup truck to their Chiang Mai guesthouses.

Figure 5.3. Pickup trucks drive trekkers from Chiang Mai to a dirt road where a footpath leads to the village. Trekkers walk for a few hours while trucks take the bags to the village. (Photo by Jean Michaud)

Figure 5.4. Foreign trekkers are the main customers and raison d'être at the village noodle shop and grocery store opened by a Thai lowlander in 1986. (Photo by Jean Michaud)

Figure 5.5. After breakfast, trekkers listen to their Thai guide giving instructions for the day. Note the pile of plastic rubbish next to the house, a distinctive feature of tourist houses in Ban Suay. (Photo by Jean Michaud)

Figure 5.6. Bamboo rafting for a few hours is an essential feature of trekking tours in the region, an activity controlled by Thai middlemen. (Photo by Jean Michaud)

Figure 5.7. In the village, tourists interact mostly with Hmong children. (Photo by Jean Michaud)

When they arrive in Ban Suay on the first afternoon of their journey, trekkers typically are taken straight to the village house where they will eat and sleep. After a cup of tea or a drink bought at the Thai grocery store, some rest, some may go for a wash in the open, while others prefer wandering the village in small groups to observe and, for most, to take photographs. The latter rarely stray from the road crossing the village and generally act respectfully toward the villagers. Encounters occur almost exclusively with Hmong kids wanting to play or have their photograph taken in exchange for a few *baht* (Figure 5.7). Hmong adults keep a distance—but that does not preclude them from joyfully commenting among themselves about how the white foreigners dress, talk, and behave. After an hour or so, around five, everyone returns to the house to eat the dinner the Thai guides have prepared from food brought from a lowland market. Darkness falls around 6:30 P.M., and thereafter trekkers rarely quit the house's immediate surroundings—mainly for fear of being severely bitten by wandering dogs that roam the village at dark. Typical activities include chatting, singing Western songs with the guides, drinking soft drinks and alcohol, and smoking opium. People settle down to sleep at various times depending on their evening activities.

Around seven in the morning, everyone is roused for breakfast, again cooked by the guides, and departure, which is around 8 A.M. After 9 A.M., no trekkers are to be seen in the village, until approximately 3 P.M., when new groups arrive.

Hmong Marginals and Thai Middlemen

In the Hmong tradition, a visiting relative is normally accommodated for free in the house of somebody belonging to the same lineage or clan. On rarer occasions, a nonrelative or even a non-Hmong may ask to stay overnight. In such cases, individuals decide whether they wish to shelter the visitor, and, usually, no compensation is expected. In 1980, the first guides and tourists taken as guests to Ban Suay were accordingly accommodated in houses belonging to friendly people with whom they happened to meet and chat. Djaleun Sae Moua, a wealthy agriculturalist, polygynist, and shaman, was the first host. He initially accepted visitors in his house merely out of curiosity and goodwill. When the prospect of bringing visitors on a regular basis was raised, a financial compensation amounting to 20 *baht* per person per night was proposed by the guides and readily agreed to by their hosts.[11] Two households were involved in this first stage of limited reception activities. The heads of these two households were mature men whose status was assured in their respective clans as well as in the community. For them, dealing with tourists was immediately seen as a rather easy way to make extra money to supplement the profits from the sale of surplus agricultural produce to which their lineages already had access. Given the importance of clan, lineage, and household economic freedom in Hmong society, no one opposed the tourist presence or the grasping of this novel business opportunity by fellow villagers, although in the evenings the lively fireside discussion throughout the village often revolved around these amazing wandering-apparently-never-working *farang* (foreigners).

According to both the original hosts and guests with whom I discussed that early situation, it was not very long before the first guides began voicing some dissatisfaction. They argued that Hmong houses were not quiet enough, that kids, dogs, chicken, and pigs would annoy the tourists, and that the latter, by staying awake late at night, would in turn seriously disturb their Hmong hosts. The guides concluded that this arrangement would not be satisfactory on a regular basis. Against the promise of more potential business, the guides convinced their Hmong partners to build, entirely at Hmong expense, two tourist houses next to their own so that accommodations could be offered without hindrance. In 1986, a lowland Thai succeeded in opening a basic grocery store in the central part of the village, with products directed toward the needs of visiting tourists. The Hmong were not willing to run a store themselves, the business opportunities were attractive from the Thai's viewpoint, and no local opposition was expressed, so the outsider stepped in smoothly.

While only three trekking agencies were active in Ban Suay between 1980 and 1984, a tourist boom in the mid-eighties attracted several more, including five agencies in 1987 due largely to the success of the Visit Thailand Year promotional campaign. During the five subsequent years, some fifteen more agencies brought trekkers to the village at least once, while an almost equal number, new as well as established firms, either temporarily interrupted or simply dropped their activities there. By the summer of 1992, five different agencies were regularly visiting Ban Suay, while three or four more were irregularly appearing or passing through the village without staying. As for the villagers, three households belonging to two different clans were actively engaged in the guesthouse business, while three special buildings were used to accommodate groups. In the decade following the arrival of the first trekkers, three households once involved no longer hosted activities and four houses specifically built for touristic purpose were abandoned or turned into storage space. We will now examine in more detail what happened during these last years.

Around 1987, crucial changes took place. First, as already mentioned, demand from agencies rose dramatically. Second, opium smoking, an activity previously confined within certain limits, led to difficulties: demand for opium from guides and tourists increased with the number of visitors. Within a short period, the number of tourists coming to Ban Suay had jumped impressively: from a maximum average of fifty persons a month prior to 1987, the flow increased to an average of ten persons daily, for a total of more than three hundred visitors a month. As a result, wealthy families with steady and extensive agricultural activities who were successfully shifting from subsistence to cash-oriented production, but who had also been hosting tourists for some years, were obliged to spend more time at home and less in the fields, and at the same time they enjoyed less and less privacy.[12] Continued involvement with tourism thus meant that a shift would have to occur in the equilibrium of their daily lives, and they disliked the idea. Some also admitted to having grown wary of potentially serious run-ins with Thai authorities if they sold larger amounts of opium to foreigners. These early partners cautiously began to withdraw from the tourist business.

Most guides then looked for more cooperative heads of households who could provide them with the whole package of services they needed. Poorer households, who had been awaiting their chance, were quick to jump at the business opportunity. A few had already hosted for agencies visiting the village on an occasional basis when available capacity had been insufficient to house all visitors during peak season. On a household basis, these families and the guides quickly agreed to deals that included the construction of new houses to accommodate guests, unlimited provision of opium, and the obligation to provide all the time required to service trek visitors. This agreement meant that the new hosts were unable to work the fields regularly and had to rely on cash and the market economy to buy whatever they ate and smoked.

These second-wave Hmong tourist business partners differ in several ways from the pioneers in the field. First, they belong to a lower economic stratum than the two other clans represented in the village, the Li and Tang clans. By Hmong standards, they labor under severe handicaps, the origins of which considerably predate their entry into the business. The majority of adult members are addicted to opium smoking, and, therefore, can do little or no work in the fields; some have ceded all their rights to the land they once worked (see Ratanakhon 1978, about land rights). As an inevitable consequence of early opium addiction, most males from these families were unable to find Hmong wives; some have opted for marrying non-Hmong women from very poor families, while two have unofficially married unregistered migrants from Burma working in a nearby forest maintenance project. The children of these latter families do not have full legal recognition and, among other disadvantages, cannot officially attend school. Household sizes are all well under the village average. Their standard of living is low, as revenues from agriculture are meager, and expenses, linked to reproduction and opium smoking, are high. For several among them, male and female, the only regular source of revenue before the advent of tourism was that derived from day labor as fuel wood collectors or porters for other villagers. Household revenues were accordingly the lowest compared to the village average. By stepping into the tourist housing business, these marginal households upgraded their financial position remarkably. A 1991 estimate of village household revenues place these families among the highest annual income earners for that year (Michaud 1997).

Table 5.1 Breakdown of Fees Paid to the Trekking Agency
by Tourists, 1992

Receipts	Amount (in *baht**)	Percentage
Cost per person for a 2-night, 3-day trek	1,400	–
Total revenue for 8 trekkers:	11,200	100
Expenditures		
To the guest houses: 300/person	2,400	21
To the travel agency: ± 10 percent	1,120	10
• Truck rental with driver, return	1,200	11
• Food	600	5
• Rental of 2 rafts at 600 each	1,200	11
• Rental of elephants for 180/person	1,440	13
• Lodging in 2 villages, 20/pers./night	320	3
Total expenditures	8,280	74
The guides' share after all expenditures:	2,920	26

*Twenty-five *baht* are equal to U.S. $1.00.

To help explain why opium-addicted families relying on cash for their survival found a niche in the new wave of the tourist business, it is useful to look at a breakdown of the profits obtained from trekking activity. My calculations show that ultimately, the average proportion of the fee paid by the trekking tourists that actually reaches the villagers' hands is meager. Several intermediaries take their cut: the travel agency, the Chiang Mai guesthouse that provided the trekking agency with customers, and the pickup drivers. Furthermore, tour operators must pay for truck rental, the purchase of food in lowland markets, and services such as elephant riding and bamboo rafting (see Table 5.1). Most of this money goes to Thai middlemen. What remains is about one-third of the money initially collected. Moreover, in normal circumstances, the portion unspent upon completion of the trek goes to the guides in the form of wages. Some 90 percent of this remaining third usually finds its way into the guides' pockets. In total, around 1.5 percent of the money paid by the customers actually reaches each of the two villages visited; the rest is skimmed off by non-montagnard middlemen.

What about the extra money spent in the villages by trekkers eager to take pictures, buy drinks and handicrafts, or try a couple of opium pipes? These reportedly common activities (Cohen 1983) apparently constitute important revenue for montagnards (Dearden 1991). Here again, field observation indicates that the middlemen, not the villagers, get the biggest share. In Ban Suay, the money paid to children for pictures is instantly spent on sweets at the grocery store, the same store that belongs to the ethnic Thai and where all the evening drinks for trekkers are bought. None of this money remains in Ban Suay, for the shopkeeper reinvests all of his profits in his lowland home village. Also, although this seems to be exceptional in the North, I neither witnessed nor heard of any significant sale of real or alleged handicrafts to trekkers.[13] As for opium, profits from sales are split fifty–fifty between Hmong suppliers and the guides. The sale of a reasonable nightly total of ten pipes to an eight-person group means close to 100 *baht* (U.S. $4) in profits for each side, in this case a tangible financial contribution from the tourist business to the hosts.

Account must be taken of further economic costs for the Hmong partners. Waiting for the arrival of the visitors and, once they have arrived, catering to their needs makes any other economic activity impossible.[14] If additional quarters have been constructed to accommodate visitors, those buildings must be watched and maintained. In addition, villagers lend blankets and provide free rice, water, fuel wood, and supplementary food if the guide has lost some on route or is short for whatever reason. And, finally, the guide must be given free food, lodging, and opium to smoke. In fact, with supply exceeding demand—in the sense that the guide can decide to patronize another house upon upcoming visits or even bypass the village altogether—keeping the guide happy is vital if the flow of customers is to be maintained, and the price to be paid for that is proportional.

When all is said and done, a realistic—but purely statistical—appraisal of daily tourism revenues for one family hosting an average eight-person group and its two guides in Ban Suay is about 260 *baht* per night (accommodation: 160 *baht*; opium sales: 100 *baht*). This amount compares with the approximate 11,200 *baht* that the group would have spent on the trekking package as a whole (1,400 *baht* per person for a two-night trek, one of them spent in Ban Suay), not including drinks and opium. With opium, it is an additional 200 *baht*

(10 pipes at 20 *baht* each), which brings the total expenses of the trekkers to 11,400 *baht*. Therefore, the share that reaches Hmong villagers in Ban Suay from what is spent by tourists climbs to about 2.3 percent (260 out of 11,400 *baht*), a minuscule share that cannot stand comparison with that of the Thai middlemen, the real winners with 97.7 percent.

But however tiny this percentage, a long tradition of frugality still makes the amount involved an important one by Hmong standards. If the flow of visitors is maintained on a daily basis, the resulting annual household revenue of 94,900 *baht* would be well above that of most households in the village, an average of 24,600 in 1991. To generate an annual income roughly equal to the average household revenue in Ban Suay, one such group per host every fourth day is sufficient. It must also be remembered that this income from tourism is for households smaller in number than the village average, making the per capita income even more significant. This income is entirely dedicated to each hosting household, and no contribution whatsoever is made to the village economy, apart from a small fraction that is exchanged for local opium to smoke and to sell to the tourists (less than 10 percent of the total village opium production in 1991).

Frontiers of Hmong Identity

In Ban Suay, the overnight profits derived from tourism by those households coming late into the business are well known among all villagers. Yet, very few express real envy. Actually, when other Hmong talk about these residents, most show simple indifference, whereas some among the wealthy traditionalists actually show a certain degree of contempt. Even those related to host families, although more sympathetic, nevertheless keep a distance. I propose the following interpretation for this response.

As is well documented in research on the Hmong, certain frontiers exist in the self-definition of Hmong identity. Overstepping those frontiers may lead to labeling as a marginal. The categories of situations and behaviors that can lead to marginalization include: membership in a family with a long-term opium addiction where addiction occurs at an early age; refusal to properly fulfill the duties of cooperation at the lineage, clan, and village levels; and total reliance on the cash economy, as opposed to work in the fields, to provide for all needs. In such cases, the individuals or families concerned may find themselves consigned by the majority to this bleak marginal zone. In these households now active in tourism, the adults have no strong interclan ties built through profitable and productive marriages. They have insufficient children either to work the land effectively, to bring in wealth through more marriages, or to care for their parents in their old age. Even the children of these families are seen as having no future. They no longer learn how to work the land, and they tend to be prone to early opium addiction, with fathers and trekkers smoking in their homes and the resulting participation in smoking as they prepare the pipes. Although individual entrepreneurship in a lucrative new business activity is normally highly valued by the Hmong, anything that a marginal person or group of persons may do is viewed with some suspicion.

In the opinion of most villagers, the imperatives of prudence and self-respect eventually left them no choice but to abandon or refuse involvement in the tourism business. Faced with a trade increasingly perceived as endangering some of the main ingredients of traditional Hmong life through increased traffic and demand, and with a growing insolence on the part of certain guides who became intolerable to several Hmong hosts, they felt it necessary to get out of the business. Only those with nothing to lose were prepared to endure such circumstances. Indeed, none of the traditionally wealthy householders initially active in the tourist trade expresses regret for having left the field. Only the loss of extra cash income is regretted.

And what of the marginals? With tourism on the decline, indeed even showing signs of being close to bust in Ban Suay, their future is in doubt. As described above, some tourist operators have quit the village, leaving Hmong families who had relied on a single agency to readjust to this setback. When asked what they will do if tourism ends, the Hmong households active as partners in tourism claim they will return to fieldwork like any other Hmong. This prospect seems rather unlikely. Their positions in their own community are marginal. They have cut contact with most of the networks of cooperation linking relatives and neighbors and have pushed further into unknown territory by severing themselves from their traditional knowledge and means of production. Having spent all their profits on opium and consumer products, they will quite probably experience further marginalization and poverty. Their fate might well be similar to that of the occasional landless Thai who come to Ban Suay in search of cheap opium to smoke and ad hoc job opportunities as trekking porters. The economic future for these villagers is most probably that of economic exile for many of the family members who can hire out as unskilled laborers. That means a life of moving around highland villages, or even Thai towns, in search of casual and sporadic labor.

The Future of Tourism in Ban Suay

Villagers say the tourist business may continue in their community as long as the incidental inconveniences do not pass the limits of acceptability, a limit which apparently has yet to be reached. According to what has been said, either directly to me or in the course of village meetings called by government agents, inconveniences perceived by the Hmong are limited to the following: the damage to the road during the rainy season when trekkers' trucks use chains; the misbehavior of drunken drivers; and the noise generated by neighboring trekkers who sing together and occasionally shout throughout the night. Typically, in this context where nondirective childraising is the custom, no one has expressed concern about the potential undesirable influences on village youth.

From a more general perspective, Ban Suay's future as a tourist destination is also linked to the influx of wealth from state-run development projects and, in this case, tourism itself. Wealth brings material changes that soon become apparent. In Ban Suay, access to the regional marketplace has improved, leading in turn to a steady increase in the circulation of merchants and merchandise. Numerous peddlers and small-time traders who quickly bridge the gap between the village and the town have brought a flood of consumer products flowing into the community. In the eyes of the tourist, the village's "authenticity" is rapidly eroded by the influx of such signs of modernity.[15] Should this authenticity fade away, the clients communicate their disappointment to the guide, and the guide reports the event to his agency. If it is foreseen that the tourists' satisfaction may decrease to the point of threatening the profitability of the venture, plans are formulated to switch to another, more promising, authentic village. A number of guides regularly visiting Ban Suay explicitly predict this move for the near future, while several others have already taken such a step. When pressed, however, several guides also confessed that harsh competition from stronger agencies was also a major motive for leaving Ban Suay. As a matter of fact, market forces do play a major role in the field of tourism as they do in agricultural production and crop circulation. Market imperatives are determined outside the village sphere and all actors, be they endogenous or exogenous, must abide by the market's coercive rules.

One potential source of serious problems with the state is opium-related activity. Selling more opium means growing or buying more. Selling it to foreigners publicly exposes the fragility of official claims of near total eradication of opium cultivation in Thailand and runs headlong into recent state efforts to comply with foreign pressure to reduce drug production and sales. The result could be a major crackdown on opium-related tourist activities in the region. But generally speaking, the Thai state has no cause to be wary of the current development of tourism-related economic activities in Ban Suay. The overall effects of tourism on local economics and politics produce results in accordance with the state's general strategies of the settlement and cultural integration of montagnards. As a specific economic activity, hosting tourists may be regarded as accelerating the pace of "Thai-ization" of highland populations by expanding the local economy and by exposing villagers to consumer products that should become available through modernization (Michaud 1993). In our study village, however, the confinement of tourist activity to a very small social and economic space may severely limit its impact as an agent of change. This situation seems to be rather unusual in Northern Thailand and takes us to our concluding remarks.

Tourism and Hmong Social Structure

As far as trekking tourism—or in Smith's terms, environmental and cultural tourism—is concerned, this case study holds interest for the general field of social research on tourism for several reasons. It shows how a cleavage has developed in this local community between, on one hand, traditionalists who can accept modernity and integrate outside influences that provoke medium-range variations in the core of the group's identity, namely agriculture, and, on the other hand, those who have departed from this very basis of Hmong identity. Commercial activities in general, and tourism hosting in particular, do not fit into the traditional Hmong set of desirable activities because they do not allow the lineage-based cooperative system of exchange of goods and services to persist. The most basic cultural institutions such as marriage, healing rituals, and funerals are affected by commercial and tourist activities, which attack the very social fabric of the group. Abandoning agriculture in order to host tourists is associated with the breaking of the community circle and isolation from the family, the most important segment of society. This case also shows that tourist revenues are not necessarily desired by locals, despite guaranteed "easy" profits. The contempt shown by Thai guides toward their hosts and the cultural loss associated with the change in the household economy are considered too high a price to pay in comparison to the accrued financial benefits.

From the perspective of cultural resistance, it can be concluded that tourism in Ban Suay does not play a major role in favoring a better or quicker integration of these non-Tai villagers into the Thai nation. When compared to the limited number of other properly conducted case studies available—namely Forsyth (1992, 1995), Toyota (1993, 1996), and Kesmanee and Charoensri (1994)—the case of Ban Suay seems atypical of the highland villages in Northern Thailand touched by trekking tourism. Extending research horizontally to other Hmong villages in Thailand, as well as comparing other montagnard groups similarly affected by state interventionism and tourism-related activities, may help to confirm to what extent the Ban Suay case is representative or to identify what makes it so uniquely resistant to economic and cultural assimilation.

But perhaps the most interesting conclusion of this case study, from an anthropological point of view, is what it reveals about the social structure upon which the tourist hosts' social organization is built. By showing villagers what may happen when they depart from an agricultural and lineage-based economy, it reveals the breakpoint beyond which the Hmong no longer consider themselves authentically Hmong. In fact, as long as the Hmong cultural system can hold together and provide workable answers to the main dilemmas and challenges of life, as it did through centuries of hardship and external influence and menace, it will not need a new set of values, be they those proposed by tourists or by the Thai state. Such cultural cohesion certainly helps to explain why tourism, as a medium of cultural change, has had so little impact on Ban Suay society as a whole, despite several years of daily contact. As to how far an explanation of cultural resistance may be linked with what has been called "Hmongness," only further research will tell (see Yang 1975, Radley 1986, Kesmanee 1989, and Tapp 1989 on the cultural resistance of the Hmong in the peninsula).

Ironically, it can thus be said that tourism in Ban Suay has revealed to the villagers the cultural limits they have implicitly fixed for their society and has perhaps planted the seeds of a collective insight into what elements of that society should be protected given the social change processes that are taking place. In this case, tourism may have had a salutary impact on these hosts, not in the form of a solution, a reason frequently invoked in the situations of other less developed countries, but rather in the form of a catalyst for self-consciousness.

Notes

I am indebted to the Fonds pour la formation de chercheurs et l'aide à la recherche and to the Fondation Desjardins of Québec, as well as to the International Development Research Centre, the Social Sciences and Humanities Research Council, and the Canada-ASEAN Centre of Canada for their financial support. I also thank Christian Culas, Jean-Claude Neveu, Erik Cohen, Michel Picard, and Robert Wood for their constructive criticism, Yann Roche for drawing the two original maps, and Geoffrey Walton for competently polishing my poor English. Additional thanks to David Hagen for reviewing a final draft of this text.

A social anthropologist, the author collected data on this village during a total of fifteen months of fieldwork in Thailand between 1991 and 1993. Detailed results and analysis can be found in the doctoral dissertation (Michaud 1994a).

1. In particular, sociologist Erik Cohen has contributed several scholarly papers dealing with related questions (Cohen 1979b, 1982, 1983, 1989). However, Cohen favored research on a larger scale and never focused on a specific highland ethnic group or one single highland community. His conclusions therefore remain general (Cohen 1983, 318) and to this day can only be partially confirmed in the field (Michaud 1994a, chap. 1).

2. In accordance with several proclamations on ethics and personal responsibility, I have chosen to give the study village a fictitious name. Specific ethics for anthropological research in highland Thailand are discussed in Wakin (1992).

3. Thailand's administrative organization divides the country into provinces *(changwat),* which are further subdivided into regions *(amphoe),* districts *(tambon),* and, finally, villages *(mooban).*

4. Among others, see Bhruksasri (1989) and Kesmanee (1989) for a survey of the governmental strategies toward the eradication of opium in the hills.

5. Hmong society is clan and lineage based and is characterized by such features as ethnic endogamy, clanic exogamy, patri-virilocality, and a household economy with a male leader in full charge. For a detailed portrait of the social structure and its implications in the economic and political spheres, see Lemoine (1972), Geddes (1976), and Cooper (1984).

6. Although widely used in the tourist industry and by several researchers on tourism, the concept of trekking tourism is not clearly defined and its significance is often taken for granted. Faced with the problem of an opera-

tional definition, I have proposed some conceptual clarifications (Michaud 1994b).

7. This typology was put forward in the first edition of *Hosts and Guests* in 1977. Smith designated five types in all: ethnic, cultural, historical, environmental, and recreational tourism. Though somewhat basic, they are useful for classifying in a general manner the predominant motivations of tourists from affluent countries. Graburn (1989) and Cohen (1979a) have also proposed typologies.

8. In 1992, the total price for a two- or three-night trek generally ran from 1,200 *baht* to 1,700 *baht* per person (U.S. $48–68) and averaged 1,400 *baht*. This price includes all meals, transportation, lodging, and guide fees, but excludes extra beverages and other personal expenses.

9. Interviews with guides and ex-guides in Chiang Mai suggest that less than 10 percent of guides working on a regular basis for trekking agencies based in the city are of genuine montagnard origin, and observations by Toyota (1993) and Kesmanee and Charoensri (1994) are similar. During my stays in Ban Suay, no guide ever proved to be of such origin, although porters occasionally did.

10. For a glimpse into pejorative ethnic Thai perceptions of montagnards, see the highly instructive review by Jean Baffie (1989) on how the latter are depicted in cheap and tremendously popular Thai comics.

11. This price, equivalent to U.S. $0.80, has not changed since in Ban Suay.

12. The peak tourist seasons in Ban Suay are July–August and December–January. The first period falls in the middle of rainy season fieldwork, the second overlaps with New Year festivities and the beginning of opium harvest time.

13. Toyota (1993) also notes that the sale of handicrafts is not an important source of revenue in the Akha village she studied. In Ban Suay, when villagers are asked why they do not sell handicrafts, the answer is that trekkers show no interest. I observed that trekkers were advised by the guides to wait until they are back in Chiang Mai to make such purchases (guides receive better commissions on sales in the city shops where they are known).

14. In the case of a Mien (Yao) village visited daily by tourist buses, Forsyth (1992) notes that the elderly take care of the stalls. But he also notes that the families involved in this trade are wealthy ones, more like the first-wave Hmong local partners in Ban Suay. It makes sense that poorer households involved in agriculture simply do not dispose of the surplus labor necessary to cope with an extra activity; in our study village, the reverse situation is also true.

15. The concept of authenticity—in particular the notion of "staged authenticity"—has been at the center of lively debate for nearly twenty years in the social research on tourism. Important texts have been devoted to the

topic, in particular the landmark works of Dean MacCannell (1976) and Victor Turner and E. Turner (1978). Malcolm Crick (1989) has published a good summary of the views of the principal authors.

References

Arbhabhirama, A., D. Phantumvanit, J. Elkington, P. Ingkasuwan
1988   *Thailand, Natural Resources Profile.* Singapore: Oxford University Press, série Natural Resources of South-East Asia.
Baffie, Jean
1989   Highlanders as Portrayed in Thai Penny-Horrible. In *Hill Tribes Today,* ed. John McKinnon and Bernard Vienne, 393–408. Bangkok: White Lotus-ORSTOM.
Bhangananda, Kachitra, and Walaya Wiwatsorn
1989   *Manuel pour guides touristiques.* Bangkok: Centre de formation continue, Université Chulalongkorn.
Bhruksasri, Wanat
1989   Government Policy: Highland Ethnic Minorities. In *Hill Tribes Today,* ed. McKinnon and Vienne, 5–33. Bangkok: White Lotus-ORSTOM.
Boulbet, Jean
1975   *Paysans de la forêt.* Vol. 105. Paris: Ecole Française d'Extrême-Orient.
Chindarsi, Nusit
1976   *The Religion of the Hmong Njua.* Bangkok: Siam Society.
Cohen, Erik
1979a A Phenomenology of Tourist Experiences. *Sociology* 13:179–201.
1979b The Impact of Tourism on the Hill Tribes of Northern Thailand. *Internationales Asienforum* 10(1–2):5–38.
1982   Jungle Guides in Northern Thailand: The Dynamics of a Marginal Occupational Role. *Sociological Review* 30:236–266.
1983   Hill Tribe Tourism. In *Highlanders of Thailand,* ed. J. McKinnon and W. Bhruksasri, 307–325. Kuala Lumpur: Oxford University Press.
1989   Primitive and Remote: Hill Tribe Trekking in Thailand. *Annals of Tourism Research* 16(1):30–61.
Cooper, Robert
1984   *Resource Scarcity and the Hmong Response.* Singapore: Singapore University Press.
Crick, Malcolm
1989   Representations of International Tourism in the Social Sciences. *Annual Review of Anthropology* 18:307–344.

Dearden, Philip
1991   Tourism and Sustainable Development in Northern Thailand. *The Geographical Review* 18(9):400–413.
Dearden, Philip, and Sylvia Harron
1994   Alternative Tourism and Adaptive Change. *Annals of Tourism Research* 21(1):81–102.
Do, Dinh Sam
1994   Shifting Cultivation in Vietnam: Its Social, Economic and Environmental Values Relative to Alternative Land Use. Report to the International Institute for Environment and Development, Forestry and Land Use, series no. 3, London.
Forsyth, Timothy J.
1992   Environmental Degradation and Tourism in a Yao Village of North Thailand. Ph.D. diss., University of London.
1995   Tourism and Agricultural Development in Thailand. *Annals of Tourism Research* 22(4):877–900.
Geddes, William R.
1976   *Migrants in the Mountains: The Cultural Ecology of the Blue Miao (Hmong Njua) of Thailand.* Oxford: Oxford University Press.
Geertz, Clifford
1963   *Agricultural Involution: The Process of Ecological Change in Indonesia.* Berkeley: University of California Press.
Graburn, Nelson H.
1989   Tourism: The Sacred Journey. In *Hosts and Guests: The Anthropology of Tourism*, 2d ed., ed. V. Smith, 21–37. Philadelphia: University of Pennsylvania Press.
Huff, L. W.
1967   The Thai Mobile Development Unit Programme. In *Southeast Asian Tribes, Minorities and Nations.* 2 vols., ed. P. Kunstadter, 425–486. Princeton: Princeton University Press.
Kesmanee, Chupinit
1989   The Poisoning Effect of a Lovers' Triangle: Highlanders, Opium and Extension Crops, A Policy Overdue for Review. In *Hill Tribes Today*, ed. McKinnon and Vienne, 61–102. Bangkok: White Lotus-ORSTOM.
1991   Highlanders, Intervention and Adaptation: A Case Study of a Mong N'jua (Moob Ntsuab) Village of Pattana. Master's thesis, Department of Geography, Victoria University of Wellington.
Kesmanee, Chupinit, and Kulwadee Charoensri
1994   The Impact of Tourism on Culture and Environment: A Case Study of the Mae Taeng Trekking Route in Chiang Mai. Report to the Office of the National Culture Commission, Ministry of Education, Bangkok.

Keyes, Charles
1987 *Thailand: Buddhist Kingdom as Modern Nation-State.* Boulder, Colo.: Westview Press.

Kunstadter, Peter, E. C. Chapman, and S. Sanga, eds.
1978 *Farmers in the Forest: Economic Development and Marginal Agriculture in Northern Thailand.* Honolulu: University of Hawai'i Press, East-West Center.

Lemoine, Jacques
1972 *Un village Hmong vert du Haut-Laos: Milieu technique et organisation sociale.* Paris: Centre National de la Recherche Scientifique.

Lombard-Salmon, Claudine
1972 *Un exemple d'acculturation chinoise: La province du Gui Zhou au XVIIIe siècle.* Vol. 84. Paris: École Française d'Extrême Orient.

MacCannell, Dean
1976 *The Tourist: A New Theory of Leisure Class.* New York: Schocken.

McKinnon, John, and Wanat Bhruksasri, eds.
1983 *Highlanders of Thailand.* Singapore: Oxford University Press.

McKinnon, John, and Bernard Vienne, eds.
1989 *Hill Tribes Today: Problems in Change.* Bangkok: White Lotus-ORSTOM.

Michaud, Jean
1993 Catalyst of Economic and Political Change: Tourism in Highland Minorities in Ladakh (India) and Northern Thailand. *Internationales Asienforum* 24(1–2):21–43.
1994a Résistance et flexibilité. Le changement social et le tourisme dans un village Hmong de Thaïlande. Thèse de doctorat en anthropologie sociale, Département d'Anthropologie de l'université de Montréal.
1994b Le trekking par les textes. *Téoros* 13(3):33–37.
1995 Frontier Minorities, Tourism and the State in Indian Himalaya and Northern Thailand. In *International Tourism: Identity and Change,* ed. M. F. Lanfant, J. B. Allcock, and E. M. Bruner, 84–99. London: Sage Studies in International Sociology.
1997 Economic Transformation in a Hmong Village of Thailand. *Human Organization.*

Mongkhol, C.
1981 Integrated Agricultural Development as a Strategy to Stabilise the Hill Tribe People in Northern Thailand. Master's diss., Rural Social Development, Agricultural Extension and Rural Development Centre, University of Reading.

Moréchand, G.
1968 *Le chamanisme des Hmong.* Vol. 64. Paris: Bulletin de l'École Française d'Extrême-Orient.

Radley, Howard M.
  1986   Economic Marginalization and the Ethnic Consciousness of the Green Hmong (Moob Ntsuab) of Northwestern Thailand. Ph.D. diss., Institute of Social Anthropology, Oxford University.
Ratanakhon, Sophon
  1978   Legal Aspects of Land Occupation and Development. In *Farmers in the Forest: Economic Development and Marginal Agriculture in Northern Thailand,* ed. P. Kunstadter, E. C. Chapman, and S. Sanga, 45–53. Honolulu: University of Hawai'i Press.
Reynolds, Craig J., ed.
  1991   National Identity and Its Defenders. Monash Papers on Southeast Asia, no. 25. Monash University, Australia.
Smith, Valene
  1989   Introduction. In *Hosts and Guests: The Anthropology of Tourism,* 2d ed., ed. V. Smith, 1–17. Philadelphia: University of Pennsylvania Press.
Stuart-Fox, Martin
  1986   *Laos: Politics, Economics and Society.* London: Frances Pinter.
Tapp, Nicholas
  1989   *Sovereignity and Rebellion: The White Hmong of Northern Thailand.* Singapore: Oxford University Press.
Tourism Authority of Thailand (TAT).
  1992   Untitled mimeo leaflet. Chiang Mai: Tourism Authority of Thailand.
Toyota, Mika
  1993   The Effects of Tourism Development on an Akha Community: The Case of a Village in Chiang Rai. Paper presented at the Fifth International Conference on Thai Studies, SOAS, University of London.
  1996   The Effects of Tourism Development on an Akha Community: A Chiang Rai Village Case Study. In *Uneven Development in Thailand,* ed. Michael J. G. Parnwell, 226–240. Aldershot, UK: Avebury.
Turner, Victor, and E. Turner
  1978   *Image and Pilgrimage in Christian Culture: Anthropological Perspectives.* Oxford: Blackwell.
Wakin Eric
  1992   *Anthropology Goes to War: Professional Ethics and Counterinsurgency in Thailand.* Monograph no. 7. Madison: University of Wisconsin, Center for Southeast Asian Studies.
Walker Anthony R. ed.
  1992   *The Highland Heritage.* Singapore: Suvarnabhumi Books.
Yang, Dao
  1975   *Les Hmong du Laos face au développement.* Vientiane: Siosavath.

KATHLEEN M. ADAMS

⫸ 6

Touting Touristic "Primadonas": Tourism, Ethnicity, and National Integration in Sulawesi, Indonesia

In 1980 Pierre van den Berghe observed that tourism is generally superimposed on indigenous systems of ethnic relations and can profoundly affect indigenous ethnic hierarchies. Only recently, however, have Pacific scholars begun to explore seriously the salience of van den Berghe's observations for countries promoting tourism as a strategy for nation-building (see Adams 1991, Kipp 1993, Picard 1993, Wood 1984). For instance, Wood (1984) discusses the politics of tourism in Southeast Asia, noting that a government's promotion of tourism not only can heighten the cultural self-consciousness and ethnic pride of indigenous groups but also can suppress those groups that are not selected for the touristic map. Ultimately, then, tourism promotion of selected groups can exacerbate ethnic tensions. Likewise, Leong (1989) has explored how, in the context of tourism promotion, the Singaporean state mines, manufactures, and manipulates ethnic cultures for the purposes of economic development and national image management.

In part, this chapter contributes to this literature by presenting a case study of the effects of the Indonesian government's tourism promotion policy on indigenous ethnic relations. The research presented in this chapter supports Wood's observation that attempts to foster national integration and development by spotlighting particular ethnic locales for domestic and foreign tourists can have ironic results. As the cases to be discussed illustrate, histories of ethnic rivalries and religious differences greatly complicate such endeavors. Ultimately, this chapter argues for the importance of situating tourism within the context of preexisting ethnic, economic, and sociopolitical scenarios.

A second, related theme addressed in this chapter is the relationship between regional political boundaries and tourism. Recently, several writers have explored the emergence of regional, pan-ethnic identities in particular provinces in Indonesia (Antweiler 1994, Robinson 1993). Given such emergent identities, what are the ramifications of the selective touristic promotion of particular ethnic groups within a province? Specifically, in this article I argue that Indonesian provincial boundaries are an often overlooked factor in shaping the discourse of tourism development and promotion.

A third theme is that of tourism and cultural resistance or contestation. A number of recent studies have explored how, in the context of touristic scrutiny, various ethnic groups have found ingenious, symbolic ways to resist or reassert control of the encounter, often in the guise of ritual humor (Evans-Pritchard 1989, Errington and Gewertz 1989, Adams 1995). While these studies tend to center on instances of resistance in what van den Berghe has termed the "tourist-touree"[1] relationship (1980), this chapter turns the lens to focus on *interethnic* contestation in the context of the touristic promotion of particular ethnic groups.

Of the various ethnic destinations promoted by the Indonesian state, my focus here is on Tana Toraja Regency in South Sulawesi, where I conducted ethnographic research from 1984 to 1985 and again in 1987, 1989, 1991, and 1992. Data are drawn from Indonesian newspaper articles, field interviews with Torajans residing at tourist sites, Buginese in Ujung Pandang, guides, foreign and domestic tourists, and Indonesian tourism officials.

Tourism Policy in Indonesia

As an archipelago nation comprised of over three hundred ethnic groups and a multitude of religions, Indonesia faces the challenge of building a shared national consciousness. In addition to ubiquitous civic education in schools and on television, one way the Indonesian government strives to instill a broader sense of national unity is by championing tourism. As early as 1969, Indonesian leaders envisioned tourism contributing to nation-building in a variety of ways: first, as a source of foreign revenue[2]; second, as a way of enhancing Indonesia's celebrity on the international stage; and third, as a strategy for fostering domestic brotherhood (see 1969 Presidential Instruction No. 9, cited in Yoeti 1985, 56–58). By 1988, tourism's role in nation-building was officially encoded into the mission statement of the Ministry of Tourism, Posts, and Telecommunications. As the statement declares:

> Development of domestic tourism is aimed at strengthening love for country, instilling the soul, spirit and high values of the nation, improving the quality of the nation's cultural life and promoting historical sites (Departemen Pariwisata, Pos dan Telekomunikasi 1990, 40).[3]

For some years now, the message that domestic tourism to ethnic (and natural) locales makes a citizen a better Indonesian has been echoed in domestic travel advertisements, journals, and guidebooks. For instance, one Indonesian-language travel poster reads, "Know INDONESIA, . . . enjoy the panoramic beauty of our beloved homeland with INDONESIA PACKAGE TOUR." Emblazoned on the poster are photographs of a Batak structure at Lake Toba in Sumatra, a row of Torajan traditional buildings, fog-swept Mt. Bromo on Java, and a Dayak building on Balikpapan (Kalimantan). In a similar vein, the first quarter of a South Sulawesi guidebook for Indonesian youths is devoted to a discussion of tourism's importance in "strengthening the bonds between Indonesian ethnic groups" (Mandadung and Kinjan 1985, I), and a variety of Indonesian newspaper articles hail youth tourism as ideal for cultivating a love of country and a sense of national pride.

Most recently, in preparation for Visit Indonesia Year (1991) and Visit ASEAN Year (1992), the Indonesian government launched a national Tourism Consciousness Campaign (Kampanye Nasional Sadar Wisata). As part of this campaign, the minister of Tourism, Posts, and Telecommunications proclaimed the *sapta pesona*, or seven charms, to which all Indonesian groups should aspire. These tourist-pleasing charms included security, orderliness, friendliness, beauty, comfort, cleanliness, and memories. According to the minister, the objectives of the *sapta pesona* were "to form a strong and sturdy identity and to maintain national discipline" (Departemen Pariwisata, Pos dan Telekomunikasi 1990, 36).

Widely discussed in Indonesian newspapers (see Faisal 1989, Kuen 1990b, Tobing 1990, Kamarto 1990, Mandadung 1990, and Mardiatmadja 1991), outlined in handbooks distributed at tourist sites (see Departemen Penerangan 1990), and posted on plaques in villages, the Tourism Consciousness Campaign prompted even remote villages in outer Indonesia to consider their own touristic charms and attracting powers. For instance, as a result of this campaign, villagers I spoke with on the remote island of Alor enthusiastically speculated that their own dances, architecture, and scenic landscape would interest both foreign and domestic tourists. Noting their "uniqueness" in Indonesia, they pointed out that their small island offered a wider array of languages and cultures than most other Indonesian islands. Since uniqueness, indigenous architecture, and dance are all key markers of touristic marketability in Indonesia, it is clear that even the Alorese have absorbed the touristic rhetoric. Moreover, as these Alorese declared, the Seven Charms were just as present in Alor as they were in Bali, if not more so, since Alor lacks the drugs and drunkenness for which Bali's Kuta Beach has become famous.

In a sense, to borrow Benedict Anderson's (1983) now-famous phrase, we might conclude that the aggressive Tourism Consciousness Campaign has laid the foundations for a new kind of "imagined community," one based on shared visions of a group's own ethnic locale as a potential tourist destination, that is, an imagined Indonesia comprised of a mosaic of equally charming yet unique tourist sites. However, the gently rivalrous tone in my Alorese acquaintance's comment about Bali merits our attention; in contemplating the state's declaration of tourism as the pathway to national solidarity, local groups cannot help but recognize, and occasionally resent, that some groups receive more attention and promotion than others. In what follows, I explore the dynamics of this paradox in South Sulawesi.

A Brief History of Tourism in South Sulawesi

Tourism in South Sulawesi cannot be disentangled from the history of ethnic relations on the island. Both international and domestic tourism to Tana Toraja are relatively recent phenomena. During the 1950s and early 1960s, Buginese-Makassarese Muslim rebellions in South Sulawesi, in tandem with poor roads, made travel to the Christianized Toraja highlands extremely difficult and sometimes dangerous (Bigalke 1981, Harvey 1974, 1977). It was not until the late 1960s, after the South Sulawesi Muslim insurrections were quashed, that the first adventurer-tourists began to travel to Tana Toraja (Crystal 1977). Hiring cars and Buginese drivers in the Buginese-

Makassarese coastal city of Ujung Pandang, these intrepid travelers embarked on twelve- to fourteen-hour journeys to the highlands in search of people who had been described by drivers as "pagans" who "celebrate death" with elaborate, "extravagant funerals."

The trickle of tourists swelled in the early 1970s when Torajan entrepreneurs recognized the touristic potential of their homeland and started to produce articles and guidebooks about Sa'dan Torajan culture (Marampa' 1974 [1970], Salombe 1972). Highlighting Torajan traditional architecture, carved effigies of the dead, funeral rituals, and the region's spectacular natural beauty, these inexpensive booklets found an audience. Moreover, the 1973 European airing of a television documentary featuring a Torajan aristocrat's funeral ritual,[4] in tandem with the Indonesian government's 1974 Second Five Year Plan, which advocated the promotion of outer island tourist destinations, prompted still more tourist traffic to the Toraja highlands. Gradually, the growing body of touristic and anthropological literature about these Sulawesi highlanders helped make Torajan culture an entity to be studied, photographed, commoditized, and consumed by both outsiders and insiders (Adams 1984, 1990, 1993a, 1993b, Volkman 1984, 1990).

Toraja fully blossomed in the national (and international) touristic consciousness in 1984, when Joop Ave, the director general of Tourism, visited South Sulawesi and declared Tana Toraja the "touristic *primadona* of South Sulawesi" and Ujung Pandang the "Gateway to Tana Toraja." For many Torajans I spoke with, this declaration, along with the selection of an image of traditional Torajan architecture to embellish Indonesia's 5,000 *rupiah* note, was a source of great ethnic pride. As many of my Torajan friends noted, for centuries the Islamic coastal Buginese and Makassarese groups had dominated the region, raiding Torajans for coffee and slaves and generally limiting Torajan access to the outside world. Now, the tables were being reversed. This newfound touristic celebrity was earning Torajans an esteemed place in the Indonesian hierarchy of ethnic groups. As Torajans noted gleefully, the word *Toraja* (not *Bugis* or *Makassarese*) dominated maps of the region, the Buginese Makassarese city of Ujung Pandang had been symbolically demoted to the status of Tana Toraja's port of entry, and the outside world was snubbing these Muslim peoples, preferring to visit the Toraja highlands (see Figures 6.1 through 6.4).

Joop Ave's selection of the word *primadona* to describe Tana Toraja is intriguing. While it is not listed in older Indonesian-English

Figure 6.1. Western tourists pause to admire a panoramic view of the Rantepao Valley, Tan Toraja, Indonesia. (Photo by Kathleen M. Adams)

dictionaries, the word does appear in a dictionary of contemporary terms as the Indonesian spelling of "prima donna" (Schmidgall-Tellings and Stevens 1981). As a borrowing from the gendered Italian expression, the precise shifts in meaning in translation can only be imagined. What is clear is that the director general of Tourism wished to convey a sense of Torajans as the premier belles of Sulawesi. I was present on the occasion when Joop Ave made this declaration to a banquet room filled with South Sulawesi tourism officials and Torajan politicians. He had just finished his first tour of Tana Toraja Regency and at dinner had waxed poetic about the allure of Tana Toraja. Within days, even Torajans far off the beaten tourist track were repeating his declaration. Some clearly had no idea what a *primadona* was, though they had divined that it was something positive. When Joop Ave returned to Jakarta, he repeated his declaration at a widely publicized event and the term rapidly became a part of tourism parlance in Indonesia.

Tourism as a New Arena for Age-Old Ethnic Battles: Does Promoting *Primadonas* Breed Envious Understudies?

By 1991, when the Toraja highlands attracted 40,695 foreign tourists and 174,542 domestic visitors[5] (most of whom spent only an

Figure 6.2. European and Indonesian tourists rest under a rice
barn in a typical Toraja village. (Photo by Kathleen M. Adams)

Figure 6.3. Tourists observe meat division at a Toraja funeral ritual. (Photo by Kathleen M. Adams)

Figure 6.4. Western tourists and their guides shop for souvenirs at To Barana village, Tana Toraja, Indonesia. (Photo by Kathleen M. Adams)

obligatory evening in the Buginese-Makassarese capital of Ujung Pandang awaiting connections to the mountains), Tana Toraja's *primadona* status was undeniable. In the eyes of Torajans, touristic preeminence was evoking the envy of their age-old rivals. As a Torajan local tourism official summed up shortly after their promotion to *primadona* status: "The Buginese are jealous of all the development tourism has brought to Tana Toraja, but it's too late for them to do anything—they just have to be content with being a 'Gateway to Toraja,' rather than a real tourist destination." Another Torajan whose livelihood relies partially on tourism invoked age-old ethnic antipathies even more directly: "in the past the Buginese raided us for coffee and slaves, now they are after our tourists." Whether or not my informants' perceptions were on the mark, shortly after the director general of Tourism's 1984 visit to Sulawesi, Buginese and Makassarese tourism officials in Ujung Pandang began attempting to upgrade the touristic experience in Tana Toraja to international standards and to add additional South Sulawesi destinations to the touristic itinerary. As I will illustrate, for Torajans, both these and other Buginese efforts to partake in the nation's tourism development program did not foster regional integration but rather further fueled intra-island ethnic antagonisms.

Case 1: Controversy over Guiding Rights

The evidence of tourism as a new arena for age-old ethnic rivalries crystallized in 1985, in a battle over the guiding rights of local Torajans. While visiting Toraja with an entourage of South Sulawesi tourism officials in 1984, Joop Ave observed that the tourist experience in Tana Toraja needed some upgrading. Several officials in the entourage noted the number of unlicensed, aspiring guides proliferating in Rantepao (the main center of tourist services in Tana Toraja) and other Torajan tourist sites. These young Torajan guides, with their villager clothes and hustler style struck officials as a potential embarrassment. From the viewpoint of the Ujung Pandang officials, the Torajan "wild guides" *(guide liar),* as they dubbed them, were not only untrained but also unprofessional. This concern with professionalism reflects the state's ideas about order and security: whereas wild guides were perceived as a threat to the state's carefully manufactured imagery of tamed cultural diversity, professionalism promised uniformity and central control. By early 1985, the South Sulawesi Provincial Tourism Office issued a decree that guides could not operate in Toraja without a license from the state. The decree provoked a great uproar from Torajans. Acquiring a license required money and schooling in distant Ujung Pandang, neither of which were available to the young and relatively poor Torajan wild guides.

The new mandate provoked an outcry from not only guides but also Torajans of all ranks and occupations. Many Torajans I interviewed declared with annoyance that the majority of the official and hence most lucratively paid guides were not Torajan but Muslim Buginese or Chinese, people whom Torajans felt knew little of their customs and frequently misrepresented the predominantly Christian Torajans as pagan and backward. For Torajans, the decree meant that they would no longer have the opportunity to represent themselves to outsiders or make money guiding those tourists that, as one wild guide put it, "had not already been snared by Ujung Pandang-based travel agencies." Local Torajan officials lobbied to have the South Sulawesi Provincial Tourism Office offer a free training workshop for guides in Tana Toraja so that aspiring Torajan guides could earn licenses. The lobbying efforts succeeded, and in late October 1985, eighty-eight Torajans participated in a two-week-long "Local Guide Training Workshop" held in Rantepao. The workshop included lessons from local elites on Torajan mythic history, architecture, dress symbolism, and ritual traditions. In addition, several professional guides from Ujung Pandang lectured on tourist etiquette and, as the token foreign anthropologist, I was asked to present a lesson on "what tourists want." At the end of the workshop, participants were tested on the material covered in the sessions, with the promise that those who passed would be granted licenses.[6]

From the outset the workshop was highly charged. Several of the Buginese travel bureau officials lecturing at the workshop confided their frustrations over Torajan demands to be granted what they deemed easy licenses. As one Buginese travel agency owner grumbled to me,

> Torajans want to politicize tourism so that they get Torajan guides—but you *can't* do this. How can they assert that just because they are Torajan, they know more about Torajan culture than outsiders who have studied it? Knowledge of Torajan culture isn't in one's blood—it's not passed down in genes—you have to study it. [A prominent Torajan elder who lectured at the workshop] is clever, but that doesn't mean his children have automatically inherited his knowledge of Torajan culture—they have to study first. I've been studying Tora-

jan culture since 1968. Also, the problem with this guide-training thing is that it has attracted people who aren't necessarily devoted to or talented for guiding. Instead, we've got people looking for free training or folks from the "tourist objects" who were ordered to attend to become explainers for their sites—and their talents weren't weighed. . . . Yeah, now we'll have to use them when we take tourists to their sites, but they're not yet ripe, and certainly not yet professional. . . . But Torajans are playing politics without considering the needs of the tourists. You *can't* politicize tourism (Adams 1985).

Ironically, in the Torajans' eyes, it was the Ujung Pandangers who, seeking to monopolize the Torajan commodity of tourism, had politicized tourism in the first place. For them, permission to sponsor a training workshop symbolized a minor victory in taking back what was rightfully theirs.

However, a number of unexpected mix-ups were to rob some Torajans of their sense of victory. When the governor of South Sulawesi did not arrive to open officially the workshop as scheduled, a few of the Torajans sitting next to me murmured their misgivings. By the second morning of the workshop, when it was announced that the anticipated funds to cover the costs of daily snacks and participants' transportation had not been received from the governor's office and the tourism office, the murmurs of doubt about the commitment of Ujung Pandang officials to the workshop erupted into a long and tense discussion. The Buginese provincial officials supervising the workshop clarified that there had never been any money committed to the endeavor, only staff participation in the lectures. Torajans in the auditorium voiced their disbelief, speculating that the Buginese had deliberately diverted the funds "because they don't want the local guides to become official guides, as their own non-Torajan guides will have a harder time competing." The workshop nearly collapsed, as the meeting deteriorated into a tense debate about where to get the necessary funds. Given their suspicions of Buginese betrayal, a number of Torajan participants were reluctant to dig into their own pockets to cover the expenses. Eventually the regent *(bupati)* of Tana Toraja donated 250,000 *rupiah,* and most participants agreed to make daily contributions for snacks.[7]

The rest of the training workshop went relatively smoothly. Following the conclusion of the workshop, the participants took their licensing exams and, to their delight, most passed. However, when I returned over a year later in early 1987, many of the wild guides were grumbling once again. Apparently, only a few of the promised licenses had arrived. Moreover, they had not expected to be charged a fee to activate their licenses and were incensed that they would have to pay for the right to guide in their homeland. As one declared, "It's the outside guides that should have to pay, not us." Again, there was speculation that the Buginese were deliberately blocking Torajan efforts to retain some of the tourism revenues in the homeland. While I suspect that many of the snafus surrounding the training workshop were rooted in miscommunication and innocent misunderstandings, it is significant that Torajans interpreted the complications as deliberately engineered and rooted in ethnic rivalries. As this case illustrates, promoting tourism does not automatically promote regional ethnic solidarity. For these historic rivals, it only exacerbated age-old tensions.

Case 2: Resentments over Lowlander Attempts to Siphon Tourism Revenues

At the same time that Torajan wild guides were lobbying for guiding rights in their homeland, Torajans involved in other sectors of the tourism industry had their own complaints, which centered on beliefs that the Buginese were attempting to horn in on the tourism cash cow. After his celebrated visit to Tana Toraja in 1984, Joop Ave, the director general of Tourism, decreed that tourist flights between Ujung Pandang and Tana Toraja be instituted on a daily basis to facilitate visits to the highlands (previous flights to Toraja were scheduled twice a week, although they were erratic at best). The Torajans I knew were thrilled—some even speculated that the flights would allow tourists to bypass Ujung Pandang altogether. However, by May 1985, Torajans active in tourism were alarmed to hear rumors of a new flight schedule that entailed changing the arrival time of the flights from Bali to Ujung Pandang from the morning to the late afternoon and scheduling the flights from Ujung Pandang to Tana Toraja to the morning. As one Torajan hotelier in Rantepao observed with irritation, "[With this plan] tourists will be forced to spend two nights in Ujung Pandang. It's Tana Toraja that's the tourist destination, but Ujung Pandang is trying to suck up our profits. Those Ujung Pandang hotels weren't built for tourists in the first place, they were built for traders and officials." He complained that the bulk of tourism development money given to the Provincial Tourism Office in Ujung Pandang is not passed on to Tana Toraja Regency, as he felt it should be; rather, the office distributes the funds all over South Sulawesi. Heaving a heavy sigh, he murmured, "It's the Ujung Pandangers who are giving us problems."

Likewise, a Torajan souvenir seller with whom I was friendly expressed similar suspicions about the rumored plan to alter flight arrival times.

> Those Ujung Pandang people [for her they were synonymous with the Buginese] are making things hard for us Torajans again. They've succeeded in changing the planes from Bali so tourists are forced to spend two nights in Ujung Pandang. Just what are tourists going to do in Ujung Pandang?! Ujung Pandang is only the "Gateway to Toraja," it's not the tourist destination, you know. Tourists aren't going to be happy about this. And eventually it'll be us who lose—tourists aren't going to want to come to Tana Toraja any more if they are forced to spend two nights in Ujung Pandang. But those Ujung Pandang folks are sly. Now they are staging dances at the Fort [site of Ujung Pandang's main museum] so that tourists will go there instead of seeing dances here in Tana Toraja. Those Ujung Pandang people are always trying to make a profit from us Torajans (Adams 1995b).

Her husband, a respected local leader, interjected that the flights were changed at the suggestion of Joop Ave, the director general of Tourism. Noting that Joop Ave proposed this so that tourists would stay longer in Sulawesi and so that Ujung Pandangers could reap the profits of tourism as well, he surmised that Joop Ave was swayed by the Buginese on his last visit to the island a month before. Turning to his wife, he speculated,

> Remember last month when he was supposed to come to a meeting here in Tana Toraja, but it didn't happen and he was stopped in Ujung Pandang? Ujung Pandangers probably deliberately arranged things that way so that they could influence him. If only he had made it to Toraja, things certainly wouldn't have turned out like this.

Returning to the issue of the Ujung Pandang dance performances, my souvenir-selling friend gave me a vigorous poke and reminded me of how, two months earlier, the prime minister of Singapore had been scheduled to visit Tana Toraja following the opening of a cement factory in lowland Sulawesi. Instead, the prime minister was whisked away to the Golden Makassar Hotel in Ujung Pandang, where he was entertained with Torajan dances. "What's more," she added in an exasperated tone, "They say the dancers weren't even Torajan! Those Bugis are always trying to profit from our Torajan cultural uniqueness." Indeed, whether or not the rumors of the flight changes and the Buginese performing Torajan dances were accurate, Torajan commentaries about the state's tourism policy in South Sulawesi were generally laden with these images of urban-rural and low-lander-highlander ethnic rivalries.

Highlanders' fears that the Buginese would attempt to siphon off tourists by replicating Toraja in Ujung Pandang mounted in the late 1980s, when plans were announced for the construction of a mini-South Sulawesi theme park in a historic fort seven kilometers south of Ujung Pandang. The park was envisioned as South Sulawesi's key contribution for the touristic promotion of Visit Indonesia Year 1991 (Robinson 1993, 230). The setting of Somba Opu Fort is significant, as the fort is the site where, approximately 350 years ago, Makassarese fighters led by Sultan Hasanudin waged one of the last battles against the invading Dutch army. Thus, several hundred years later, in 1989, the fort was being unearthed and restored as a sacred site where various South Sulawesi groups would once again encounter outsiders. However, this time the invading outsiders were not Dutch soldiers but coveted tourists bringing economic rewards.

South Sulawesi tourism developers regaled the selection of this site for Taman Miniatur Sulawesi (Miniature Sulawesi Park) as an opportunity to restore Somba Opu to its former position of glory. As the writers of a book promoting investment in South Sulawesi proclaimed, "Somba Opu is therefore nothing else than a fortress of defense mythologized as a symbol of greatness, courage and pride of the South Sulawesi people at that time" (Wahab 1992). This seemingly semiconscious transformation of a place of Makassarese resistance into a sacred site embodying the (presumably unified) greatness and pride of all South Sulawesi peoples is evocative of Hobsbawm and Ranger's (1983) now-classic notion of "the invention of tradition." In short, through its selection as the locale for Taman Miniatur Sulawesi, the fort is being refashioned into a key symbol of a pan-regional identity. Although South Sulawesi regional identity is only recently emergent and far from seamless, this mythologizing of the fort lends it the authority of a glorious past.

A brief mention of recent anthropological discussions of the assertion of a South Sulawesi regional identity is appropriate at this point. Observing the national political context for the construction of regional identities in Indonesia (the economic development agenda of the New Order and the instillation of national integration through the cultivation of common national values), several writers have suggested that there is growing evidence of the forging of a pan-ethnic provincial identity in South Sulawesi. Antweiler (1994), for example, points to the dwindling ethnic residential segregation in Ujung Pandang, the growth of ethnic intermarriage (particularly between lowland Islamic groups), and the increasingly frequent references to common South Sulawesi cultural traits by Ujung Pandang academics, journalists, and ordinary people. However, in discussing how riots between city youth groups are often couched in ethnic terms and in noting the endurance of powerful ethnic stereotyping between these groups, he also offers ample evidence for the persistence of strong ethnic sentiments, despite the state's orchestrated moves to tame them. Likewise, in Robinson's exploration of the emergence of the platform house as a symbol of South Sulawesi regional identity (1993), she is careful to note that this symbol of common identity has salience only for the Islamic groups in South Sulawesi (the Buginese, Makassarese, and Mandarese), not for the Toraja or the Chinese. Thus, while the foundation for a common regional identity may be salient for some groups at some times, it is not yet sturdy, and some groups (for example, the Toraja and Chinese) are more likely to be set apart from this identity. In part, this separation reflects the fact that, at the provincial level, political power remains in the hands of the Islamic Buginese.

Returning to Taman Miniatur Sulawesi, the park was deliberately modeled after Ibu Suharto's[8] celebrated Mini-Indonesia in Jakarta. In fact, the name of the park was ultimately changed to Taman Budaya Sulawesi[9] because of concerns about detracting from the "uniqueness" of Ibu Suharto's park in Jakarta (Stanislaus Sandarupa, personal communication). Taman Budaya Sulawesi was designed to feature traditional architecture and cultural displays from the four main ethnic groups in South Sulawesi province (Bugis, Makassar, Mandar, Tana Toraja). As Robinson has noted, despite the strong presence of the Torajan traditional house in the park's promotional brochures, the park represents the "first real attempt to establish everyday vernacular architecture of the Islamic peoples of South Sulawesi as an aspect of the province's attraction for visitors" (1993, 230).

As noted earlier, a number of Torajans were aware of the park's potential to displace them from their position as the most celebrated group in South Sulawesi and felt that they had little say in the matter. In Tana Toraja, rumors circulated that Torajans were not represented on the park's planning committee (which turned out to be untrue). On the occasion of the park's opening in the summer of 1991, the governor of South Sulawesi declared that: "It wouldn't be in the least bit astonishing if Miniature Sulawesi Park one day becomes the most interesting tourist object in all of eastern Indonesia. The issue now is how we can develop and improve the services and facilities at the site" (anon. 1991a, 10). For many Torajans these were ominous signals that Ujung Pandangers were promoting Mini-Sulawesi to compete with their title as "*primadona* of South Sulawesi."

To make matters worse, as opening day approached, a number of Torajans felt they had little control over how they were represented in the displays or how their rituals were presented in the park.[10] One Torajan student studying in Ujung Pandang told me of how irked he was to learn that the park officials planned to alter significantly the Torajan house consecration ritual *(mangrara tongkonan)* that was to accompany the opening festivities of the park. "The Bugis said there'd be no live pigs at the ceremony! But pigs are essential for the *mangrara* ritual—how can you have a house consecration without pigs? Just because they are Muslim and uncomfortable with pigs doesn't mean they should be allowed to change our rituals." According to the student, he and many of his Torajan friends residing in Ujung Pandang decided to boycott the opening ceremony at the park to protest this issue.

Taman Miniatur Sulawesi (as it was then known) opened to coincide with South Sulawesi's Second Annual Festival of Culture. Indonesia's minister of agriculture opened the festivities with a speech stressing the festival's importance to achieving the nation's tourism goals and to fertilizing a love for the homeland. Moreover, he emphasized that:

> Up until now, the tourist destination of South Sulawesi is only known for its primadona, Tana Toraja. But actually there are other tourist sites here with great potential for development. With this Festival of Culture, these other regions of South Sulawesi have the opportunity to showcase their touristic potential and become better known (anon. 1991b, 1).

Undoubtedly, the minister's words resonated with the Sulawesi groups at the festival. Partly as a result of the state's tourism promotion policies and partly through witnessing Torajans basking in touristic celebrity, people from the lesser-known regions of Sulawesi have already begun pursuing touristic fame. Local scholars are researching and listing potential tourist destinations, and local newspaper columnists have helped to promote interest in finding alternative tourist locations so that, as one writer put it, "the province is not dominated by already known locations such as Tana Toraja and the like" (Amier 1993).

In fact, since the late 1980s, South Sulawesi newspaper articles have regularly featured headlines announcing the new *primadonas* in South Sulawesi. As one 1990 South Sulawesi newspaper headline proclaimed, "South Sulawesi Doesn't Only Have Tana Toraja" (Kuen 1990). Other headlines heralded "Lemo, the Hidden Primadona" (Huka 1990) and reminded South Sulawesi residents that Ujung Pandang's central market was "still a primadona" (anon. 1993). Still other newspaper articles hailed Jambu Mete (a predominantly Muslim locale near Maros) the "Primadona of the Grilled Fish Region" (anon. 1992) and declared "The Kuri Coast and Batimurung the Tourist Primadona of Maros [a Buginese region of South Sulawesi]" (Basir 1991). By the early 1990s, *primadona* fever had caught on so that even *tamorilla* fruit and crab were being hailed as *primadonas* of South Sulawesi in local newspaper headlines and articles (anon. 1990, Amin 1991).

It is noteworthy that these articles announcing the new *primadonas* of Sulawesi are appearing in Indonesian-language South Sulawesi newspapers. The immediate audience is not foreign tourists, nor even Javanese tourists, but residents of South Sulawesi, many of whom are already familiar with these areas and foods. Thus, it is important to ask what purpose these articles serve. Aside from encouraging Ujung Pandangers to reacquaint themselves with an array of cultures and foods in their own province, this profusion of *primadonas* symbolically deflates the preeminence of Toraja's *primadona* title.

A similar move to promote other lowland regions of South Sulawesi, thereby diminishing Tana Toraja's preeminence in the province, can also be discerned in a recent English-language video produced by the South Sulawesi Provincial Tourism Office. This thirty-five-minute video, entitled "South Sulawesi, Land of Surprises," begins with a lengthy segment heralding the touristic charms of Ujung Pandang and its offshore islands. A second elaborate segment focuses on the southern coastal region of the peninsula. The segment addressing Tana Toraja is buried toward the end of the video and lasts only about ten minutes. As a friend commented, "If you blinked you could almost miss Toraja!" While she was exaggerating, the video makes it clear that the Ujung Pandang-based officials at the Provincial Tourism Office are no longer heralding Toraja as the central attraction in South Sulawesi.

Building Bridges and Boundaries: Torajans' Encounters with Domestic Tourists

How do actual touristic encounters figure into this picture of nation-building and regional integration in South Sulawesi? What are the effects of domestic tourism on interethnic relations and nation-building? Ironically, while there is a rapidly growing literature on tourism in South Sulawesi, it gives but passing attention to domestic tourists (for example, Crystal 1977, Volkman 1984, 1990, Yamashita 1994). That is surprising, as domestic tourists greatly outnumber foreign tourists. In 1989, for example, five out of six visitors to Tana Toraja Regency were domestic tourists (Razaq 1991). Based on interviews as well as on a perusal of guest registries at tourist sites, the majority of domestic visitors to Tana Toraja are urban Buginese, Javanese, and Chinese Indonesians. Many Sulawesi lowlanders visit Toraja as part of a school group *pesantren* or government entourage.

The majority of the lowland Muslim tourists I interviewed in Tana Toraja appeared ambivalent about their highland neighbors. While many commented that the Toraja were "less backward" than they had anticipated and some even observed a few linguistic or mythological similarities, most focused on aspects of Torajan culture that they found disturbing. A few Buginese tourists commented that although the mountains were lovely, Torajans were not very friendly. Other lowland Sulawesi Muslim visitors expressed their disdain for the Torajan affinity for pigs and dogs. Still others complained of the food, the mud, or the sanitary conditions. Not surprisingly, such ambivalent feelings were often mutual. Torajan souvenir sellers often grumbled with disappointment when Buginese descended from the tour buses, declaring them "stuck-up" and "stingy." Several vendors observed that, unlike visitors from other islands, Muslim tourists from lowland Sulawesi did not buy many carvings as gifts for their friends back home. Instead, they bought small, inexpensive bamboo items. (Indeed, very few of the middle-class Buginese I knew in Ujung Pandang decorated their homes with Torajan souvenirs. This general lack of interest in Torajan carvings may again convey the cultural ambivalence that typifies Toraja-Buginese relations). Other souvenir sellers claimed that whenever Buginese youth groups browsed in their souvenir shops, they would tell their relatives to help them keep an eye on their goods, because "Buginese kids don't buy, they shoplift."

Of all the visitors to Tana Toraja, Toba Batak tourists appear to be the most successful in fulfilling the Indonesian government's aims of fostering common bonds between different ethnic groups via domestic tourism. Like the Toraja, the Toba Batak of Sumatra are a strongly Christianized mountain people who receive much attention from tourists. Moreover, both in Tana Toraja and in Toba Batak, the touristic attractions are non-Christian cultural and religious elements. Finally, both groups are experiencing indigenous cultural revivals. Batak tourists I spoke with were particularly struck by the similarities between Torajans and themselves. As one Batak exclaimed, "It's just like home! The carved houses, the water buffalo, everything." And as an eighteen-year-old Batak woman recorded on my tourist survey, "Generally, Torajans and Bataks are just the same, both in terms of their attitudes and their dialects." This feeling of Batak-Toraja kinship appears to be mutual. Torajans I interviewed spoke of enjoying their encounters with Batak tourists. They commented on the similarities in language (unapparent to me) and cultural style. Moreover, they noted that Toba Batak, like themselves, were Christian and hence comfortable around the pigs and dogs that make up the Torajan landscape.

The Indonesian government's strategy of using tourism to forge ties between different ethnic groups also appears to be somewhat more successful with Balinese visitors to Tana Toraja. Although I did not encounter large numbers of Balinese tourists, those Balinese I spoke with commented on the resemblance of Torajan scenery to their own and observed that Torajans, like themselves, were acclaimed as talented carvers. Moreover, Balinese and Torajans alike noted that *aluk to dolo* (Torajan indigenous religion) is also "classified by the government as a branch of Hindu Bali." Notably, they did not dwell on the many differences between their religions, but contrasted them with Islam.

Clearly, ethnicity, religion, and local histories all color such encounters between Torajans and domestic tourists from other regions. In short, such face-to-face encounters between Indonesian domestic tourists and tourees can both bolster nation-building—fostering recognition of commonalities between diverse groups—and reignite ethnic and religious antipathies.

Provincial Political Boundaries and the Discourse of Tourism Development

The cases discussed here underscore the importance of situating tourism within the context of preexisting ethnic, economic, and sociopolitical processes. As we have seen, the history of ethnic and religious tensions between lowland Buginese-Makassarese and highland Torajans has greatly complicated the state's efforts to forge national unity through tourism. The promotion of Tana Toraja to touristic *primadona* of the province has added new fuel to long-simmering ethnic antagonisms. Rather than fostering pan-provincial bonds between ethnic groups in South Sulawesi, tourism promotion has intensified interethnic competition, rivalry, and mutual suspicion between some South Sulawesi groups. In short, van den Berghe's observations about tourism's effect on social relations in San Cristobal, Mexico hold true for the situation in South Sulawesi: it has rendered even more complex a preexisting system of ethnic relations (van den Berghe 1994, 145).

Moreover, this chapter has championed the importance of attending to regional political boundaries in researching tourism. Drawing attention to provincial boundaries enables us to perceive new dimensions of the state's effects on indigenous peoples' perceptions of their own identities. In addition, by focusing on the framing of tourism at the provincial level, we are better able to understand how the state's manipulation of local and ethnic markers fosters a sense of regional, rather than simply Torajan, entitlement to tourists (and, more importantly, to the accompanying political celebrity and economic rewards). Briefly put, provincial political boundaries play a critical role in reshaping the discourse of tourism development in South Sulawesi.

While I have devoted much of this chapter to tracing the ethnic rivalry that resurfaced in the context of tourism promotion in South Sulawesi, I do not wish to suggest that the Indonesian government's attempts to foster national integration through tourism have been entirely unsuccessful. Spotlighting Toraja as a touristic *primadona* has clearly spurred other areas in South Sulawesi to refashion themselves as aspiring *primadonas,* and in that sense has encouraged economic development and local cultural efflorescence. Moreover, the touristic promotion of Tana Toraja has enhanced infrastructure in South Sulawesi, making travel within the region easier and more common, and it has fostered a sense of ethnic pride and centrality to the nation for Torajans. In addition, as I have argued elsewhere

(Adams 1991), face-to-face touristic encounters between Torajans and Bataks, as well as other Christian Indonesian groups, have generally fostered new appreciations of commonalities and enhanced national pride.[11]

Likewise, the state's celebration of traditional cultures in South Sulawesi serves to bolster Indonesians' pride in their own cultural resilience after years of colonialism and cultural imperialism from the West. As one South Sulawesi column declared:

> As Indonesians we should thank God for having given us a country so beautiful and rich in cultures. If before independence foreigners came to our country and oppressed and exploited our race, now after freedom it's just the opposite . . . their coming here [as tourists] is making our country rich (Faisal 1989).

In this sense, tourism can foster nation-building by reminding Indonesians of their common identity vis-à-vis foreigners. The columnist's invocation of Indonesians' shared colonial struggles against the Dutch does just that, while stimulating readers to think triumphantly about the latest wave of outsiders penetrating their country.

Finally, as Rita Kipp (1993) has astutely observed, the Indonesian cultural policy of encouraging ethnic pride masks the imbalances of wealth and power in Indonesia. In a similar vein, Torajans' promotion to *primadona* status effectively highlights local provincial ethnic rivalries and diverts attention from the economic and power imbalances between inner and outer Indonesia. By inadvertently fueling competition between Buginese and Torajans, tourism deflects attention from common resentments of Jakarta's advantaged position and authority. It is perhaps in this sense that the *primadona* policy contributes most forcefully to national integration.

Notes

A shorter version of this essay was originally presented at the 1994 World Congress of Sociology in Bielefeld, Germany. I am grateful for the thoughtful suggestions made by Greg LeRoy, Michel Picard, and Robert Wood. I also wish to extend my thanks to Mary McCutcheon for sending me the South Sulawesi promotional video.

1. "Touree" refers to the ethnic group member who is the object of the tourist's gaze.

2. For more on the relationship between tourism, economic development, and nation-building, see Wood (1979, 277) and Booth (1990).

3. Also see Departemen Kepariwisata, Pos dan Telekomunikasi (1992, 41).

4. According to Toby Volkman (1985, 165), this documentary was produced by Ringo Starr, which presumably added to its cache.

5. These are the most recent figures available. The domestic figures may be slightly inflated, as the government determines this figure by counting hotel and homestay registers. Thus, some traders and businesspeople are inadvertently added to the pool. However, during my twenty-two month stay in Ke'te' Kesu' (the most visited tourist site in Tana Toraja), I found that domestic tourists far outnumbered the foreign tourists. Many of the domestic tourists came on group tours, often organized by schools, scout clubs, and so forth.

6. By 1991, a tourism and hotel studies high school had opened in Tana Toraja, effectively eliminating the need for local guide training workshops.

7. A few participants made a show of bringing their own snacks and refusing to contribute to the donation basket, steadfastly noting that the funds should come from the Buginese-run provincial tourism office, not their own pockets. It was unclear whether this was a strategy to conceal the fact that they could little afford to make a donation, or whether it was truly a matter of principle—a refusal to be taken advantage of by people they perceived to be their rivals.

8. President Suharto's wife.

9. This translates as Sulawesi Culture Park. It is noteworthy that, although the park showcases the different cultural traditions of South Sulawesi, "culture" is singular and not plural.

10. A number of Ujung Pandang Torajans worked as consultants on the Torajan section of the park. Moreover, a ritual specialist from the highlands officiated at the consecration of the *tongkonan* (traditional house) erected in the park (Sandarupa 1994).

11. However, perhaps not surprisingly, Buginese tourists I interviewed following their visits to Tana Toraja generally did not return with a new appreciation of their many regional commonalities with Torajans. Rather, most of the Buginese I spoke with, after noting Tana Toraja's refreshing mountain climate and scenery, made negative comments about the ubiquitous mud and pigs. For most Buginese, their touristic experiences in Tana Toraja reaffirmed their sense of superiority.

References

Adams, Kathleen M.
  1984 "Come to Tana Toraja, Land of the Heavenly Kings": Travel Agents as Brokers in Ethnicity. *Annals of Tourism Research* 11(3): 469–485.

1985 Field notes. Carving a New Identity: Ethnic and Artistic Change in Tana Toraja, Indonesia. Ph.D. diss., University of Washington, Seattle.

1990 Cultural Commoditization in Tana Toraja, Indonesia. *Cultural Survival Quarterly* 14(1):31–34.

1991 Touristic Pilgrimages, Identity and Nation-Building in Indonesia. Paper presented at the 1991 Association for Asian Studies Annual Meeting, New Orleans.

1993a Club Dead, Not Club Med: Staging Death in Contemporary Tana Toraja (Indonesia). *Southeast Asian Journal of Social Science* 21(2):62–72.

1993b Theologians, Tourists and Thieves: The Torajan Effigy of the Dead in Modernizing Indonesia. *Kyoto Journal* 22:38–45.

1995a Making Up the Toraja? The Appropriation of Tourism, Anthropology and Museums for Politics in Upland Sulawesi (Indonesia). *Ethnology* 34(2):143–153.

1995b Field notes.

Amin, Lukman
1991 Kepiting Sang Calon Primadona. *Pedoman Rakyat*, 3 March.

Amier, Mansur
1993 Wisata Baharu Sulsel, Peluang dan Masalahnya. *Pedoman Rakyat*, 14 February, 9.

Anderson, Benedict
1983 *Imagined Communities: Reflections on the Origin and Spread of Nationalism*. London: Verso.

Anon.
1990 Membangun Tana Toraja Tanpa Akronim Macam-Macam. *Pedoman Rakyat*, 11 March, 9.

1991a Miniatur Sulawesi Siap Menyambut Pekan Budaya Sulsel. *Pedoman Rakyat*, 16 June, 1, 10.

1991b Prosesi Kultural Awali Pekan Budaya Sulsel. *Pedoman Rakyat*, 18 July, 12.

1992 Jambu Mete "Primadona" dari Daerah "Ikan Bakar." *Pedoman Rakyat*, 23 April, 9.

1993 Pasar Sentral UP Tetap Primadona. *Pedoman Rakyat*, 11 March, 2.

Antweiler, Christoph
1994 South Sulawesi: Towards a Regional Ethnic Identity? Current Trends in a "Hot" and Historic Region. In *Nationalism and Ethnicity in Southeast Asia*, ed. Ingrid Wessel. Berlin: Humboldt University.

Basir, Ardhy M.
1991 Pantai Kuri dan Batimurung Primadona Pariwisata di Maros. *Pedoman Rakyat*, 13 January, 9.

Bigalke, Terance
1981   A Social History of Tana Toraja 1870–1965. Ph.D. diss., University of Wisconsin, Madison.
Booth, Anne
1990   The Tourism Boom in Indonesia. *Bulletin of Indonesian Economic Studies* 23(3):45–73.
Crystal, Eric
1977   Tourism in Toraja (Sulawesi, Indonesia). In *Hosts and Guests: The Anthropology of Tourism,* ed. Valene Smith, 109–125. Philadelphia: University of Pennsylvania Press.
Departemen Pariwisata Pos dan Telekomunikasi
1990   *Annual Report.* Jakarta.
1992   *Annual Report.* Jakarta.
Departemen Penerangan
1990   *Pedoman Penerangan Kepariwisataan.* Jakarta.
Errington, Frederick, and Deborah Gewertz
1989   Tourism and Anthropology in a Post-Modern World. *Oceania* 60: 37–54.
Evans-Pritchard, Deidre
1989   How "They" See "Us," Native American Images of Tourists. *Annals of Tourism Research* 16(1):89–105.
Faisal
1989   Sadar Wisata Sebagai Satu Nilai Perjuangan Kemerdekaan. *Pedoman Rakyat,* 6 August, 9.
Harvey, Barbara
1974   Tradition, Islam and Rebellion in South Sulawesi 1950–1965. Ph.D. diss., Cornell University.
1977   *Permesta: Half a Rebellion.* Ithaca: Cornell Modern Indonesia Monograph Series.
Hobsbawm, Eric, and Terence Ranger, eds.
1983   *The Invention of Tradition.* Cambridge and New York: Cambridge University Press.
Huka, Amus
1990   Lemo, Primadona yang Tersembunyi. *Pedoman Rakyat,* 30 September, 9.
Kamarto, Kobu'
1990   Kampanye Sadar Wisata Propinsi Sulawesi Selatan. *Pedoman Rakyat,* 18 February, 9.
Kipp, Rita
1993   *Dissociated Identities: Ethnicity, Religion and Class in an Indonesian Society.* Ann Arbor: University of Michigan Press.
Kuen, Fredrich C.
1990   Sulsel Tidak Hanya Miliki Tanatoraja. *Pedoman Rakyat,* 6 May.

Leong, Wai-Teng
1989 Culture and the State: Manufacturing Traditions for Tourism. *Cultural Studies in Mass Communication* 6(4):355–375.

Mandadung, Arianus
1990 Mengenal Kampanye Sadar Wisata 1989–1991. *Pedoman Rakyat*, 24 February, 9, and 4 March, 9.

Mandadung, Arianus, and Syahran Kinjan
1985 *Penuntun Wisata Remaja Sulawesi Selatan*. Ujung Pandang: Himpunan Penulis Pariwisata Indonesia.

Marampa', A. T.
1974 *A Guide to Toraja*. Ujung Pandang.

Mardiatmadja, B. S.
1991 Wawasan Wisata. *Kompas*, 12 January, 4.

Picard, Michel
1993 Cultural Tourism in Bali: National Integration and Regional Differentiation. In *Tourism in South-East Asia*, ed. Michael Hitchcock, Victor King, and Michael Parwell, 71–98. London: Routledge.

Razaq, Nurzaman
1991 Tana Toraja dan Masalah Keparawisataannya. *Pedoman Rakyat*, 3 February, 9.

Robinson, Kathryn
1993 The Platform House: Expression of a Regional Identity in the Modern Indonesian Nation. In *Culture and Society in New Order Indonesia*, ed. Virginia M. Hooker, 228–242. Kuala Lumpur: Oxford University Press.

Salombe, C.
1972 *Orang Toraja Dengan Ritusnya: In Memoriam So' Rinding Puang Sangalla'* (The Toraja and their rituals). Ujung Pandang.

Sandarupa, Stanislans
1994 Personal communication with the author, 28 May.

Schmidgall-Tellings, A. Ed., and Alan M. Stevens
1981 *Contemporary Indonesian-English Dictionary*. Athens: Ohio University Press.

Tobing, D.
1990 Tana Toraja Belum Mewujudkan Sapta Pesona. *Pedoman Rakyat*, 22 April, 9.

van den Berghe, Pierre
1980 Tourism as Ethnic Relations: A Case Study of Cuzco, Peru. *Ethnic and Racial Studies* 3(4):375–392.
1994 *The Quest for the Other: Ethnic Tourism in San Cristobal, Mexico*. Seattle: University of Washington Press.

Volkman, Toby
1984 Great Performances: Torajan Cultural Identity in the 1970s. *American Ethnologist* 11(1):152–169.

1985   *Feasts of Honor: Ritual and Change in the Toraja Highlands.*
       Urbana and Chicago: University of Illinois Press.
1990   Visions and Revisions: Torajan Culture and the Tourist Gaze.
       American Ethnologist 17(1):91–110.
Wahab, Cholik, ed.
1992   *Investment, Trading and Tourism Potential in South Sulawesi.*
       Ujung Pandang: PT. Wahyu Promospirit and the Governor's Office
       of South Sulawesi.
Wood, Robert E.
1979   Tourism and Underdevelopment in Southeast Asia. *Journal of
       Contemporary Asia* 9(3):274–287.
1984   Ethnic Tourism, the State and Cultural Change in Southeast Asia.
       Annals of Tourism Research 11(3):353–374.
Yamashita, Shinji
1994   Manipulating Ethnic Tradition: The Funeral Ceremony, Tourism,
       and Television Among the Toraja of Sulawesi. *Indonesia* 58:69–
       82.
Yoeti, Oka A.
1985   *Pengantar Ilmu Pariwisata.* Bandung: Penerbit Angkasa.

⟫ 7

Cultural Tourism, Nation-Building, and Regional Culture: The Making of a Balinese Identity

Bali's fame and fortune is due to its success as a tourist destination. Not only has tourism made Balinese dances and ceremonies famous worldwide, but the promotion of their culture as a tourist attraction has also conferred on the Balinese a special prominence within the Indonesian nation. Furthermore, most foreign observers appear to agree that, unlike other regions of Indonesia, the island of Bali has retained the vitality of its traditional culture in the modern world and many of them willingly credit tourism for providing the Balinese with an incentive to nurture their cultural heritage. Such a flattering opinion not only is commonly held among the Balinese themselves but also is widespread among other Indonesian ethnic groups, who look with unconcealed envy upon the Balinese and take them as a model for asserting their own ethnic identity and assessing their own cultural worth in Indonesia.

Yet, in the early 1970s, the arrival of increasing numbers of tourists on their island shores had caused patent apprehensions among the Balinese. This intrusion was the result of a decision made by the Indonesian government in 1969 to open the country to international tourism, primarily to address a pressing national balance-of-payments deficit. Banking on Bali's prestigious image as a tourist paradise, which was first cultivated in the 1930s, the government decided to make the province the focus of tourism development in Indonesia. Following the advice of the World Bank, a team of foreign experts was commissioned to compile a master plan for tourism development in Bali. The report, published in 1971 and revised in 1974 by the World Bank, proposed to confine the bulk of the tourists to the south of the island, while providing for a network of excursion routes linking major inland attractions (SCETO 1971, IBRD/IDA 1974). Meanwhile, the number of foreign visitors multiplied from fewer than 30,000 in 1970 to over 1.5 million in 1994 (for a local population approaching three million on an island spanning only 5,600 square kilometers). As for domestic tourism, which is being actively promoted by the state with the aim of fostering national integration, there are no statistics available, but a common estimate puts the figure at roughly half that of international tourism. During the 1970 to 1995 period, the total number of accommodations increased from less than five hundred to over thirty thousand rooms.

There is no question that tourism, and the activities it has generated, such as handicrafts and other cottage industries, has boosted the economic growth of Bali, to the point of displacing agriculture as the leading sector of the gross domestic regional product. Yet, the uneven distribution of its economic benefits within the population and throughout the island, the growing encroachment of foreign interests, and the severe degradation of the environment, which is rapidly eroding the island's touristic appeal, remain matters of serious concern. The question of tourism's social and cultural implications also appears to have raised contradictory expectations and appreciations among the Balinese.[1]

It is important to know that tourism policy in Bali is taken out of the hands of the provincial government and vested in the hands of the central government. Thus, the Balinese authorities had little say in the Jakarta government's decision to trade in Bali's charms to refill the coffers of the state, and they were not even consulted about the master plan. Faced with a fait accompli, they nevertheless attempted to appropriate tourism as a tool for regional development. In response to the master plan, the Balinese authorities proclaimed in 1971 their own conception of the kind of tourism they deemed the most suitable to their island—namely, what they termed "cultural tourism" *(pariwisata budaya)* (Seminar 1971).

From the start, the Balinese evinced an ambivalent attitude toward tourism, which they perceived as being both fraught with danger and promising prosperity. On the one hand, the artistic and religious traditions that had made Bali famous worldwide provided its main attraction as a tourist destination, thus turning Balinese culture into the most valuable "resource" for the island's economic development. On the other hand, the invasion of Bali by foreign visitors was seen as posing a threat of "cultural pollution." Hence, the Balinese regarded tourism as a challenge to be taken up with caution: How to develop tourism without debasing Balinese culture? Such was the task assigned to cultural tourism—to take advantage of Balinese culture to attract tourists while using the economic benefits of tourism to foster Balinese culture.

A decade or so later, it seemed that cultural tourism had achieved its mission, at least based on the declarations of provincial authorities extolling tourism as an agent of the cultural renaissance of Bali. According to most opinion leaders, the money brought in by tourists had revived the interest of the Balinese in their artistic traditions, while the admiration of foreign visitors for their culture had reinforced the Balinese sense of identity. By patronizing Balinese culture, tourism was said to have contributed to its preservation and even to its revitalization, to the extent that it had turned culture into a source of both profit and pride for the Balinese.

Here is not the place to dispute such allegations, as I have already dealt with the subject in numerous publications (Picard 1990b, 1992, 1993, 1995). Suffice it to say that tourism neither polluted Balinese culture nor entailed its renaissance. Far from being an external force striking a local society from without, tourism—or, rather, what I am inclined to call the *touristification* of a society—proceeds from within by blurring the boundaries between the inside and the outside, between what is "ours" and what is "theirs," between that which belongs to "culture" and that which pertains to "tourism." That is what I mean when I say Balinese culture has become a "touristic culture." Therefore, instead of asking whether or not Balinese culture has been able to withstand the impact of tourism, we should ask how tourism has contributed to the shaping of Balinese culture.

The decision to promote cultural tourism has elicited from the Balinese a particular form of reflexivity, in which they oscillate between anxiety and self-admiration with regard to their culture. It is as if tourism had convinced the Balinese that they were the owners of something at once precious and perishable called "culture" *(kebudayaan)*. And as it was distinguished and enhanced by the "tourist gaze" (Urry 1990), their culture became reified and externalized in the eyes of the Balinese, transforming into an object that could be detached from themselves in order to be displayed and marketed for others.

Once it had become a tourist asset, the Balinese resolved to preserve and promote their culture, while taking advantage of its prestige abroad and its economic importance at home in order to obtain full recognition of their ethnic identity from the state and to improve their position within Indonesia. That is how culture, by becoming Bali's *brand image*—that which distinguishes its tourist product in a highly competitive international market—has also become, indissociably, an *identity marker* for the Balinese, that which characterizes them as a particular ethnic group within the Indonesian multiethnic nation. No wonder, then, that their culture became such a sensitive issue for the Balinese, who have reflected and debated its authenticity in numerous reports and seminars as well as in articles published by the *Bali Post,* the daily newspaper of the province. If we concur with Edward Bruner that "in multiethnic Indonesia, . . . to write about one's own culture is to establish one's ethnic identity" (Bruner 1987, 9), this very fact is worth some consideration.

Now, in the discourse of cultural tourism, we are confronted with two different conceptions of Balinese ethnic identity. On the one hand, Balinese culture *(kebudayaan Bali)* is invariably portrayed as a bounded and homogeneous entity comprised of three components: it takes its source in the religion; it permeates customary practices and institutions; and it inspires artistic creations of great beauty. Thus epitomized by the specific combination of religion *(agama),* custom *(adat),* and art *(seni),* for the Balinese their culture embodies their identity as Balinese—what they call their "Balineseness" *(keBalian).* On the other hand, when explaining why tourism did not corrupt Balinese culture, contrary to what had been initially feared, prominent members of the intelligentsia are prone to declare that as long as the Balinese are aware of the indivisible unity of religion *(agama),* custom *(adat),* and culture *(budaya),* their identity is not at risk.

My purpose here is neither to account for this discrepancy nor to assess the veracity of these claims. Rather, it is to deconstruct the contemporary expression of Balinese identity by retracing the history of its construction, not unlike what has recently been done by Rita Kipp (1993), Joel Kahn (1993), and John Pemberton (1994b) with respect to the Karo, the Minangkabau, and Java. The issue I am addressing, then, relates to ethnic consciousness rather than cultural history, in that I am not concerned with the evolution of what has been called, by anthropologists and travel writers alike, "Balinese culture," but with the dialogical fashion in which a certain image of their culture came to be used self-consciously by them as an identity marker. In other words, I treat Balinese culture itself as being a cultural artifact. In this respect, the allegedly immutable and primordial unity of religion, custom, and art/culture, through which the Balinese presently define their identity, is the outcome of a process of semantic borrowings and of conceptual reframings in response to the colonization, the Indonesianization, and the touristification of their island.

For the sake of clarity, I shall divide my analysis into three historical periods: (1) from the Dutch conquest in 1908 to the proclamation of Indonesia's independence in 1945; (2) the first period of the Indonesian republic, which ended in the "coup" of 1965; and (3) the New Order, which has been ruling the country since the the coup.

The Netherlands East Indies

The island of Bali was one of the last regions of the Indonesian archipelago to be absorbed into the colonial empire of the Netherlands East Indies. Initiated in 1846, the military conquest of Bali was finally completed in 1908 with the ritual suicide of several royal houses, who chose a glorious end rather than a surrender to a foreign master. The protests raised over the military's brutality were a source of international embarrassment to the Dutch, who attempted to atone for the carnage by displaying a more worthy image of their colonial policy in Bali—an image based on the preservation of Balinese culture and its promotion as a tourist attraction.[2]

Dutch Colonial Policy

The Dutch authorities understood poorly the society over which they stretched their empire, but they certainly had an idea about what it should be and endeavored to make it conform to that image. They were greatly influenced by an Orientalist vision, which regarded the island of Bali as a "living museum" of the Hindu-Javanese civilization, the only surviving heir to the Hindu heritage swept away from Java by the coming of Islam.[3] In their view, Hinduism was the foundation of Balinese society and the warrant of its cultural integrity. Accordingly, it had to be protected by the enlightened paternalism of colonial tutelage from the encroachment of Islam, which had fastened its grip on the major part of the archipelago.

If this idea of a "living museum" was so willingly taken up by the colonial administrators, it is not only because of a genuine concern that the uniqueness of Balinese culture might be destroyed by indiscriminate contact with the wider world, but also because it neatly fit the Dutch political agenda. In the early 1920s, the Dutch came to regard Bali as the cornerstone of their effort to contain the spread of Islamic radicalism and the various nationalist movements that had recently arisen in Java and Sumatra.[4] The Dutch realized that the Balinese nobility, whom they saw as the vehicle of the Hinduization of the island and the pillar of its traditional order, was the best barrier against the threat of Islam and of nationalism. Thus, despite the suspicion and low esteem in which they held the Balinese princes, the Dutch resolved to ensure their loyalty, first by upholding the so-called caste system and legalizing its hierarchy[5] and then by reinstating the former royal houses in the trappings of their previous glory.

In order to govern the island effectively, the colonial state introduced a uniform administration throughout Balinese society, which had previously been characterized by the diversity of its customs. Dutch officials simplified the village administration, which led them to study Balinese customary law with a view to codifying and institutionalizing the "traditional" order. A new type of administrative village was created, usually consisting of several customary villages grouped together under a new name. By thus introducing a dichotomy between customary authority, left to the Balinese, and administrative authority, which they appropriated, the Dutch could rule Bali, while pretending to restore its traditional order.

As for this traditional order, it was not enough that it be rescued from the onslaught of modernization and insulated from disturbing outside influences, but the Balinese people had to be taught by their new overlords how to continue to be authentic Balinese. Such was the aim of the cultural policy launched in the 1920s and known as the "Balinization of Bali" *(Baliseering),* which was expected to produce a state-sponsored renaissance of Balinese culture. Designed by Dutch Orientalists, this policy was specifically intended for the native youth, who had to be made conscious of the value of their cultural heritage through an education focusing on the Balinese language, literature, and arts.

The Orientalist vision of Bali as a Hindu island surrounded by a sea of Islam was to have long-lasting consequences, for two related reasons. On the one hand, by looking for the singularity of Bali in its Hindu heritage, and by conceiving of Balinese religious identity as formed through opposition to Islam, the Dutch set the framework within which the Balinese were going to define themselves. On the other hand, by attempting to preserve Bali's singularity from the rest of the East Indies, they ultimately emphasized and reinforced it far more than they had ever envisioned.[6]

The Emergence of a Balinese Ethnic Identity

It appears to have been the Dutch predicament that they wanted to maintain Balinese society in a fixed, traditional order, at the same time that Bali underwent rapid and profound changes due to increasing interference by the colonial government in native affairs. The requirements of a modern administration prompted the formation of a Balinese intelligentsia, as the colonial state needed bilingual educated natives to mediate between the colonized peoples and their European masters. This intelligentsia strove to make sense of of their newly opened-up world, at a time when foreign interest in Balinese culture was growing. As Western-educated Balinese began to ponder the foundations of their identity, they were in the novel position of defining what it meant to be Balinese in terms comprehensible to non-Balinese.

During the 1920s, modernist organizations were established in North Bali,[7] which, in addition to opening schools and religious foundations, began to publish periodicals, a complete novelty for Bali. Written in Malay with occasional articles in Dutch, these publications were devoted mostly to issues pertaining to religion and social order. The use of Malay—the language of education and administration, soon to become that of Indonesian nationalism—to address thoroughly Balinese topics indicates that the intelligentsia were conscious of being an integral part of an emerging national entity. Thus, the same movement that prompted the Balinese to question their identity was dispossessing them of their own words by compelling them to think about themselves in languages not their own.

In these periodicals, for the first time, the Balinese viewed themselves as a singular entity, as a "people." Specifically, they described themselves both as a religious minority, the stronghold of Hinduism threatened by the aggressive expansionism of Islam and Christianity, and as a particular ethnic group, characterized by their own customs. That is to say, they construed their identity—what they called their "Balineseness" *(keBalian)*—as being based simultaneously on religion *(agama)* and custom *(adat)*. The very fact of the Balinese resorting to these terms testifies to the epistemological revolution occurring on the island after its takeover by an alien power.

The word *adat* is of Arabic origin, borrowed by Islamized populations in the archipelago to refer to indigenous "customary law" as opposed to imported "religious law." Introduced to Bali by the Dutch, *adat* replaced an existing terminology of locally variable customs that had "a field of meanings covering ritual obligation, social institution, legal regulation, and ancestral evocation" (Warren 1993, 4) and that infused the Balinese sense of communal solidarities in the villages. The word *adat* created a new conceptual domain of "custom," in contradistinction not of "religion" but of "administration." Furthermore, the incorporation of miscellaneous local terms into one generic word altered the meaning of "custom" for the Balinese: what had until then been an interplay of significant differences deliberately fostered between villages soon became the locus of the Balinese ethnic identity, in the sense of a customary body of regulations and institutions that the Balinese inherited from their ancestors.

As such, in Bali "custom" was not clearly distinguished from "religion." Indeed, *adat* is for the Balinese a truly religious matter, in that it refers both to an immutable divine cosmic order and to the social order instituted by ancestors, at once defining the ideal order and prescribing the behavior required to achieve that order. Unlike the world religions that have a core of abstract basic tenets and symbols meaningful to people of diverse cultural backgrounds, Balinese religion consists of rites that relate specific groups of people to one another, to their ancestors, and to their territory. Thus, religion in Bali is highly localized, and its gods—their Hindu denominations notwithstanding—are deified ancestors and forces of nature. Moreover, religion is a customary obligation for the Balinese; participation in the rites is a consequence of membership in both a local community and a descent group. Hence, it is doubtful that religion was a marker of ethnicity for the Balinese before they began to view Islam as a threat. Until then, religious differences were signs that helped to differentiate groups otherwise seen as having basic similarities. Before their traumatic encounter with the Dutch, the Balinese did not conceive of a different system of social organization, and so there was no absolute category of the Other, but only a distinction between people of the same island and people from overseas. Given this perspective, Islam was conceived as belonging to the same cultural sphere as Bali (Vickers 1987).

In any case, the definition of "religion" in terms of *agama,* which the Balinese intelligentsia resorted to in their publications, opened a significantly different semantic field. *Agama* is a Sanskrit word, referring originally to a traditional religious teaching, a meaning similar to that of *adat*. Over the centuries, *agama* came to be related in the archipelago to an Indic model of divine kingship, Sanskrit literature, and Hindu (as well as Buddhist) theology, that is, to literacy and power attributed to a prestigious foreign civilization (Atkinson 1987). By the eighteenth century, through its association with Islam, *agama* had taken on the meaning of "religion" (Hoadley and Hooker 1981). For the Balinese intelligentsia of the 1920s, the discourse of *agama* bore the imprint not only of Islam but also of Christianity. Proponents of both faiths, by appropriating the term *agama*, had shaped new associations for it, mainly an emphasis on a supreme deity, the requirement of conversion to a foreign doctrine with teachings contained in a holy book, and an ideal of societal progress.

Reading through their publications, it is clear that the main concern of the Balinese intelligentsia was to ensure that their religion could stand beside Islam and Christianity, and thus resist the thrust of their proselytism. Although the Balinese reformers shared a common reference to Hinduism, a conflict arose between commoners and aristocrats regarding the name of their religion. While the latter argued that it should be called "Hindu Balinese religion" *(agama Hindu Bali),* thus emphasizing the Balinese aspect in their attempt to preserve the traditional order, the former, stressing the Hindu element, wanted to call it "Balinese Hindu religion" *(agama Bali Hindu).* The conflict escalated, focusing on the religious justification of the castes and their place in contemporary Balinese society. The commoners challenged the alliance between the Dutch and the Balinese nobility, aiming to overturn the old feudal ties of caste in the name of progress.

The tension between commoners and aristocrats receded in 1928, thanks to the combined efforts of leading Balinese aristocrats and Dutch officials, who labored to defuse what they saw as a political threat. That same year, in Singaraja, the Dutch resident opened a foundation that was dedicated to the preservation of traditional Balinese culture and that was to publish a monthly magazine financed partly by the colonial state. Its main contributors were former leaders of the two feuding groups of commoners and aristocrats, who now worked together under the leadership of Dutch Orientalists toward the politically safe goals of education and culture.

The magazine articles were markedly different than those in previous journals. A significant proportion were in Balinese, as the colonial government had an obvious interest in fostering the consciousness of a Balinese cultural identity, as opposed to an identity based on caste difference or on national unity. In addition to numerous articles on religion and custom, there were articles on Balinese art *(seni)* and culture *(budaya)*;[8] mainly about music and dance for the former and language and literature for the latter. Art and culture as specific topics had been conspicuously absent from Balinese reflections on their identity in the 1920s. Indeed, unlike Malay, the Balinese language has no word for "art" or for "culture." In keeping with their marked preference for concrete verbal forms as opposed to abstract concepts, the Balinese have always been concerned with specific activities, inseparable from their context, which were therefore not perceived as belonging to a domain coming under a generic label, such as "art" or "culture." For example, even though the Balinese consider dance as the yardstick of their artistic creativity par excellence, there is no word in Balinese that could translate the English word *dance*. Instead, there are as many names as there are different genres of dance and drama, and the choreography of a performance is not conceptually distinguished from its theatricality. Dances are usually performed in the context of a religious ceremony, as an offering—an act of personal devotion for the dancers and a customary obligation for the congregation responsible for its organization. Hence, for Bali's unique dances to be recognized as an art form, they first had to be detached from the context of their performance, which required the intercession of an external gaze. In other words, for the Balinese to perceive their dances as art, these dances had to be recognized as such by non-Balinese (Picard 1990a, 1996).

The Coming of the Tourists

Tourists enter the picture as the most dedicated proponents of an aesthetic vision of Balinese culture. In 1908, the year in which Bali's last unyielding royal house fell to Dutch superior military might, the colonial government opened a tourist bureau in its capital of Batavia, with the aim of promoting the East Indies as a tourist destination. Initially focusing on Java, the bureau extended its scope to Bali in 1914, as soon as control of the island by the army allowed for safe traveling. Guidebooks for tourists soon began to appear. But it was not until 1924 that tourism expanded in Bali, after the Dutch shipping company established a weekly steamship service connecting Singaraja with Batavia and Makassar. In 1928 a proper tourist hotel, the Bali Hotel, was built in Denpasar, the main town in the southern part of the island, seen as the heartland of Balinese culture. To entertain their guests, the management of the hotel arranged weekly performances of Balinese dancing, which soon became one of the most popular tourist attractions on the island.

The performances presented at the Bali Hotel consisted of a series of short dances, strung haphazardly together and suited to the taste and attention span of a foreign audience. The very conception of this tourist program was made possible by the advent of a new style of dance, the *kebyar,* which allowed the dance to be detached from both its theatrical content and its ritual context and presented as an art form in its own right.[9] Indeed, dance had to become autonomous before it could be exploited for commercial ends. Once freed of the constraints that hindered its autonomous development, Balinese dance could be made accessible to spectators unfamiliar with the linguistic codes, dramaturgic conventions, and literary references of the traditional dance dramas. Besides, with *kebyar* a dance performance became a much more expressive and narrative event, dynamic and linear instead of static and cyclical, hence more likely to be appreciated by Westerners than traditional styles of music and dance.

Not only did the troupes performing for the Bali Hotel become famous with foreign visitors, but this fame also conferred upon the troupes considerable prestige among the Balinese. The commercial success of *kebyar* dances greatly accelerated their spread and popularity across Bali in the 1930s.

Along with the tourists, special mention should be made of the small community of artists and scholars who resided in Bali between the wars. The accounts, paintings, photographs, and films that recorded their sojourn on the island contributed to a sensational image of native life, an image eventually relayed through the promotional services of the nascent tourist industry (Boon 1977, Vickers 1989). Among the numerous clichés which they initiated, none proved more pervasive than the claim that "the Balinese are the greatest artists of this age, and still more, that every Balinese, man or woman, is an artist" (André Roosevelt, in Powell 1930, x). "Coolies and princes, priests and peasants, men and women alike, can dance, play musical instruments, paint, or carve in wood and stone" (Covarrubias 1937, 160).

No wonder, then, that the first articles written in the 1930s by Balinese about their own arts took obvious pride in evoking the artistic reputation of their island abroad.[10] Given the fame of Balinese dance as both a major artistic achievement and a pervasive tourist attraction, it is significant that the tourist accounts of Balinese dances preceded their academic study. Even so, it was only after the Bali Hotel began to entertain their guests with performances of "native dancing" that Balinese dances were deemed worthy of being recommended to tourists in guidebooks and travel accounts.

The Independence of Indonesia

The Japanese invasion in 1942 opened an era of violent turmoil that ended in a bloodbath in 1965 and that stifled tourism in Bali for nearly three decades. The return of the Dutch in 1946, after the period of chaos that followed the capitulation of Japan, was backed by most of the Balinese nobility, who hoped to restore the traditional order. Against them stood the nationalists, struggling to achieve the independence of Indonesia, which had been proclaimed by Sukarno in 1945. Diplomatic pressures finally forced the Dutch to acknowledge in 1949 the sovereignty of their former colony, which a year later became the Republic of Indonesia, with Sukarno its president. From then on, the Balinese were expected to identify themselves primarily as Indonesian citizens, something which was far from obvious, given that the primordial loyalties of kinship, ethnicity, religion, and language made far more sense to them than the claims of the remote and abstract nation-state.

Ethnicity and Nation-Building

After Indonesian sovereignty had been internationally recognized and the colonial adversary had been removed, ethnic and religious tensions threatened to tear the fabric of the newly imposed and still fragile sense of national unity. In the 1950s, Indonesia experienced serious rebellions in several regions. The central government eventually quelled all rebellions, an achievement that strengthened the role of the armed forces within state and society. The unity of the nation-state was given first priority, to which all other interests were subordinated.

Indonesia is a country of extreme ethnic diversity and is geographically fragmented over an island arc of about five thousand kilometers. However, the problem of governance is not so much the sheer magnitude of ethnic diversity but the imbalances caused by the cultural and political dominance of the Javanese (who comprise over 40 percent of the population) and by the economic dominance of the Chinese. Among the some three hundred acknowledged ethnic groups in the archipelago, it is necessary to distinguish between the ethnic minorities proper and approximately a dozen major ethnic groups (including the Balinese, with less than 2 percent of the population), each occupying its own particular region, speaking its own language, and possessing its own forms of social organization and cultural expression (Geertz 1963, Anderson 1987).

In order to manage such a plural society, the state's founders undertook to forge a national identity by building a national culture composed of the highest cultural achievements of all the regions of Indonesia. In actual fact, only the major ethnic groups (with the exclusion of the Chinese), those showing evidence of "civilization," were taken into account. Ethnic minorities, seen as being imprisoned in their own narrow customary horizon of *adat,* were not really perceived as specific cultures, but rather were lumped together as if they shared an overriding common cultural pattern, that is, their alleged "primitive" nature (Colchester 1986). Thus, in the definition of the national culture, a few superior cultures—among which the Javanese culture is the highest valued—are distinguished from inferior cultures, which are excluded from contributing to the national culture.

Balinese Religion: From Ethnic to Universal

Religion was another, far more controversial, source of tension in the newly independent Indonesia, further complicated by its link with ethnicity. Unlike the colonial state, the Indonesian state does not register ethnicity in its population censuses. It does, however, register religion. According to census figures, nearly 90 percent of the Indonesian population embraces Islam, which makes Indonesia the single largest national community in the Muslim world.[11] However, Indonesia did not become an Islamic state because of Sukarno's opposition, backed by both Christian and secular nationalists, who argued in favor of a state in which religious and secular affairs would be kept separate. A compromise resulted in the famous "Five Principles" *(Pancasila)*—the Indonesian state placed the "Belief in the One Almighty God" first, without making Islam an official, or even privileged, religion. This ambiguous formulation led to later disagreement over which religions, other than Islam and Christianity, fostered such a belief and, hence, would qualify for the protection and support that the Constitution guaranteed to genuine "religions" *(agama)*. Shortly after the compromise, the Ministry of Religion, dominated by Muslims, drastically restricted the official acceptation of *agama* by stipulating that a religion must be monotheistic, possess a holy book and a prophet, and, further, its congregation should not be limited to a single ethnic group.

Such stipulations struck dismay in Bali. Indeed, while changes in Balinese religion had been advocated in the last decade of colonial rule, no consensus had been reached on the overall direction of reform. Even the proper name for Balinese religion remained in question. Now that Bali was integrated in the Republic of Indonesia, the social pressures under which Balinese reformists had first opened their religious enquiries were growing into an undisguised threat, lending urgency to the debates on religion among the intelligentsia. The peril was undoubtedly very real. Balinese religion was classified as "tribal" by the Ministry of Religion because its rites were considered to belong to the domain of custom *(adat)* and not to that of religion *(agama)*—that is, the Balinese were regarded as people who "do not yet have religion." Consequently, if the Balinese did not want to be a target of Muslim or Christian proselytizing, they had to invest their religion with the attributes of *agama*.

During the 1950s, the Balinese kept pressing the Ministry of Religion to recognize their religion and a number of new reformist religious organizations appeared. Whereas some reformers attempted to find in their own indigenous tradition the seeds of regeneration, the majority endeavored to have Balinese religion acknowledged as the local manifestation of a universal religion, on a par with Islam and Christianity. They enjoined the Balinese to return to Hinduism, presented as the source of their rites, by renewing their contacts with India, whose freshly acquired independence had increased its international prestige. On their initiative, classical texts of Hindu theology were translated into Indonesian, Indian scholars were invited to Bali to teach their religion, and scholarships to study in India were granted to several young Balinese.

In 1958, the main Balinese religious organizations finally enlisted the support of Sukarno (whose mother was Balinese) to have their religion officially recognized as monotheistic by the Ministry of Religion. It was called "Hindu Balinese religion" *(agama Hindu Bali)*, the name advocated by the conservative faction in the 1920s. The following year, these diverse organizations merged into a single representative body, the Hindu Balinese Council (Parisada Dharma Hindu Bali), which became the official liaison between the Hindu Balinese congregation and the Ministry of Religion. The council compiled a theological dogma to standardize ritual practice and to normalize the priesthood (Bakker 1993).

While the council's use of the name *Hindu Bali* implied a clear recognition of the distinctive indigenous component of Balinese religion, its leaders were increasingly pressured to universalize. At the same time, some Javanese groups, conscious of their own Hindu heritage, began investigating the possibility of associating with Balinese Hinduism, as the Balinese introduced their religion to other islands, where they moved as transmigrants or civil servants. As a result, in 1964 the council changed its name to Parisada Hindu Dharma (the Hindu Council), thus forsaking any reference to its Balinese origins. When President Sukarno announced the names of the religions that were to qualify for official government sponsorship in 1965, the Hindu religion *(agama Hindu)*, not the Hindu Balinese religion *(agama Hindu Bali)*, was included.

In summary, during Sukarno's time a combination of internal changes and external pressures led to a conceptual separation of religion and society. This movement of religious rationalization began during the colonial period, when the Balinese reformers were attempting to name their religion. Previously, religion had not been seen as something distinct and in need of a specific name. It was not singled out as "religion," or as a set of systematically coherent beliefs and practices that could be isolated from other aspects of life. Although the Dutch had depoliticized *adat* by dissociating political power from ritual authority, in the colonial days religion was still merged with custom. Now, after Indonesia's independence, the Balinese were compelled to distinguish explicitly between religion and custom. In order for their rites to accede to the status of *agama*, they had to be detached from the domain of *adat*. However, the distinction between religion and custom, by transferring all that is sacred to the side of *agama*, ends in desacralizing *adat*. This secularization—besides raising inextricable epistemological problems—has caused widespread incomprehension and resentment among the Balinese ever since.[12]

As a result of the increasing marginalization of *adat*, through its depoliticization cum desacralization, the locus of Balinese identity has clearly tipped in favor of *agama*. Here we are no longer referring to the communal identity Balinese could secure from practicing their customary religion—bounded as it is to both a territory and a genealogy—but to its reformed persuasion, which characterizes the Balinese people as a non-Muslim (and non-Christian) minority within the Indonesian multiethnic and multireligious nation. This rationalized version of Balinese religion bears little resemblance to everyday religious practice in houseyard and village temples, which is ritual-focused rather than text-focused. Yet, by the very same token that the Balinese reformers have reworked their beliefs into a transcendental religion and shaped their ethnic community into a religious congregation, they have used Hinduism as an ethnic boundary marker.

Thus, somehow paradoxically, Hinduism became the prime marker of Balinese ethnicity precisely when religion was being severed from its ethnic origin to become a means of national integration.

The New Order: Unity in Diversity

Since coming to power after pushing aside Sukarno in the aftermath of the "coup" of 1965, Suharto's "New Order" regime has struggled to build a strong unitary state. Backed by the armed forces and sustained by the massive inflow of funds from the oil boom of the 1970s as well as from foreign aid, Suharto's government proved able to impose its authority and establish its legitimacy over the country. Political stability was restored by severely restricting any form of partisan activity, while economic recovery was achieved through the launching of ambitious development plans. Long held in check by regional interests, the sovereignty of the state finally asserted itself, and national integration became an undisputable reality through a steady centralization of state power (Drake 1989). National integration efforts have focused on promoting a national language through education, framing all individuals into standard structures and networks nationwide, incorporating remote communities into the mainstream of the national economy, and imposing universal religions in order to eradicate "animist" attitudes deemed harmful to national development. Once national unity could be taken for granted, the emphasis on centralization might be relaxed somewhat and instead placed on the country's diversity, in accordance with the state motto, "Unity in Diversity," engraved on the Indonesian coat of arms. In addition, the directorate general of Tourism eagerly advertises Indonesia as "a destination of endless diversity."

Since the 1980s, ethnicity has become the fashion in Jakarta, to the extent that the media now talk of an "ethnic revival." There have been numerous exhibitions on the arts and crafts of the outer islands, accompanied by the publication of glossy coffee-table books. Traditional textiles provide a constantly renewed source of inspiration in Indonesian haute couture and interior design, and the new international airport proudly exhibits a variety of decorative patterns borrowed from the country's diverse ethnic groups. Ethnic handicrafts are sold as souvenirs to domestic and foreign tourists and are extensively exported abroad. Dance troupes from the provinces perform in the capital city, and the national television offers regular regional cultural shows. In short, Indonesia appears to be going ethnic, as witnessed by the motto of the Visit Indonesia Year 1991 program, "Let's Go Archipelago."

Some scholars have lent academic validity to this "ethnic revival" by asserting that the state might use cultural mobilization based on ethnic identity to prevent mobilization based on class interests (Magenda 1988). In addition, a focus on ethnic identity would provide a welcome counter to Western-style consumer culture, which has flooded Indonesia since it opened its gates to international capital, giving rise to an affluent urban middle class. If there is some truth in this position, it is far from telling the whole story. Rather than denying the appeal of ethnicity as a focus of allegiance and identity by suppressing its manifestations, the New Order has resorted to the more cunning strategy of disempowerment and incorporation. In short, not only have ethnic identities been domesticated by the state, but they are also being enlisted to contribute to the process of nation-building.[13]

As several scholars have rightly pointed out, while the expression of ethnic identity appears to be officially sanctioned, it will be so only as long as it remains at the level of cultural display—and even then, the kinds of cultural differences that can be displayed are strictly defined by the state (Alexander 1989, Hooker 1993, Kipp 1993, Liddle 1989, Pemberton 1994b, Rodgers 1993). Thus, the visual and decorative aspects of Indonesian ethnic cultures—such as dance and music, costumes, handicrafts, and architecture—have benefited from an unprecedented degree of official promotion and are what the Indonesians call the "cultural arts" *(seni budaya)* and what Greg Acciaioli (1985) has termed "culture as art." Here we have a folkloristic vision of ethnic cultures, targeting two audiences: first and foremost, Indonesians themselves, expected to endorse a state-contrived version of their national cultural heritage; and, second, foreign visitors, enticed into the country to admire its famed tourist objects. Needless to say, this showcase vision does not acknowledge that which forms the core of a culture—language, religion, legal system, economic practices, social organization, and so on—and that which sustains the sense of identity of the participants in this culture. On the contrary, the destruction of traditional economic patterns, the plundering of the environment, and the depreciation of local knowledge that ensue from the policy of national "development" are conducive to the deculturation of religion and the erosion of the ritual function of the arts (Dove 1988, Foulcher 1990). In Indonesia, there is no room whatsoever for diversity which asserts competing economic and political interests of different ethnic groups. In this respect, the New Order is proceeding just as the former colonial state had proceeded in order to prevent ethnic differences from taking on political force: by culturalizing those differences as far as possible (Geertz 1990).

But even that is only one view, as we are not really dealing with Indonesia's "ethnic cultures," but with what Indonesian officials call "regional cultures" *(kebudayaan daerah)*, the implications of which seem to be lost on most foreign observers.[14] Some semantic clarification is required here. The acceptance of the word *kebudayaan,* commonly translated as "culture," is at once normative and evolutionist, in that it refers to the process through which the diverse ethnic groups are expected to acquire the qualities necessary to institute the order and civilization consonant with the ideal of the Indonesian nation. Therefore, we should not expect to find in this word the idea of a cultural specificity characteristic of each ethnic group or the idea of cultural relativism. The term *daerah*, which translates as "region," carries an ambiguity as to the nature (ethnic or administrative) and geographic scope (local or regional) of the cultural entity under consideration.

Now, through the pervasive use of the set syntagma *kebudayaan daerah*, what we actually are witnessing, in conjunction with the process of national integration, is a policy emphasizing *provincial* differentiation. The Indonesian state is aiming to induce in each of its provinces a distinctive homogeneous provincial identity, grounded on a single distinct set of unique cultural features, at the expense of the diverse ethnic cultures enclosed within their boundaries. Such provincial identities are promoted by the regional governments and supported by synthetic images based on a notion of culture stripped down to the "cultural arts." These images are proposed to the nation for consumption and to the local populations they allegedly represent for authentication.[15] Thus, in promoting the so-called regional cultures, the state is playing the provinces not only against the various ethnic groups that compose them, but also against the regions proper, which, as political entities rooted in a specific history, are considered a threat to national unity.

Just as "culture" (read "cultural arts") is used to defuse potential political problems, the risks inherent in ethnic mobilization are defused by focusing on the "region" (read "province"), that is, by shifting the locus of identification from a primordial to an administrative entity. In addition to the rather conspicuous folklorization of culture, there is a more discrete, yet no less crucial, *provincialization of ethnicity.* In this perspective, the promotion of provincial cultural identities can be interpreted as a safe way for the state to bridge the gap between ethnic identities—regarded as being either irrelevant or detrimental to the process of nation-building—and the still remote national identity.

This situation bears critical implications for Bali, where the issues are obscured by the singular fact that the signifier "Bali" refers simultaneously to a geographic, an ethnic, and an administrative reality—and also designates the touristic showcase of Indonesia. Thus, unlike the Dayak in Kalimantan, who speak either for their specific ethnic group or for a pan-Dayak regional entity (which, being contested by the Indonesian state, is divided into four provinces), when the Balinese speak in the name of their "Balineseness," they refer more often than not to Bali as either a province or a tourist destination.

Balinese Culture as Regional Culture

I now return to "Balinese culture"—understood in the sense of a duly acknowledged "regional culture"—by briefly relating what is happening to each of its three professed components.

Starting with religion, the paradoxical trend alluded to earlier has been continuing unabated, in that Hinduism has become the main pillar of Balinese ethnic identity, although it is becoming ever more detached from its Balinese origin. There are two distinct reasons for this. On the one hand, the government ban on political mobilization has strengthened religious loyalties across the country, while the social and cultural dislocation engendered by rapid economic growth and modernization has prompted people to cling more tightly to their faith. On the other hand, the New Order has greatly enhanced the prestige of Hinduism in Indonesia by celebrating the glorious Hindu-Javanese kingdoms of the past and upholding the traditional sources of authority. Thus, shortly after the anticommunist massacres of 1965, numerous Javanese groups "converted" to Hinduism for fear of being branded as "atheists," an accusation synonymous with "communist" in Indonesia. In the following years, the Balinese and Javanese Hindus were joined by several ethnic minorities who took refuge in the Hindu fold, hoping to conserve their ancestral rites, Hinduism reputedly being more accommodating than Christianity or Islam. This steady growth of Hindu followers continued to such an extent that, even if the Balinese have managed to dominate the decision-making positions of the Parisada Hindu Dharma, they are threatened with becoming a minority within the religion they themselves established.

This concern has been mounting since 1986, when the council, with sections in every province of the country, became the Parisada Hindu Dharma Indonesia. The "Indonesianization" of what had initially been the council of the Balinese religion was reaffirmed in 1991 during the latest Parisada congress, which was held in Jakarta rather than Bali, as had been traditional. The proceedings focused on transferring the seat of the council to the capital city, a move advocated by the majority of provincial delegates (but blocked by the veto of the Parisada's founding members) in order to place Hinduism on an equal footing with the other official religions. In response to the creation of the influential Indonesian Muslim Intellectuals' Association, a group of Balinese living in Jakarta recently founded the Indonesian Hindu Intellectuals' Forum. Its leaders are highly critical of the Parisada, whom they accuse of being a conservative pressure group of the Balinese nobility who aim to further the interests of Bali rather than a genuinely religious body. These radical Hindu intellectuals are striving to universalize their religion even more by breaking its ties to Bali and aligning it with the allegedly "genuine" Hinduism of India.

As we have seen, this Balinese investment in religion has occurred mainly to the detriment of custom, which has consequently become secularized and ever more marginalized by the state. After the chaos of the revolution and early independence, which completely disorganized the local administration, the New Order renewed state control of village government in Bali based on the Dutch model: a dual structure of administrative villages and customary villages. In 1979, the Village Government Law established uniform local administrative structures across Indonesia, with the objective of transforming village administration into an arm of the central bureaucracy. This law undermined the authority of the customary village by narrowing the sphere of relevance of *adat*, despite the fact that Indonesian law formally acknowledges the existence of *adat* institutions as independent of administrative matters.

Shortly before the Indonesian state curbed the prerogatives of *adat*, the provincial government of Bali began to establish itself as the guardian of *adat*, as much to ward off the central government's grip on Balinese customary autonomy as to enhance its own authority over local institutions. In 1979, the Forum for the Development of Customary Institutions (Majelis Pembina Lembaga Adat)[16] was established under the governor's office to reinforce the role of customary institutions and to systematize and reform local customs. The forum is formalizing the status of customary law and promoting the written codification of village regulations. While aiming to strengthen the legal standing of *adat* in the judicial system, this campaign does so by severing it from local knowledge and practice and then submitting it to a centralized administrative authority. In the process, the locus of Balinese custom has become the province, in effect creating a provincial *adat* (Schulte Nordholt 1991, Warren 1993).

While Balinese *adat* is rendered vestigial and appropriated by the state, Balinese cultural arts are thriving, to the point that local and foreign observers alike have felt entitled to speak of a cultural renaissance on the island. And indeed, the provincial government has spared no effort to preserve and promote the Balinese *seni budaya*. The government has two interwoven goals in its patronage of the Balinese arts (particularly the performing arts): the promotion of a regional culture that contributes to the national Indonesian culture and that may be used to celebrate and legitimize the New Order; and the use of cultural performances to attract tourists and thus boost the regional and national economies. While such cultural policy is applied to some extent in most provinces, Bali enjoys a privileged position with respect to each of these goals. First, as the prime tourist destination of the country, its arts symbolize not so much Bali as Indonesia as a whole and are expected to enhance the prestige of Indonesian culture abroad;[17] second, as the acknowledged heir to the Hindu heritage of the great Hindu-Javanese kingdoms, Balinese arts benefit from the neotraditional leanings of the New Order, in that the official rehabilitation of the traditional values associated with Javanese "high culture" also applies to Balinese court arts.

Since the 1960s, a host of institutions have been established by the provincial government to cultivate, develop, and preserve the Balinese arts (specifically the performing arts), in accordance with the instructions of the Ministry of Education and Culture (Soebadio 1985): the Conservatory of Music, the Academy of Dance, the Council for the Development of Culture, and the Art Centre. To a certain extent, these institutions have taken over the patronage formerly exerted by the royal courts: the creation of styles and the establishment of norms for their execution, the training of dancers and musicians, and the organizing and financing of performances. Contrary to the courts, however, which always maintained their own distinctive styles, the Indonesian government, through its provincial apparatus, is deliberately centralizing, normalizing, and decontextualizing the Balinese performing arts (Hough 1992, Ramstedt 1992). Such institutionalization of the arts goes hand in hand with their professionalization, as witnessed by the following statement by the head of the Academy of Dance: "The motivations for the performing arts, so far, have been religious ones. But now, we cannot isolate ourselves from globalization any more. . . . We have to live with overseas and domestic tourists. Therefore, now is the time for our artists to conduct themselves like professionals" (Bandem 1991, 24).

Undoubtedly, the best example of this official version of the Balinese arts is the Bali Arts Festival, a month-long event held annually since 1979 at the Art Centre in Denpasar. Among the various events—including parades, exhibitions, competitions, seminars, and stage performances—the performances by far attract most of the public attention. Significantly enough, even though the Bali Arts Festival was initially presented by the governor as the perfect exponent of cultural tourism, it was never convincingly promoted on the tourist market and soon became a thoroughly Balinese affair. Extensively publicized by both regional and national media—and made compulsory by a provincial regulation in 1986—the festival has evolved into the most prominent showcase for the Balinese arts. And its recognition by the central government in 1987 was interpreted as a signal for other provinces to explore, filter, edit, and promote their arts in order to organize their own festivals modeled on the Balinese example.

Thus, year after year at the Bali Arts Festival, a selection of the Balinese "cultural arts" is taken from its original context and reformulated into an officially approved image for the urbanized Balinese who flock to the Art Centre. Indeed, only those Balinese who are already isolated from their rural roots can recognize themselves in an idealized image that projects the authorized version of their cultural identity on the national stage. As the most illustrious exponents of Bali's regional culture, the arts presented at the festival are therefore less the product of an ethnic group than of a social group, namely, the emerging Indonesian middle class of Bali. But to the extent that art forms conceived in the provincial capital of Denpasar are then presented to the villages by former students of the Indonesian artistic institutions—and broadcast on the cultural programs of Indonesian television—they are ultimately recognized as being Balinese by the island's rural population.

Tourist Sites as Contested Domains

Admitedly, I have given the impression that Balinese cultural identity has been imposed by the Indonesian state on the Balinese people. In fact, the politics of culture in Indonesia is a contested domain, the locus of debate and conflict between ethnic groups and the state. At times, the folkloristic vision promoted in the guise of regional cultures is countered by a more politically vigorous version of ethnic identities. Two recent events concerned with tourism development on Bali are worth recalling in this respect.

To understand the significance of these events, it should be borne in mind that since the Indonesian government began developing international tourism, after the slump in oil revenues in 1986, tourist arrivals in Bali have registered a sharp increase, followed by an even faster rise in hotel investment fueled by deregulation of the banking system. In 1988, alleging the pressure of demand, the governor of Bali scheduled fifteen areas for development as tourist zones,[18] thus essentially lifting the restrictions imposed by the master plan on the construction of large hotels and facilities outside the initial southern seaside resorts. Since then, there has been noticeable unrest among the Balinese, who are apprehensive about outsiders usurping their island—perhaps not so much foreign and domestic tourists as Javanese migrant workers and wealthy Jakarta investors. At the same time, Balinese involved in the tourist industry have been voicing concerns that, with the growing tourist presence on the island and the subsequent degradation of the environment, the quality of the Balinese tourist product is declining, and have been urging that something be done to enhance the appeal of Bali as a tourist destination.

Given these concerns, in 1993 the Garuda Wisnu Kencana, better known in Bali by its acronym GWK, was proposed. GWK is a monumental statue of Wisnu (Vishnu), the Hindu god preserving and restoring the universe, riding his mount, the celestial bird Garuda, which is bedecked with golden *(kencana)* ornaments. Proudly labeled "the biggest and highest statue in the world" by its promoter—a Balinese artist established in Java, who likens his creation to such eminent sights as Borobudur, the Egyptian pyramids, and the Eiffel Tower and who nevers omits to specify that it will surpass the Statue of Liberty—the monument will be 125 meters high. It will be on a site covering over one hundred hectares on the southern peninsula, near the airport, and will be visible from the main tourist resorts in the area. Costing an estimated $200 million (in U.S. dollars) and capable of accommodating twenty thousand visitors a day, the monument will provide various facilities and will be "the most prominent tourist attraction for those who visit Bali" (GWK 1994, 1).

Presented by its creator as a gift to his home province and enthusiastically backed by both the Indonesian minister of Tourism and the governor of Bali, the GWK is designed as a landmark to welcome visitors on their arrival at the airport, and destined to become a prime item of "cultural heritage" for future generations of Balinese. Taking into account the role of Bali as the main gateway to Indonesia, this landmark is envisioned by the minister as the "image of Indonesian tourism," while for the governor it epitomizes the "image of Balinese culture."

As soon as it was made public, the project hit the headlines, giving rise to heated controversy. Endorsed by the provincial government and the tourist industry, the GWK is approved by a significant portion of the intelligentsia and public opinion. Its partisans advance the glory of Indonesia and the pride of the Balinese, capable of building a colossal monument—complete with the latest technology and worthy of the prestigious heritage of their ancestors—which cannot fail to fill with admiration the crowds of tourists rushing to visit it. As for its opponents, they are mostly from the ranks of artists and intellectuals, swollen with students and activists from various nongovernmental organizations. Accusing their adversaries of megalomania, they assert that famous historical monuments were not meaningless objects like the GWK but had a religious purpose. They note that tourists do not come to Bali to see a statue bigger than the Statue of Liberty but, to the contrary, are interested in discovering the Balinese traditional way of life in all its authenticity.[19] In a particularly striking appeal, a group of critics asked: "Does Bali have to become a Disneyland, a Hindu Theme Park where everything is made quaint and neatly packaged for sale? Is this what is called Culture?" (Helmi, Suarnatha, and Suasta 1993, 3). The GWK is indeed what is called "regional culture" in Indonesia and in this respect is certainly the best example of the construction of a provincial identity in Bali.

Hardly had the passions enflamed by the GWK (whose construction started in early 1995) cooled when the *Bali Post* published news about the Bali Nirwana Resort (BNR), a luxury tourist resort—complete with a five-star hotel, hundreds of private villas and condominium units, and an eighteen-hole golf course—scheduled for construction near Tanah Lot, one of Bali's holiest temples and most famous tourist spots. This 121-hectare resort, developed by a Jakarta-based international investment firm, was only the first of six other similar hotel complexes planned for a 600-hectare site on the same coastal strip. Since then, Bali has been shaken by unprecedented protest—the first time that so many Balinese have dared publicly to express discontent not only with tourism development on their island but more generally with the government.

Although some villagers in the vicinity resisted selling their rice fields to the developers, ultimately it was religion, not land, that became the primary focus of the controversy. Outraged by the prospect of a tourist resort rising next to their revered temple, hundreds of readers throughout the island submitted letters to the editor of the *Bali Post*. With impressive unanimity, they insisted that Tanah Lot was a symbol of Bali throughout the world and that the Balinese saw it as the very symbol of their identity. It was under this banner that they rejected the BNR, claiming that the sanctity of the temple was in jeopardy and accusing the government of selling off their faith in the name of development and national interest.

The fact is that religion proved to be the most effective—as well as the most emotionally charged—means of mobilizing public opinion against the project, as witnessed by the immediate support received from groups of Hindu students and intellectuals across the country. Among the most vocal were the leaders of the Indonesian Hindu Intellectuals' Forum, who admonished the Parisada's central board to defend their religion, accusing that organization of being a rubber stamp for government decisions. In January 1994, the council finally decreed that a distance of two kilometers must be maintained between the Tanah Lot temple and any development unrelated to religious purposes. Approved by President Suharto, this decree, had it been applied, would have stopped the BNR project; but, as is often the case in Indonesia, it was more a face-saving maneuver than a measure likely to be implemented. Rather than risk an outright confrontation, the council compromised. The developers agreed to change the resort's logo—the temple's famed silhouette—to soothe concerns that religion was being used for commercial ends. The resort's location, however, a few minor alterations notwithstanding, remained unchanged, with the hotel still situated less than five hundred meters from the temple. Meanwhile, the military had suppressed the protests and student demonstrations, and the daily front-page stories in the *Bali Post* covering the BNR issue promptly ended. By May the central government confirmed its approval for the resort, and the construction, interrupted in January, finally resumed in September 1994.

Beyond the immediate outcome of the protest, which looks as though the petitions and demonstrations have come to naught, the lesson to be learned from the BNR affair is twofold. On the surface, the Balinese intelligentsia are becoming increasingly critical of tourism while pushing for a greater role in shaping public policy on their island. At a deeper level, though, the powerlessness of the provincial authorities in matters of tourism development is construed by the Balinese as a threat against their identity, to which they react by closing ranks behind their religion.

Touristification and the State

As the example of Bali clearly attests, ethnic identities should not be seen as static primordial identities but as dynamic responses to new situations brought about by the state. Accordingly, it is important to avoid interpreting locally asserted identities and those prescribed by the state as two separate domains, one characterized by inherent authenticity and the other by contrivance.

Since the subjugation of their island at the turn of the century, the Balinese intelligentsia have attempted to circumscribe the foundation of their identity, which they considered should remain the preserve solely of the Balinese. To do so, they had to cut through the living fabric of their culture and draw boundaries where they perceived only a continuum. Thus, they proceeded to a series of conceptual discriminations, separating custom from politics, religion, and art. In the process, by having to relinquish its former political and religious prerogatives while some of its outward signs were praised for their artistic qualities, Balinese custom has seen its sphere of authority secularized and relativized. As a result, the Balinese have rooted their ethnic identity in the Hindu religion, which owes its official recognition to the condition that it not be restricted solely to the Balinese. At the same time, they have displayed the image of their ethnicity through cultural manifestations, which are acknowledged as long as they can support nation-building and tourism development.

In this respect, the role of tourism cannot be neatly set apart from that of the state. Indeed, while the touristification of Bali can be said to have furthered the culturalization of Balinese identity by promoting Balinese culture as art, such a trend is being implemented by the New Order for its own purpose, following in this instance, as in many others, the colonial state. Furthermore, as the GWK and the BNR affairs illustrate, the development of tourism in Bali fosters a provincial identity on the one hand and a religious identity on the other, frames of reference deliberately provided by the state as safe outlets for the expression of ethnicity in Indonesia.

Notes

This chapter is based on observations gathered during numerous trips to Bali since 1974, particularly on research undertaken in 1981 and 1982. The fieldwork was accomplished under the auspices of the Indonesian Institute of Sciences, and it benefited from the institutional patronage of Dr. I Gusti Ngurah Bagus, head of the Department of Anthropology at Udayana University. I am indebted to Robert Wood for critical comments as well as for assistance in conveying my French thoughts in proper English.

1. When I talk about "the Balinese," I refer in fact to the culture-producing people who formulate, propagate, and explain contemporary issues and emergent ideas to the rest of the population. Besides the personnel of the provincial government proper, these opinion makers comprise the intelligentsia at large—such as academics and journalists, bureaucrats and technocrats, entrepreneurs and professionals. These are the Balinese who are *authorized* to speak for society and who are thus in a position to monopolize legitimate discourse on Bali. Although it would be mistaken to suggest that they all share the same views or interests—particularly considering recent developments, which widen the gap between those who do and do not benefit directly from tourism—we nonetheless find that the members of this modern Balinese elite, most of whom live in the provincial capital, Denpasar, tend to share an outlook regarding the place of Bali within Indonesia. They mediate between the village and the state by speaking on behalf of the Balinese to Jakarta and by conveying the instructions of the center to the province, which allows them to affirm their ethnic identity while furthering the integration of Bali within the Indonesian nation.

2. Thus writes Vicki Baum in the preface of her novel *A Tale from Bali:* "I would like to believe . . . that the self-sacrifice of so many Balinese at that time had a deep significance, since it impressed upon the Dutch the need of ruling this proud and gentle island people as considerately as they have, and so kept Bali the paradise it is today" (Baum 1937, x).

3. According to local chronicles, the island of Bali was conquered in the fourteenth century by the Hindu-Javanese kingdom of Majapahit. Allegedly, after the sixteenth-century fall of Majapahit, Javanese priests and aristocrats bundled up what they could of the great Hindu tradition and transfered it to Bali, where they inaugurated an era of grandeur that is now regarded as the golden age of the island.

4. In the late nineteenth century, a protonationalist consciousness had taken shape around Islam that formed a common bond among natives from many different ethnic backgrounds and distinguished them from their Christian overlords. After the turn of the century, it was in the guise of Muslim organizations that Indonesian nationalism was given its first concrete expression.

5. The division of Balinese society into four hierarchical groups (incor-

rectly termed "castes" due to a misleading lexical analogy with the situation prevailing in India) is justified by the Balinese in reference to Majapahit. According to this myth of origin, the descendants of different groups of Javanese invaders collectively compose the nobility, as opposed to the commoners, who form the bulk of the population.

6. The cultural policy of the colonial authorities in Bali is still in need of thorough investigation, and its implications cannot be reduced to the simplified account given here. A reliable presentation is provided by Henk Schulte Nordholt (1986) and by Geoffrey Robinson (1992).

7. North Bali had come under direct Dutch administration in the 1880s, and the town of Singaraja was made the seat of the colonial government. This area had been the scene of repeated attempts to introduce Christian missions, and branches of Islamic associations had recently opened in Singaraja. Founded in the 1910s in Java, these associations had rapidly expanded throughout the archipelago, where they not only sowed the seeds of Indonesian nationalism but also set the trend for reform among followers of other religions.

8. A neologism of Sanskrit origin, the word *budaya,* which refers to the development of the reason or the character of an individual, replaced the Dutch word *cultuur* during the 1930s. The Malay word *seni,* which tended to replace the Dutch word *kunst,* meant "fine" or "refined" before assuming its modern sense of "art."

9. The circumstances surrounding the birth of *kebyar* during the 1910s in North Bali remain obscure, and the social situation that resulted from its integration into the Dutch Indies has yet to be investigated. For all that we know, it was initially a purely instrumental composition, displaying the virtuosity of the musicians with extremely fast and complex rhythms, full of sudden stops and starts, in a profusion of contrapuntal ornamentation. In line with this stylistic innovation, musical compositions took on a life of their own, independent of any ritual celebration, literary recitation, or dramatic performance. This newly conceived, "concert" music combined into one single composition piece borrowed from various repertoires. To adjust to the new musical style, certain instruments were transformed and a new orchestra was created, while dances were choreographed to interpret its rhythms. In these new creations, instead of the musicians following the lead and clues of the dancers, who were themselves strictly bound to the conventions defining the character they impersonated as in most dramatic dances, the *kebyar* tended toward the opposite in that the dancer was expected to embody the tempo and mood of the music, thereby acquiring a wider range of personal expression. On Balinese music, see Tenzer (1991) and on dance, see Bandem and deBoer (1981).

10. It is noteworthy that one of the few references to tourism I found in the Balinese periodicals of that time—an article published in 1927 by the commoners' mouthpiece—was a vehement diatribe against precisely such an

artistic vision of Bali. Its author not only reproached the Balinese for allowing themselves to be seduced by the glamour of their island abroad, but also rejected the image of a "living museum" propagated by the Orientalists and denounced the colonial government's policy of cultural conservatism. Advocates of progress, the commoners wanted Bali to renounce its archaic reputation and build a modern society that would contain nothing to arouse the curiosity of tourists in search of the exotic.

11. In fact, a fair proportion of them are only "statistical Muslims," notably among the Javanese majority.

12. Such a situation is neither particular to Bali nor due only to a movement of religious rationalization, but it testifies more generally to the suspicion in which the Indonesian state holds *adat*. On the one hand, *adat* proved a useful ideological weapon in the nationalist struggle, inasmuch as it symbolized the common and distinctive cultural heritage of the Indonesians. On the other hand, after independence the very diversity of *adat,* if allowed to develop freely, threatened dissension among the various ethnic groups. In independent Indonesia, therefore, *adat* has duly received the honored place that its ideological usefulness won for it; but its scope and legal import have been steadily curtailed by the state.

13. This should be understood only as a very general statement, which does not hold true for either ethnic minorities or the Chinese or regions where independence movements are threatening the unity of the nation, such as Aceh, East Timor, and West Irian.

14. The only notable exceptions that I am aware of are due to Bernard Sellato (1990) and Christoph Antweiler (1993), who expose the implications of this phenomenon in Kalimantan and South Sulawesi, respectively.

15. The process is twofold: selecting those elements of ethnic traditions considered representative of the province and, from those, selecting the elements that can also be considered pan-Indonesian. The most conspicuous illustration of such an official image of the country's cultural diversity is President Suharto's pet project, the Beautiful Indonesia-in-Miniature Park (Taman Mini Indonesia Indah), a grandiose theme park built in the early 1970s in Jakarta that displays the domestic architecture and cultural artifacts attributed to each of Indonesia's twenty-seven provinces (Pemberton 1994a). That same official image is also reproduced in the regional museums in the provincial capitals (Taylor 1994) and in numerous schoolbooks, where the culture of each province is, as a rule, reduced to a "traditional" house, a pair of costumes, a dance, and a ceremonial weapon.

16. The word *development* cannot but imperfectly render the idea conveyed by the Indonesian terminology, which implies an intention, a concerted effort to shape, to build up, and to promote a quality, which is not taken for granted but should be cultivated and developed in a certain direction. Clearly, the aim is to stress the mobilization of society to serve the needs of the state. In this respect, the New Order emphasis on development

involves far more than economics—*agama, adat,* and *seni budaya* should also be "developed."

17. Here "cultural tourism" merges into "cultural diplomacy," a concept advanced by the minister of Foreign Affairs in the early 1980s with a view to using the country's arts to convey Indonesia's image as a highly sophisticated culture to the world. Given its prestigious touristic reputation, the province of Bali was particularly required to contribute its performing arts to represent Indonesian culture abroad. Accordingly, Balinese music and dance groups sent on overseas tours are regarded as "cultural diplomats," expected to stimulate international tourism to Indonesia and promote Indonesia's cultural image.

18. From fifteen in 1988, the tourist zones became twenty-one in 1993 and now cover one-quarter of the total area of the island, deemed utterly excessive by some Balinese observers.

19. Whatever its promoters might say, it is clear that the public for which the GWK is intended—like that of Taman Mini Indonesia in Jakarta—is Indonesian, and particularly Balinese, rather than foreign.

References

Acciaioli, Greg
   1985   Culture as Art: From Practice to Spectacle in Indonesia. *Canberra Anthropology* 8(1, 2):148–174.
Alexander, Paul, ed.
   1989   *Creating Indonesian Cultures.* Sydney: Oceania Publications.
Anderson, Benedict R. O'G.
   1987   The State and Minorities in Indonesia. In *Southeast Asian Tribal Groups and Ethnic Minorities,* 73–81. Cambridge: Cultural Survival.
Antweiler, Christoph
   1993   South Sulawesi: Towards a Regional Ethnic Identity? Paper presented to the conference on Nationalism and Ethnicity in Southeast Asia, at Humbolt University, Berlin.
Atkinson, Jane M.
   1987   Religions in Dialogue: The Construction of an Indonesian Minority Religion. In *Indonesian Religions in Transition,* ed. R. Smith Kipp and S. Rodgers, 171–186. Tucson: University of Arizona Press.
Bakker, Frederik L.
   1993   *The Struggle of the Hindu Balinese Intellectuals: Developments in Modern Hindu Thinking in Independent Indonesia.* Amsterdam: VU University Press.
Bandem, Made
   1991   Bali's Art Czar: Interview with Dr. Made Bandem. *Nusa Tenggara,* 23 November, 24.

Bandem, Made, and Fredrik E. deBoer
1981 *Kaja and Kelod: Balinese Dance in Transition.* Kuala Lumpur: Oxford University Press.
Baum, Vicki
1937 *A Tale from Bali.* Garden City, N.J.: Doubleday.
Boon, James A.
1977 *The Anthropological Romance of Bali 1597–1972: Dynamic Perspectives in Marriage and Caste, Politics and Religion.* Cambridge: Cambridge University Press.
Bruner, Edward M.
1987 Introduction: Experiments in Ethnographic Writing. *Journal of the Steward Anthropological Society* 17(1, 2):1–19.
Colchester, Marcus
1986 Unity and Diversity: Indonesian Policy towards Tribal Peoples. *Ecologist* 16(2, 3):89–98.
Covarrubias, Miguel
1937 *Island of Bali.* New York: Alfred A. Knopf.
Dove, Michael R., ed.
1988 *The Real and Imagined Role of Culture in Development: Case Studies from Indonesia.* Honolulu: University of Hawai'i Press.
Drake, Christine
1989 *National Integration in Indonesia: Patterns and Issues.* Honolulu: University of Hawai'i Press.
Foulcher, Keith
1990 The Construction of an Indonesian National Culture: Patterns of Hegemony and Resistance. In *State and Civil Society in Indonesia,* ed. A. Budiman, 301–320. Clayton: Centre of Southeast Asian Studies, Monash University.
Geertz, Clifford
1990 "Popular Art" and the Javanese Tradition. *Indonesia* 50:77–94.
Geertz, Hildred
1963 Indonesian Cultures and Communities. In *Indonesia,* ed. R. T. McVey, 24–96. New Haven: Yale University Press.
GWK
1994 *The Blue Chip in a Tropical Tourism World.* Bandung: Yayasan Garuda Wisnu Kencana.
Helmi, Rio, Made Suarnatha, and Putu Suasta
1993 Tanggapan mengenai Garuda Wisnu Kencana (Reaction to the Garuda Wisnu Kencana), trans. Carol Warren. Mimeo. Bali.
Hoadley, Mason C., and M. B. Hooker
1981 *An Introduction to Javanese Law: A Translation of and Commentary on the Agama.* Tucson: University of Arizona Press.
Hooker, Virginia M., ed.
1993 *Culture and Society in New Order Indonesia.* Kuala Lumpur: Oxford University Press.

Hough, Brett
  1992 *Contemporary Balinese Dance Spectacles as National Ritual.*
    Clayton: Centre of Southeast Asian Studies, Monash University.
IBRD/IDA
  1974 *Bali Tourism Project: Appraisal Report.* Washington: Tourism
    Projects Department.
Kahn, Joel S.
  1993 *Constituting the Minangkabau: Peasants, Culture and Modernity
    in Colonial Indonesia.* Providence and Oxford: Berg.
Kipp, Rita Smith
  1993 *Dissociated Identities: Ethnicity, Religion, and Class in an Indone-
    sian Society.* Ann Arbor: University of Michigan Press.
Liddle, R. William
  1989 The National Political Culture and the New Order. *Prisma* 46:
    4–20.
Magenda, Burhan D.
  1988 Ethnicity and State-Building in Indonesia: The Cultural Base of the
    New Order. In *Ethnicity and Nations: Processes of Interethnic
    Relations in Latin America, Southeast Asia, and the Pacific,* ed.
    R. Guidieri, F. Pellizi, and S. J. Tambiah, 345–361. Austin:
    Rothko Chapel.
Pemberton, John
  1994a Recollections from "Beautiful Indonesia" (Somewhere Beyond the
    Postmodern). *Public Culture* 6(2):241–262.
  1994b *On the Subject of "Java."* Ithaca: Cornell University Press.
Picard, Michel
  1990a "Cultural Tourism" in Bali: Cultural Performances as Tourist
    Attraction. *Indonesia* 49:37–74.
  1990b *Kebalian Orang Bali:* Tourism and the Uses of "Balinese Culture"
    in New Order Indonesia. *Review of Indonesian and Malaysian
    Affairs* 24:1–38.
  1992 *Bali: Tourisme culturel et culture touristique.* Paris: L'Harmattan.
    English revised translation, 1996, *Bali: Cultural Tourism and
    Touristic Culture.* Singapore: Archipelago Press.
  1993 "Cultural Tourism" in Bali: National Integration and Regional
    Differentiation. In *Tourism in South-East Asia,* ed. M. Hitchcock,
    V. T. King, and M. J. G. Parnwell, 71–98. London: Routledge.
  1995 Cultural Heritage and Tourist Capital: Cultural Tourism in Bali.
    In *International Tourism: Identity and Change,* ed. M. F. Lanfant,
    J. B. Allcock, and E. M. Bruner, 44–66. London: Sage Studies in
    International Sociology.
  1996 Dance and Drama in Bali: The Making of an Indonesian Art Form.
    In *Being Modern in Bali,* ed. A. H. Vickers. New Haven: Yale Uni-
    versity Southeast Asian Studies.

Powell, Hickman
    1930   *The Last Paradise.* London: Jonathan Cape.
Ramstedt, Martin
    1992   Indonesian Cultural Policy in Relation to the Development of
           Balinese Performing Arts. In *Balinese Music in Context,* ed.
           D. Schaareman, 59–84. Winterthur: Amadeus, Forum Ethnomusi-
           cologicum 4.
Robinson, Geoffrey B.
    1992   The Politics of Violence in Modern Bali, 1882–1966. Ph.D. diss.,
           Cornell University.
Rodgers, Susan
    1993   Batak Heritage and the Indonesian State: Print Literacy and the
           Construction of Ethnic Cultures in Indonesia. In *Ethnicity and the
           State,* ed. J. D. Toland, 147–176. New Brunswick: Transaction
           Publishers.
SCETO
    1971   *Bali Tourism Study. Report to the Government of Indonesia.*
           Paris: UNDP/IBRD.
Schulte Nordholt, Henk
    1986   *Bali: Colonial Conceptions and Political Change, 1700–1940:
           From Shifting Hierarchies to "Fixed Order."* Rotterdam: Erasmus
           University.
    1991   *State, Village, and Ritual in Bali.* Amsterdam: VU University
           Press.
Sellato, Bernard
    1990   Indonesia Goes Ethnic: Provincial Culture, Image, and Identity:
           Current Trends in Kalimantan. Paper presented to the conference
           on Centres and Peripheries in Insular Southeast Asia, Paris. CNRS-
           DEVI.
Seminar on Cultural Tourism in Bali
    1971   *Hasil Keputusan Seminar Pariwisata Budaya Daerah Bali*
           (Proceedings of the seminar on cultural tourism in Bali). Den-
           pasar.
Soebadio, Haryati
    1985   *Cultural Policy in Indonesia.* Paris: UNESCO.
Taylor, Paul M.
    1994   The *Nusantara* Concept of Culture: Local Traditions and National
           Identity as Expressed in Indonesia's Museums. In *Fragile Tradi-
           tions: Indonesian Art in Jeopardy,* ed. P. M. Taylor, 71–90. Hono-
           lulu: University of Hawai'i Press.
Tenzer, Michael
    1991   *Balinese Music.* Berkeley: Periplus.
Urry, John
    1990   *The Tourist Gaze.* London: Sage.

Vickers, Adrian H.

1987　Hinduism and Islam in Indonesia: Bali and the Pasisir World. *Indonesia* 44:31–58.

1989　*Bali: A Paradise Created.* Berkeley: Periplus.

Warren, Carol

1993　*Adat and Dinas: Balinese Communities in the Indonesian State.* Kuala Lumpur: Oxford University Press.

≫ 8

Consuming Cultures: Tourism and the Commoditization of Cultural Identity in the Island Pacific

> [B]y its transformation into a commodity a thing, of whatever
> type, has been reduced to a means for its own consumption.
> . . . The objects of the commodity world of capitalism . . . shed
> their independent "being" and intrinsic qualities and come to
> be so many instruments of commodity satisfaction: the famil-
> iar example is that of tourism—the American tourist no longer
> lets the landscape "be in its being" . . . but takes a snapshot of
> it. . . . The concrete activity of looking at a landscape . . . is
> thus comfortably replaced by the act of taking possession of it
> and converting it into a form of personal property (Jameson
> 1979, 131).

This chapter explores the relationship between state-promoted tourism and local perceptions of cultural identity in some
Pacific Island societies. A considerable literature has documented the
growing touristic appeal of "staged authenticity" and cultural performances (Adams 1990, Greenwood 1977, Jolly 1982, MacCannell
1976, Picard 1990, Volkman 1982, 1984) that accompany the emergence of ethnic tourism (Dearden and Harron 1992, Harron and
Weiler 1992, Smith 1989, Wood 1984). As Jameson described a landscape transformed into an object and appropriated as property by a
tourist gazing through a camera, so other authors have argued that
culture is commoditized—reified and transformed into a marketable
item—when customs become tourist attractions (Greenwood 1977).
Several writers, observing the long-term development of tourism in
developing nations, have noted that tourism has some subtle but pro-

found consequences for self-perception. The "tourist gaze" in effect presents local people with a distorted mirror for viewing their own lifeways. Increasingly, ethnographers are arguing that interaction with touristic representations, which are promoted by states for economic reasons, causes people to reevaluate their customs and to reconceptualize their group identity (Linnekin 1982, 1990, MacCannell 1984, Picard 1990, Volkman 1982, 1990, Wood 1993, Wood and Deppen 1994).

This volume focuses on links between the state, which propagates particular images of local cultures when it promotes tourism, and the "dialogic construction" (Picard 1990, 74) of cultural identity among peoples who are visited by tourists. The discussion presented in this chapter extends the argument from ethnic tourism and cultural performances to another venue for cultural commoditization—the design and marketing of consumer goods. I will attempt to outline connections between touristic representations of culture, local constructions of cultural identity, and consumption. Western elite and middle-class travelers comprise a market for reified, stereotypic, packaged cultures; ethnic tourism both responds to and stimulates this market demand. Touristic discourse objectifies and essentializes customs and the people who practice them (see Adams 1984). With a growing tourist presence and increasing engagement with the tourist market, local discourse about culture and ethnicity may increasingly resemble touristic discourse in its premises and narrative style—as has happened in Hawaii.

In Hawaii, identity merchandise has become tremendously popular over the past five years. By identity merchandise, I mean consumer products that represent cultural groups by means of graphic paragons, archetypes, and key symbols (see Ortner 1973). Typically these items combine naturalized representations of ethnic exemplars, in purportedly traditional attire, with slogans asserting ethnic strength, "blood" purity, and cultural authenticity. T-shirts adorned with slogans and place names have long been popular in the Island Pacific, but the trend toward explicitly ethnic representations and depictions of "tradition" on consumer goods, especially apparel, appears to be growing in the region. Such products are designed to appeal primarily to local people, not to tourists. But I suggest that the Euro-American tourist gaze—with its vision of naturalized ethnicity and objectified culture—has shaped the context in which the designs are created and has stimulated the demand for such merchandise.

Volkman (1982, 1984, 1990) and Picard (1990), among others,

have argued convincingly that tourism has transformative effects on local identity concepts and self-definition, particularly when culture is marketed as an attraction. I contend that the consumption of identity merchandise arises and flourishes in an economic context in which culture and ethnicity have been objectified and commoditized—conceptually transformed into products that can be bought and sold in the marketplace. State-sponsored cultural or ethnic tourism (see Wood 1984) accomplishes precisely such reification. This argument extends Volkman's (1990, 91) assertion that, " 'Collection'—in the form of souvenirs, postcards, photographs, artifacts, tales, experiences, or memories—presupposes processes of objectification that extend . . . to 'culture' itself."[1] The immense popularity of identity merchandise in Hawaii, where the tourist industry has a hegemonic presence in the economy and public discourse, illustrates how local people may also come to objectify culture in such settings. In Hawaii, local people have become collectors of culture—but of their "own" culture, in the form of stereotypic artifacts and stylized, essentialized ethnic archetypes displayed on consumer goods.

In the Pacific Islands as in many other postcolonial venues, however, it must be noted that cultural commoditization has historical and conceptual origins that considerably predate the rise of tourism. Modern ethnic tourism derives its appeal from the Western fascination with the exotic and the primitive—a preoccupation traceable at least to eighteenth-century Europe (see Smith 1960)—and thus represents the continuing legacy of Orientalism (Said 1978). Moreover, ethnic tourism—with its passion for collecting different cultural experiences and artifacts—rests on the Western paradigm of ethnicity, which sees a cultural group as a naturally bounded, biologically self-perpetuating entity (Linnekin and Poyer 1990). In this view, ethnic groups maintain discrete boundaries through time and inherit an enduring cultural core or essence—a "tradition." The underlying model of ethnic tourism, in other words, could be likened to a human zoo. In contrast, to speak of the "construction" of cultural identity or the "invention of tradition," as many writers now do, is to emphasize that culture is a dynamic product of human consciousness and is constantly being reformulated in the contemporary context. The argument advanced in this chapter reflects the constructionist perspective (see Linnekin 1992), which Davydd Greenwood (1982, 27) enunciated succinctly in *Cultural Survival Quarterly*'s first special issue on tourism:

All societies create traditions, accept elements from outside, invent ceremonies, and reinvent themselves for both sacred and secular purposes. All viable cultures are in the process of "making themselves up" all the time.

State-promoted tourism establishes an economic setting in which cultural forms are readily packaged as market commodities. Local people participate in the tourist industry out of economic necessity and/or political pressure, but such participation has consequences for self-definition and for general concepts about the nature of human groups and ethnic affiliations. Multiple historical and political-economic determinants are of course at work in postcolonial and "Fourth World" (where indigenous peoples have been conquered and outnumbered in their own homelands), settings, and it is impossible to isolate tourism's particular role in transforming local constructions of cultural identity. Consumption patterns may, however, offer clues to changing public notions about group identity.

A caveat is warranted before proceeding. Most writers use the term "the state" to refer to a centralized national government, but it is important to particularize "the state." At several points this chapter will challenge assumptions of overarching state control and hegemony where tourism and local cultural representations are concerned. We must ask, what is the operational referent of "the state" in Hawaii, Western Samoa, and other Pacific Island societies, and to what extent does the state promote tourism? How does the role of the state compare to that of regional organizations, such as the Tourism Council of the South Pacific? In the Island Pacific, the scope and effectiveness of central governmental control is highly variable and is typically more uneven than in either the advanced capitalist or socialist nations. Swain (1990, 26) has reported: "The role of the state is critical in defining China's ethnic tourism industry through its regulation of tourism investment, production, and consumption." By contrast, central governments are far weaker in the small island nations of the Pacific, and in general have a minimal role in directing the course of tourism, mercantile capitalism, and consumerism.

Even in Hawaii, where the legislature allocates millions of dollars annually to the state's tourist promotion agency, tourism cannot be said to be state controlled. On the contrary, the State of Hawaii frequently loses in disputes with major businesses, such as airlines, over routing and development decisions. The state-funded Hawaii Visitors Bureau promotes Hawaii in general to the nation and the world, but specific initiatives and marketing decisions are largely in the hands of entrepreneurs and Japanese or mainland-based corporations. Most of the factors affecting tourist volume are not under any government's control; in recent years such factors have included the Gulf War, a hurricane, recessions in America and Japan, the cancellation of airline routes, the Kobe earthquake, and the dollar's fall against the *yen*. Through its advertising and promotion efforts the state does, however, "position the product." State-level marketing establishes certain dominant themes that are likely to be reproduced by independent brokers. As Adams (1984) has shown, such representations significantly shape tourist expectations and set precedents for future discourse about a place.

Why is identity merchandise so popular in Hawaii today, and why is it becoming prevalent in consumer markets elsewhere in the Pacific? An answer to the first question would have to include a sketch of Hawaii's colonial history, in which a racist, naturalistic model of ethnicity founded a strategy of labor control, and an understanding of recent ethnic politics. After tracing the historical formation of Hawaii's tourist economy, I will offer an abbreviated comparison with the development of tourism in other Pacific Island societies, focusing particularly on the relative appeal of culture in marketing these destinations. I will then discuss the emergence of identity merchandise and analyze some examples drawn from Hawaii and Samoa.

While the state promotes and endorses certain types of cultural representations, I suggest that entrepreneurial capitalism disseminates these images and their conceptual premises far more efficiently and effectively than could any governmental body. Profit seeking, in other words, takes up where the state leaves off in purveying commoditized culture to the public. Both tourist promotion materials and identity merchandise purvey commoditized representations of cultural groups. Tourism and consumer markets are, at most, imperfectly under state control. My emphasis on the market rather than the state follows from Jameson's (1979, 131) characterization of "the commodity world of capitalism" as one "in which everything, including labor power, has become a commodity." The state encourages and expedites market processes in capitalist societies but does not control the specific media and commodity expressions that result. Moreover, entrepreneurial capitalism is indiscriminate in the sense that merchants will target local consumers as well as tourists and will develop products that local people find attractive. Thus, in Hawaii, cultural motifs that have long been a mainstay in tourist advertising have been adopted and artistically transformed by designers and silk-screen printers, who are competing to meet the local demand for fashions exalting ethnic strength and tradition.

Sugar, Ethnicity, and Tourism

In the Pacific Islands, Hawaii represents the extreme in its economic dependence on tourism and in the volume and commercialization of its "hospitality industry." As sugar's profitability declined after World War II, Hawaii was transformed from a largely rural plantation colony into a highly urbanized tourist mecca, with much of the boom occurring during the 1960s (see Cooper and Daws 1985, Farrell 1982, Kent 1983, Nordyke 1989). Hawaii has more tourists annually, more hotel rooms, more tourist-oriented retail shops, and more rental-car agencies than any other location in the Island Pacific. To many who live elsewhere in the Pacific, Hawaii illustrates a cautionary tale of tremendous economic success gained at the price of indigenous dispossession, wholesale social transformation, and cultural loss, not to mention a high cost of living. Arguably, nowhere else in the Island Pacific was the indigenous culture so effectively suppressed by colonialism, short of the eradication of the native people. As commodity agriculture has died a slow death, tourism has been defended as the only alternative for generating jobs and state tax revenues. This argument has never been successfully challenged, at least as far as the state government is concerned. A steep downturn in tourism in the early 1990s and an unprecedented budget shortfall have resulted not in a drive for economic diversification but in accelerated planning for a state-sponsored convention center and increased funding for the Hawaii Visitors Bureau.[2]

A dependency analysis would categorize postcontact Hawaii as the periphery of the world system (see Wallerstein 1974, 1979, Kent 1983). For several decades after Captain Cook's arrival in 1778, most rural Hawaiians continued to live by farming and fishing, while residents of Honolulu and a few other port localities became heavily involved in mercantile capitalism and the provisions trade. Meanwhile, the Hawaiian chiefs became conspicuous consumers of imported luxury goods—clothing, silver service, liquor, boats, furnishings—usually purchased on credit. Initially the chiefs paid with sandalwood, which Western merchants shipped to China to sell at a handsome profit. But the sandalwood gave out in the 1820s, leaving a legacy of debt that the kingdom would never be able to repay.

By the 1840s a small but influential group of resident foreigners—

missionaries, businessmen, and self-made political advisers—were pressuring the Hawaiian monarchy to institute major changes in the land system. In the indigenous economy land was inalienable; people acquired use and access rights from the chiefs through a rank hierarchy of tenancy relationships. In return, commoners gave the chiefs tributary gifts of food and domestic necessities at ritually prescribed times and were expected to work for the chiefs when commanded. Although the chiefs had the right to evict the people under them, in practice most commoners lived undisturbed and were able to pass on their lands to family members. Westerners argued from several fronts that this tenancy system should be changed to one of private property. Missionaries claimed that tenancy was a disincentive to industry, that the commoners would be more productive and less inclined to wander if they owned their own land. Businessmen saw the land as potential capital going to waste while the native population dwindled through disease. (The Hawaiian people declined in numbers by at least 75 percent in the first seventy years of foreign contact; see Schmitt 1968, 18–24, 74.) Would-be entrepreneurs wanted the right to buy, own, and sell land and to develop it as they saw fit. During the 1840s, the Hawaiian Kingdom was beset by threats and intimidation from European consuls and foreign creditors and had weathered one abortive invasion. Western political advisers argued that establishing private property would enhance Hawaii's stature in the international arena of "civilized" nations.

Private real estate was instituted in Hawaii through a process known as the Great Mahele, a "division" of rights that occurred between 1848 and 1855. During the Mahele all landholders in the kingdom had to present and defend their claims to land, and, if successful, they later received a private, fee simple title. Initially, the king and principal chiefs divided all the lands in the kingdom among themselves. In 1850, a statute gave commoners the right to receive private titles to their own small holdings; that same year, another statute gave foreigners what they had long petitioned for—the right to buy, own, and sell land in the kingdom. Another 1850 law made mandatory the payment of taxes in currency rather than in produce or pigs, thus forcing subsistence cultivators to engage in the cash economy. And the Masters and Servants Act, also passed in 1850, made it legal to import foreign workers as contract laborers.

These four statutes could not have been better designed to facilitate the demise of the Hawaiian subsistence economy and the growth of commodity agriculture. Hawaiians were free to sell their lands precisely as foreigners were permitted to buy them; the labor force problem, which dogged contemporary foreign planters in Samoa, was solved by the Masters and Servants Act. In the aftermath of the Mahele, the king and the chiefs also sold off lands in large tracts. To list and discuss all of the factors in Hawaiian land alienation during the latter half of the nineteenth century would consume several pages (see Linnekin 1987). Suffice to say, Hawaiian dispossession enabled the phenomenal growth of the sugar industry during this period. By the end of the century Hawaiians were a minority in their own homeland. The denouement speaks for itself: in 1893 Hawaiians lost their political sovereignty as well as the remaining publicly held lands when a small clique of resident foreigners, most of them sugar planters, overthrew Queen Liliʻuokalani. Although Grover Cleveland's administration investigated and condemned the overthrow, the American government would not intervene by force. The revolutionaries held out until Cleveland left office, and the United States annexed Hawaii as a territory in 1898.

Sugar was Hawaii's principal export by the end of the Civil War, and the plantations' profitability soared after the 1875 Reciprocity Treaty, which allowed tariff-free exports to the United States. Planters began in earnest to recruit Asian (and some European) contract workers to fill their labor needs. Hawaii became the archetypal plantation colony. As in Wallerstein's model of the capitalist periphery, Hawaii supplied commodities to the core state by harnessing *"cheap* labor *far away"* (Wallerstein 1974, 86; emphasis in original). The sugar planters constituted a white ("haole") minority elite, tightly knit through intermarriage and the interlocking directorates of Hawaii's Big Five corporations. Ever in search of more tractable "races," they recruited first Chinese, then Portuguese to act as overseers, then Japanese and Okinawans, then Filipinos. Smaller numbers of workers were recruited from Spain, Puerto Rico, Korea, Russia, Germany, and Scandinavia (see Nordyke 1989).

The haole elite profoundly feared that imported Asian workers would overwhelm them, hence the tactic of recruiting from different nations sequentially in order to "dilute" the influence of any one group (Reinecke 1979). The planters' strategy for controlling sugar workers relied on paternalism—controlling every aspect of the laborers' lives—combined with a thorough system of ethnic stratification (Takaki 1983). Plantation workers lived in ethnically segregated residential camps. Wage scales were calibrated by ethnicity, with Europeans receiving more than Asians for the same work, and

Japanese receiving more than Filipinos (Takaki 1983, 77). Social status was reflected in each group's location along the camp's latrine trench: the haole manager's house stood on the highest point. The Filipino camp was at the end of the system. In the words of novelist Milton Murayama (1975, 96): "Shit too was organized according to the plantation pyramid." Managers encouraged interethnic competition in the form of contests to reduce absenteeism and increase productivity (Takaki 1983, 68–69).

Not surprisingly, racialist and racist rhetoric abounded in the Territory of Hawaii, not only in the haole elite's communications but also in ethnic community newspapers and labor activists' speeches (Reinecke 1979). The Chinese, Japanese, and Filipinos in Hawaii stereotyped and maligned one another in the early territorial period. Ideas of ethnic exclusiveness are not unique to Europe and America, of course. But nascent ideologies of ethnic separateness were exacerbated by the planters' "divide and conquer" strategy, federal laws and classifications, and the aggressively Americanizing public school system. The ethnicities were conceptualized as clearly bounded, enduring groups, racially and culturally distinct, and were maintained as such on the plantations. Labor unions in Hawaii were bounded by ethnicity. Portuguese were enumerated as a separate "race" in the census until the 1930s, when they were reclassified as Caucasians. The framers of the 1920 Hawaiian Homes Act, an attempt to restore some land to Hawaiians, stipulated that only those with 50 percent Hawaiian "blood" should be eligible for the leasing program. Until 1952, federal law barred Asian immigrants from becoming naturalized citizens. "English standard" public schools effectively segregated white children from the pidgin-speaking children of immigrant laborers.

Though overused in contemporary scholarship, the term "hegemony" seems justifiable when describing public ideology in territorial and present-day Hawaii. Decades of political and economic control by a minority elite framed local discourse about ethnicity long before Hawaii became a tourist destination. Many residents use the terms "race" and "ethnicity" interchangeably, and most local college students cannot distinguish the two concepts. In Hawaii today, well-defined ethnic stereotypes are entrenched in local discourse and ethnic jokes are still socially acceptable. When asked, any long-time resident of Hawaii can attest that Japanese are short, quiet, shy, smart, and polite, while Chinese are smart, industrious, and *pake,* a pidgin word meaning thrifty or stingy. Portuguese are loud and talkative. Filipinos are hardworking, hot tempered, and colorful dressers. Hawaiians are large, easygoing, and loving. And haoles are smart, outspoken, pushy, and aggressive.[3]

Rooted in the hierarchy of plantation society, these stereotypes reveal some of the tensions and antagonisms of modern Hawaii. Some local people in Hawaii will defend the objective validity of ethnic behavioral stereotypes. Nonetheless, the valence of Hawaii's multiculturalism has shifted since the 1950s. Concurrent with the drive for statehood and the rise of tourism, suspicion and separation have been replaced—or masked—by a prevailing public ideology of interethnic harmony, or aloha. In the 1920s and 1930s plantation workers eventually recognized their common interests and forged an interethnic labor movement (Takaki 1983). The more significant political benchmark was the Democratic "revolution" of 1954, when a coalition of working-class haoles and Japanese Americans won control of the territorial legislature from the Republican oligarchy. The Democratic political leaders and their supporters vigorously promoted both tourism and statehood. Hawaii's new economic elite was soon comprised of real estate developers, contractors, and lawyers—many of whom had close ties to the new political leadership (see Cooper and Daws 1985).

The decline of commodity agriculture in Hawaii since World War II has been gradual but irreversible. Tourism became the surrogate, "a new kind of sugar," as an early volume on Pacific tourism called it (Finney and Watson 1974). The transition from plantations to tourism as an economic base has reproduced the dependency relationship between Hawaii and external metropolitan centers. Most hotels and the major shopping centers in Hawaii are owned by Japanese or mainland corporations; the service staff is local, but the top managers are outsiders and the profits go elsewhere. Job growth in Hawaii has been stagnant for many years, except in low-paying service occupations such as hotel cleaning and food service. Despite Hawaii's high cost of living, professional salaries are generally lower than for similar jobs on the mainland. As a comparative case, Hawaii represents the mature development of the colonial periphery. In its transition to a tourist economy, Hawaii still offers "cheap labor far away." Many developing nations in the Pacific and elsewhere have suffered from declining world prices for tropical commodities such as sugar, copra, and cocoa. Many are seeking economic recovery by encouraging tourists from the industrial nations. But Pacific Islanders cite Hawaii as a negative example of tourism's impacts, and the cultural consequences provoke the greatest concern.

Selling Hawaii

*Maybe it was the magical sunset or the emerald-green gardens
and brilliant, colorful flowers. Perhaps it was the gentle philos-
ophy of "aloha" in every smile of those who are from here.
Whatever it was that brought people to Hawaii in the first
place, you'll find it at the Hyatt Regency Kauai (advertisement,* Islands *magazine, April 1995).*

The advertisement quoted above aptly reflects the mix of nature and
culture in the marketing of Hawaii as a destination. Since the 1950s,
Hawaii's primary touristic appeal has been of the tropical island
variety: scenery, beaches, and sun. From the perspective of mainland
Americans and Japanese, Hawaii is reasonably priced and Americans
do not need a passport. Many tourists who come to Hawaii do not
object to Waikiki's tacky commercialization and crowded streets, but
seem to find the carnival atmosphere fun, the fast-food restaurants
reassuringly familiar.

Culture, however, is a strong second as a distinctive marketing
point for Hawaii, especially for mainland tourists who have even
closer and cheaper options for sun and sand. There is, primarily, the
appeal of a romanticized Hawaiian culture. Even in the early 1900s,
tourists were greeted with flower leis, ukulele serenaders, and hula
troupes. The Hawaiian greeters of that era were probably landless
city dwellers attempting to eke out a living, but their aloha nonetheless seemed sincere and spontaneous. Most of them were working
independently for themselves and their families. By the 1960s, large
tour companies had taken over the visitor industry, and representations of Hawaiian culture had become routinized, formulaic, and
cheapened. Every one of the thousands of tourists arriving by jet
could expect to experience the lei greeting, the Hawaiian warrior in
red loincloth and ersatz feather helmet at the airport, incantations of
"aloha," the hula show, and the obligatory luau.

While the above is still the typical Hawaiian vacation for many
visitors (especially those on low-priced package tours), in the 1980s
and 1990s the industry has generally attempted to upgrade the tourist experience. Marketing and hotel design have emphasized local history and have attempted to present a more "authentic" Hawaiian culture. The shift was prompted, in part, by the observation that Hawaii
was attracting predominantly low-budget travelers intent on spending as little as possible during their stay. At least, this was the trend
in the westbound market; Japanese tourists have always vastly out-

spent mainland visitors and are much more interested in shopping for high-priced goods during their Hawaiian vacation. However, declining tourist arrivals in the early 1990s heightened concerns over the aging of Hawaii as a destination. Placing more emphasis on culture and history is one strategy for enhancing Hawaii's competitiveness vis-à-vis myriad other sun-and-sand tourist spots.[4]

By offering a higher quality tourist experience, the state and the industry hope to attract a higher class of tourist and to refresh Hawaii's image. Plastic hula skirts are out; respectful performances of ancient *(kahiko)* hula are in. In keeping with recent trends in Western tourism (see, for example, Weiler and Hall 1992), Hawaii's marketing has increasingly sought to portray the vacation as an opportunity for personal growth and learning rather than a purely hedonistic experience. An *Islands* magazine (April 1995) advertisement for the upper-bracket Ritz-Carlton Resorts features *kahiko* dancers silhouetted against a sunset in a volcanic landscape, with the copy: "When you return, you'll bring back memories of a place where your family discovered another civilization, as well as each other." Some developers have incorporated archaeological sites into hotel layouts and feature them in their advertisements to suggest a more culturally sensitive experience. The Hotel King Kamehameha, in Kona on the island of Hawai'i, has reconstructed a historic *heiau* (pre-Christian temple) located on the hotel grounds. The *heiau* and Hawaiian cultural history form the centerpiece of the hotel's self-presentation. Hawaiian artifacts are displayed in museumlike cases in the lobby. The treatment is careful, respectful, and informed and the preservation is commendable. Nevertheless, in this context Hawaiian culture is also a marketing vehicle whereby the hotel portrays itself as a guardian of tradition.

Importantly, Hawaii's cultural marketing is not restricted to indigenous Hawaiian culture. The Islands' ethnic diversity is a major selling point. To the average visitor, Hawaii's social environment and street scenes appear foreign and full of local color (see Wood 1984). A special advertising supplement in *Forbes* magazine (28 September 1992) claimed that Hawaii offers the most exotic vacation available without leaving the United States. I have been with a group of Elderhostel participants—older mainland Americans on a study tour—who viewed local children walking to school as a fascinating cultural performance. I have also had the opportunity to experience the other side of the observer/observed relationship in Hawaii. On more than one occasion when my children were younger and we were at the beach, I was asked by young Japanese women if they could photo-graph us. These defamiliarizing encounters provided valuable instruc-tion in how it feels to be "collected"; in someone else's vision, my blond children were natives and we were part of Hawaii's local color.

Hawaii's tourist marketing has long conveyed a pointed message about this multiculturalism. Hawaii is unlike most other places in the world, the message runs, in that the different ethnic groups retain their uniqueness while living together cooperatively, in a spirit of aloha. Long before the rise of mass tourism, visitors to Hawaii were attracted to this positive vision of ethnic coexistence. A more critical historical interpretation might note that Hawaii's relative peaceful-ness was founded on decisive power disparities in the plantation colony: Hawaiians had been dispossessed and outnumbered, Asian immigrants were barred from full citizenship, and the plantation structure set up formidable barriers to interethnic alliances. Though historically debatable, the notion that Hawaiian society had over-come ethnic divisiveness became a dominant public ideology during the territorial period and was reflected in scholarly and popular writ-ing about Hawaii (see, for example, Michener 1959). As a public ideology in and about Hawaii, aloha became particularly salient after World War II (Farrell 1982). The rise of mass tourism and lobbying for statehood were more-or-less concurrent movements in the 1950s, and the ideal of interethnic harmony was advantageous for both. As the descendants of immigrants moved off the plantations, local people too came to share this sanguine vision of Hawaii as a unique place, and aloha became the normative ideal for civil behavior. Local discourse today likens Hawaii not to a melting pot, but to a beef stew or tossed salad: in this model, the different cultures mix but retain their individuality. Ethnic diversity is generally assumed to be a public good and is celebrated on a daily basis in the local media. Hawaii's schools are especially active in promoting this ideology, valorizing Hawaii's "rainbow" of cultural traditions through pag-eants, programs, field trips, and subjects such as Hawaiiana.

A broader American ideology also holds that cultural diversity is a positive and enriching force for the nation—when expressed in approved ways. Again, it is impossible to separate constructions of culture and ethnicity in Hawaii from their historical context. In Hawaii even more so than in mainland America, the unremitting public celebration of multiculturalism has effectively co-opted cul-tural practices as a mode of resistance. Two generations ago, to dance and teach the hula in a private, religious manner (rather than for commercial ends) was a subversive act. Today, the hula is vaunted as an affirmation of Hawaii's native culture, one of several traditions that make up the social rainbow. In an earlier era, the *kahiko* hula style was cast as anti-Christian and dangerous; today *kahiko* is celebrated as an "authentic" tradition revived, even though most of the dances performed have been newly created. And as indicated at the beginning of this section, *kahiko* is now as likely to be featured in resort advertisements as the ersatz, commercialized hula was a few decades ago.

Industry publications report that tourists are attracted to Hawaii because of the friendly people, the high standards for service and accommodation, and a sense of personal safety. From the state's point of view, the ethic of aloha is a precious economic resource and a social norm to be guarded with care. Threats to Hawaii's public image of ethnic harmony are potentially disastrous for the state's economy. Aloha—meaning interethnic cooperation and celebratory multiculturalism—has been a hegemonic ideology in Hawaii for several decades and has successfully *contained* cultural revival as a form of political resistance. Over the past several years, however, growing resentment of tourists has combined with ethnic activism to shake the normative effectiveness of aloha. Since the 1970s, Hawaiian political organizing has accelerated dramatically. Demands for redress have become more vocal and have won unprecedented recognition from such established political leaders as Senator Daniel Inouye. Recently the state has made partial efforts to redress Hawaiian claims with large monetary payments and the return of some lands to the Hawaiian Homes trust. But in the past decade the call for some form of Hawaiian sovereignty has attained such credibility and momentum that an eventual Hawaiian nation seems inevitable, though its form is a subject of much debate.

Although Hawaii represents an extreme degree of engagement with tourism, the processes that formed Hawaii's particular nexus of tourism, ethnicity, and the state are common to several other Pacific and Asian societies. Hawaii represents the plantation colony turned tourist destination—a historical transition that has occurred in many other developing nations on the capitalist periphery. Given certain conditions—ready access to a metropolitan tourist market, attention from foreign entrepreneurs, well-funded marketing efforts—Hawaii's present could be the future of some Asian and Pacific societies that are now only beginning to develop a tourist industry.

In Hawaii as elsewhere, tourism's commoditization of culture has conceptual roots in colonial history. In Hawaii, both plantation management strategies and tourist marketing techniques have purveyed a naturalistic concept of ethnicity that conflates race and culture. It has often been noted that Fourth World nationalist movements tend to represent ethnic groups similarly, as primordial, clearly bounded, biologically self-perpetuating entities maintaining separate cultural traditions. In Hawaii the plantations, the tourist industry, and Hawaiian nationalism tend to dovetail in how they represent human groups. In line with the global resurgence of micronationalism, contemporary political activism in Hawaii emphasizes ethnic distinctiveness and exclusivism over the state-promoted ideology of aloha. As I will elaborate below, consumer markets have responded rapidly to this new spirit of the times.

Marketing Pacific Cultures

Western Samoa. In these quintessentially Polynesian isles of glorious blue water and towering palms . . . a hearty tradition of hospitality   (Islands *magazine, April 1995).*

Reporting on the decline in Hawaiian tourism during the Gulf War, a newswriter for *Pacific Islands Monthly* invoked "image fatigue" (1 September 1991, 45). Increasingly since the 1970s, special interest tourists and those desiring a less crowded and commercialized experience have flown directly to the outer islands, bypassing Waikiki and the island of Oahu altogether. Many independent tourists no longer come to Hawaii at all but seek more culturally "authentic" and exotic vacation settings in the Island Pacific. As in the case of Hawaii, the primary attractiveness of South Pacific destinations lies in the familiar tropical allure of sun, beach, and sea. But native cultures are a strong secondary attraction, as suggested in the above characterization of Western Samoa.

Until recently tourism had a relatively low profile in most of the Island Pacific. Tahiti and Fiji were the first Pacific societies beyond Hawaii to attract large numbers of tourists. From the late 1950s to the mid-1980s, Fiji's tourist business grew from an annual total of $5 million to $150 million (*Islands Business Pacific,* 1 December 1986, 17). Fiji became to Australians and New Zealanders what Hawaii has been to mainland Americans: a relatively inexpensive tropical getaway, not too far away, offering a foreign—but not *too* exotic—cultural backdrop together with a high standard of comfort and service. Tahiti, which remains a French colony, is more dependent on tourism than Fiji and has experienced some significant environmental degradation in resort areas. In the 1980s, Rarotonga, in the Cook Islands, had the fastest-growing tourist business in the Island Pacific, but many other locations—Tonga, Vanuatu, the Solomons—have been bypassed. Connell (1991, 265), citing Britton (1987), observes that Tonga's lack of a colonial past has actually been a hindrance to tourist development: "Access to metropolitan states is critical because there is minimal indigenous tourism."

But the unevenness of tourist development in the Pacific Islands has partly been due to variable governmental and popular support. Many Pacific Islanders are, at best, ambivalent about tourism (for a Vanuatu example, see Jolly 1982). Western Samoa's political leaders have long debated its costs and benefits and have been particularly concerned that the presence of large numbers of visitors could corrupt the nation's young and threaten the *fa'aSamoa,* "the Samoan way." In a brochure published by the Western Samoa Visitors Bureau, the minister for Tourism highlights Samoan culture as a primary attraction for visitors but underscores the country's conservatism:

> We believe our country is very special. We are a traditional society with a distinctive Polynesian cultural heritage which we wish to preserve. However, at the same time, we know that our unique culture *(Fa'asamoa)* provides one of the principal attractions for our visitors.

Island governments may not directly impede tourist development, but they can be very bureaucratic. Individual department heads can make it difficult for outsiders to obtain permits, approvals, and visas for key personnel. In most Pacific Island societies, unlike Hawai'i, communal land tenure is legally protected and finding development sites is difficult, frequently requiring lengthy negotiations with local authorities. As in Hawai'i, states do have an important role to play in tourist promotion through international advertising and the funding of travel offices in major market centers. After experiencing modest growth in visitors during the 1970s, Papua New Guinea closed its state tourist office in 1982, partly because of concerns about tourism's impact on indigenous peoples (see Lea 1980); only 37,000 adventurous tourists visited the country in 1987 (*Islands Business Pacific,* October 1989, 45). By the 1980s, however, most Papua New Guinea political leaders were convinced that they had few economic alternatives. In 1993 Prime Minister Paias Wingti established a new Tourism Promotion Authority and made a personal commitment to support the industry (*Islands Business Pacific,* November 1993, 38).

Projections of astronomical growth in tourism to the Island Pacific have, for the most part, been wildly inaccurate. From the foreign tourist's perspective, visiting a less developed island has drawbacks that may override the attractions of pristine settings and exotic cultures. Papua New Guinea has been plagued by civil disorder and random violence for more than a decade. Ten years ago the capital of Western Samoa had only two hotels that foreign visitors would have found reliably clean and comfortable; even today, the quality of smaller establishments can be unpredictable. For years regional magazines have touted Western Samoa's impending tourist boom. In 1987 a United Nations study team prepared a ten-year plan for tourism in Western Samoa, optimistically predicting 200,000 visitors annually by the 1990s (*Islands Business Pacific,* July 1987, 35). But the boom has yet to materialize. The actual visitor count for 1990 was 47,600 (*Pacific Magazine,* March 1992, 23). A more recent estimate predicts 102,000 tourists annually by 2001 (*Pacific Magazine,* October 1992, 15), but that, too, seems unlikely.

There are cultural and infrastructural impediments to the growth of tourism in small island countries as well as a dearth of local expertise in marketing, finances, and management. The deference, respect, and assiduous service that may be tendered to indigenous visitors are not automatically extended to foreign tourists, whose status is ambiguous and who are usually ignorant of local etiquette. Flush toilets and hot water are typically nonexistent in rural villages. Sunbathing and recreational swimming are for the most part Western pastimes, and many Pacific Islanders find it offensive for women to appear publicly in scanty dress such as shorts and bikinis. Moreover, in many island cultures the beach is a liminal setting, a place to throw rubbish and relieve oneself. Indigenous authorities usually oversee the tidiness of rural villages, but Pacific towns have grown haphazardly and responsibility for public sanitation is ambiguous. Furthermore, island governments with scant resources are likely to give commitments such as education a higher priority than street cleaning. A Samoan writer summed up a tourist's reaction to Western Samoa in the title of a news article: "Friendly, Unique but Filthy" (Aiavao 1991).

Though their primary interests may be sun, sand, and sea, most tourists to the Pacific are also strongly attracted to the mystique of island cultures. Touristic representations of Polynesia emphasize sensuality and a tradition of hospitality, while adding that tourists to Polynesia can still enjoy a world-class level of comfort. In what could be called the older model of Pacific tourism, exemplified by Hawaii, Fiji, and Tahiti, indigenous culture provided an exotic backdrop with an occasional special event or performance such as hula or Fijian firewalking. Most older resorts in the Pacific maintain this balance. The hotel or resort becomes a surrogate for home, with familiar creature comforts. The weekly "Polynesian show" is a fixture at many hotels, often combined with a buffet dinner featuring local foods. In the typical Polynesian show, a small troupe performs a selection of dances from various Pacific Island groups—the hula, the Samoan *siva pati* (slap dance), and always the flashy, hip-gyrating dances identified with Tahiti and Rarotonga. Styling and subtleties may be lost, but for many tourists this reader's digest approach is sufficient as an experience of island cultures.

Sunbathing and first-class accommodations are typically less important to tourists in Melanesia, who may resemble those who attend funeral rituals in Toraja in that cultural performances are a primary attraction. These travelers want authenticity. They tend to see staged entertainment events as tacky and spurious and seek out cultural performances in their "original" context. For the more adventurous tourist, Melanesia offers experiences that border on the otherworldly—the highland New Guinea *singsing,* performed by painted, feathered men chanting in close array, or the death-defying land divers of South Pentecost in Vanuatu (who were the inspiration for Western bungee jumping; see Jolly 1982). Cultural tourism in Melanesia is still in a relatively early stage, and the situations are too diverse to detail here. But many Melanesian societies would be ideal settings in which to study tourism's emergence and transformation over time, as Volkman and Adams have done for Toraja.

It is important to note that Wood's (1984, 361) taxonomy of primary and secondary ethnic and cultural tourism has a temporal dimension. A tourist destination has a career; as infrastructure and accessibility improve, a location's market tends to shift from adventurous individual travelers to mainstream mass tourists. Primary ethnic tourism, to use Wood's term, may be superseded by one of the other types as visitor traffic increases and facilities improve. As an example, Western Samoa's initial appeal to foreign visitors (coming largely from New Zealand and Australia) was similar to that of Fiji: another tropical refuge from the antipodean winter, somewhere new, different, and exotic. But secondary cultural tourism in Samoa was slowed by the scarcity of international-standard hotels and swimming beaches and by Samoan inexperience in dealing with tourists.

In recent years entrepreneurs as well as state promotion efforts have been positioning Western Samoa to attract what Wood might call primary cultural tourism, in which Samoan culture is a center-stage attraction rather than a quaint and exotic backdrop. As *Islands* magazine notes, Western Samoa is "quintessentially" Polynesian. Western Samoa Visitors Bureau posters and brochures refer to the country as the "cradle of Polynesia."

Such characterizations cannot simply be dismissed as touristic manufactures; they resonate in complex ways with other ideas prevalent in both popular and scholarly discourse. Most cultural anthropologists have portrayed Western Samoa as a bastion of tradition—an estimation shared by many Samoans themselves. Since the Lapita finds of the early 1980s, archaeologists have come to regard Samoa as the likely launching place for the colonization of eastern Polynesia. In present-day public discourse, scholarly constructions interact with older, indigenous ideas about Samoan cultural identity. Oral history suggests that Samoans had a sense of themselves as a distinct (and superior) people long before European contact. For several generations Tonga subjugated Samoa, and the expulsion of the Tongans is vaunted as a pivotal event in Samoan national history. Western Samoa was the first Pacific Island colony to achieve independence, in 1962, and its citizens tend to see themselves as practicing Samoan tradition *(fa'aSamoa)* more fully and more authentically than Samoans in American Samoa, Hawaii, and elsewhere.

In Western Samoa, tourist marketing has selected for emphasis themes that were already present to some extent in Samoan self-definition. However, tourist promotion accentuates and crystallizes nascent forms of cultural objectification. From the tourist's point of view, every day in Western Samoa is a cultural performance. Yet tourists have tended to spend most of their time in and around Apia. Aggie Grey's Hotel has long been the most desirable and successful lodging establishment in Western Samoa. Aggie and her managers (all part-Samoans and family members) overcame the ethical breach between wage labor and culturally mandated service by emulating the normative organization of a Samoan village. In Samoa untitled men are at the beck and call of family elders and titled chiefs *(matai)*. Every village has an association of untitled men, the *'aumaga,* who are expected to perform service *(tautua)* for the chiefs and the village. Aggie Grey's famed crew of solicitous young men is known as "Aggie's *'aumaga.*" The young women and men on Aggie's staff double as singers and dancers in the weekly *fiafia,* which reproduces the energy and sincerity of a homegrown performance by a Samoan village troupe. Aggie's entertainment avoids the ersatz quality of the typical South Seas Polynesian show—no Tahitian-style gyrations here.

To foreign tourists, Aggie's epitomizes the *fa'aSamoa,* the Samoan way. Aggie's workers also seem to feel that their service is culturally authentic, for to all appearances the alienation and resentment often found among resort workers are absent here. The success of Aggie's hotel operation points to the dual valence of cultural objectification: if indigenous culture is presented with pride and celebration in commercial contexts, is it commoditized nonetheless? As in the wearing of identity merchandise, the answer must be yes, but in local estimation there may be more and less demeaning forms of cultural commoditization. Nevertheless, the problem with cultural tourism remains, as Margaret Jolly (1982, 352) phrases it, "that the economic benefits of tourism are rarely enjoyed equally, least of all by those whom the tourists have come to watch."

Cultural tourism in Western Samoa also takes the form of guided visits to rural villages. Aggie's hotel runs some of these; others are conducted by local tour operators and entrepreneurs. A popular destination for such trips is the small island of Manono, off the western end of Upolu. Manono has no automobiles, no electricity (except for a few family generators), and no running water. Manono's tidy villages and houses without walls *(fale)* look very "traditional" and the island has a long-standing reputation for cultural conservatism. In the recent past the chiefs forbade the wearing of long pants on the island; young men were always to wear lavalavas. Strangers of any variety are highly conspicuous on Manono. The public pathway around the island lies essentially in people's front yards, between the houses and the sea. Samoans engaged in their daily activities comprise a living cultural performance for visitors, and the human zoo analogy seems inescapable. As they walk around the island, the tourists gaze into the open-sided houses at Samoans eating, sleeping, dressing, or engaged in meetings and ceremonies. There is, at best, ambivalence among the Manono people toward these visits. Tourists may stop to swim at beaches that are not "public" in Samoan conceptualization, and foreign women on vacation frequently dress in a manner that the Samoans find offensive. In the past the Manono people also resented the fact that they were not making any money from these visits, and most regular tour operators now pay a "cut" to the villages.

For many Western Samoans, the rise of cultural tourism has been accompanied by a heightened sense of relative deprivation. This awareness is by no means solely or even primarily due to tourism, but it is accentuated by the increasing presence of foreign visitors. In the early 1990s Western Samoa was devastated by two cyclones that flattened breadfruit, banana, and coconut trees as well as houses. The subsistence economy was battered further by a taro blight that has all but annihilated the staple root crop. Taro was also an important export and one of the few sources of cash available to rural people, other than remittances. In the wake of the cyclones many Samoans were eating white rice (donated by foreign nations and aid organizations) three times a day; four years later, the more fortunate supplemented the rice with potatoes from New Zealand. Paradoxically, however, the destruction caused by the cyclones was followed by a building boom, financed by remittances, foreign aid, and a new goods and services tax that provoked the first public demonstrations in many years.

Consumerism has also blossomed. Along with Western Samoa's first high-rise office building, first elevator, and first traffic lights, Apia has seen many retail shops, restaurants, and a flea market open in the past few years. However, most of the new businesses are oriented toward tourists, Western expatriates, and elite Samoans. Samoans whose incomes derive only from the local economy are less and less able to buy the consumer goods now available in Apia. The new foreign-style restaurants are prohibitively expensive for the average citizen. As a taxi driver commented to me outside an incongruous new pizzaria: "You won't see any brown people in there." The public market in Apia has long been a place for Samoans to buy and sell produce and home-produced specialty items such as cocoa, woven sennit cord, coconut oil, and kava strainers. The market has also been a tourist attraction where Samoans offer craft items for sale—miniature kava bowls and outrigger canoes, coconut-leaf fans, shell necklaces, and woven pandanus leaf *(lau fala)* handbags. Tourist-oriented stalls and vendors selling "Samoan strength" apparel became more numerous in the market in the early 1990s, and an outdoor flea market was established a few blocks away. In its first location the flea market consisted of ramshackle plywood-and-tarpaulin booths crowded together in a lot often flooded with rainwater. In 1995, however, the public produce market was moved to a new pavilion a few blocks inland, and the flea market, greatly expanded, took over the food market's old quarters. The relocations effectively segregated the produce market, where few tourists are now seen, from the trade in apparel and crafts. The flea market offers shoes, toiletries such as soap and Western shampoos, hair barrettes and jewelry, a wide selection of identity merchandise, and the latest island fashions, such as tie-dyed lavalavas. The market for these articles appears to be a mix of tourists and elite Samoans. Designs and slogans celebrating Western Samoa's national rugby team, Manu Samoa, are particularly popular. Some tourists buy Samoan identity merchandise as novelties, but most prefer sloganless items such as printed lavalavas.

In 1985 I spent the better part of an afternoon searching Apia's shops for a T-shirt with some sort of Samoan slogan or design to take home as a gift for a child—without success. Today hundreds of different Samoa-theme T-shirts are sold in Apia's markets. It is tempting to discern parallel forms of cultural commoditization in the side-by-side sale of Samoan crafts (for tourists) and "Samoan strength" T-shirts and lavalavas (for local people). However, in Samoa, as elsewhere on the colonial periphery, tourism is only one factor generating consumer demand for products that objectify culture. Most Western Samoans have family members in New Zealand and Hawaii and transnational visiting is very frequent. In Hawaii, Samoans are economically disadvantaged and subject to discrimination. In both Hawaii and New Zealand the indigenous people are engaged in Fourth World nationalist movements. Indeed, Hawaiian identity T-shirts are very popular on the streets of Apia and Pago Pago. While not the whole story, tourism contributes to a context in which essentialized cultural representations are seen as legitimate and are used in consumer marketing. In the next section I will examine some identity images in detail and will explore the implications of representing people, rather than cultural artifacts, as traditional archetypes.

Consuming Cultural Identities

I suggested above that Western ethnic categorization, cultural tourism, and Fourth World activism converge in the ways that they represent human groups. Cultural affinities are presumed to coincide with biogenetic ancestry; groups are seen to be clearly bounded by custom as well as by race. The crucial affiliation—the one represented as legitimate and emotionally compelling—is rootedness in a primordial homeland. In Hawaii today, this model of ethnicity has become a successful marketing formula, evidenced by an explosion in identity merchandise over the past several years. Slogans associating ethnic pride with hypermasculinized graphic paragons are ubiquitous on T-shirts in Hawaii's shopping malls, classrooms, and public places. Most items are worn by young men and boys. Importantly, the identity merchandise targets Hawaii's disadvantaged groups, primarily Hawaiians, but there are also Samoan and Filipino variants. There are no analogous articles touting Chinese, Japanese, or haole identity. The messages represent the cultural authenticity and autochthonous power of subordinated groups as a foil to the economic success of these other ethnicities in Hawaii.

The tourist's "Hawaiian T-shirt" was the immediate forerunner of today's identity apparel. For decades the T-shirt has been the cheapest and most widely available Hawaiian souvenir. Local people also wear T-shirts more than any other garment; they are cheap, cool in the semitropical climate, and emblematic of the working-class background of most Hawaii families. However, there are clear semiotic distinctions between tourist T-shirts and the ones that locals wear, and they are sold at different retail outlets. Tourist T-shirts tend to feature stereotypic tropical beach and surf scenes labeled "Hawaii." The least expensive genres proclaim the year of the visit ("Hawaii 94") or include vulgarities such as "I got lei'd in Hawaii." Local people do sometimes wear inexpensive tourist-style shirts, but only when engaged in dirty work—fishing, gardening, fixing the car. Since the 1970s many T-shirt companies have emerged, but they tend to target either tourists or the local market. Crazy Shirts is a well-known, upscale brand that features evocative motifs such as geckoes and sumo wrestlers. Nevertheless, local students have told me that they would wear a Crazy Shirt only if it were given to them; similarly, they would buy one as a gift, but not to wear themselves. Lines such as Cane Haul Road, on the other hand, were designed to appeal specifically to Hawaii people. Popular in the 1970s and 1980s, Cane Haul Road shirts featured in-jokes that relied on a knowledge of pidgin or an intimate familiarity with local lifeways.

Cane Haul Road designs were not ethnically exclusive and could be enjoyed by any longtime Hawaii resident. But in the 1990s, messages on distinctively local T-shirts have become less subtle, more ethnically specific, and more politically charged (see Figure 8.1). This trend parallels Hawaiian political resurgence, notably the sovereignty movement, and a growing local disenchantment with tourism. Today's most popular genres explicitly celebrate particular disadvantaged ethnicities and symbolize group strength by means of hypermasculine traditional archetypes. The designs have become formulaic

Figure 8.1. Total sovereignty. (Photo by Jocelyn Linnekin)

in their similarities; clearly, the juxtaposition of ethnic slogans and steroidal paragons is a combination that sells. Ikaika, the name of one series, means "strong, powerful" in Hawaiian; it is currently a very popular name for Hawaiian boys (see Figure 8.2). Although some Hawaiian strength T-shirts are aimed at women—some feature the volcano goddess Pele—the identity fashions are overwhelmingly gendered. Ethnic strength is graphically identified with male potency and prowess. This gendering of ethnic assertiveness clearly deserves an extended analysis, but that is not possible here.

Figure 8.2. Ikaika. (Photo by Jocelyn Linnekin)

A near-universal symbol in Hawaiian identity merchandise is the warrior helmet shown in the Ikaika logo and on the figure on the back of the shirt (see Figure 8.3). In the past decade this helmet has become the quintessential symbol of Hawaiian identity, evoking connotations of spiritual power, mystery, and cultural revival (see also Figure 8.1). It is incorporated into the logos of numerous T-shirt lines, with trademark titles such as Kapu—Forbidden Territory and Local Boyz Rule. Kiosks in shopping malls sell helmet reproductions made from polished coconut shells and dyed feathers, in a wide range of sizes and color schemes. These icons dangle from the rearview mirrors of hundreds of pickup trucks. Muscular helmeted warriors were also a popular motif for milk cap designs during Hawaii's recent pog craze (see Figure 8.4). The helmet's modern redefinition bears little resemblance to its indigenous cultural standing, however, illustrating the creativity of modern identity representations. Fashioned from a gourd, with a tuft of ferns on top and tapa cloth strips dan-

Figure 8.3. Lono Maku. (Photo by Jocelyn Linnekin)

gling from the lower edge, the helmet was observed and described only once, during Captain Cook's visit, and only on the island of Hawai'i. John Webber, the artist on the voyage, produced two engravings of men wearing such headgear. They were believed to be priests of Lono, a peaceable god whose ritual time specifically proscribed warfare. Nevertheless, today the warrior helmet is a formulaic symbol of Hawaiian cultural superiority and ethnic assertiveness, and it is often combined with other contemporary symbols of aggressiveness such as pit bull dogs and sword-and-sorcery weapons. On one shirt, a menacing helmeted warrior rides a bulky motorcycle. The most popular background color is black, with images predominantly in silver or white. In a representative example, a hypermuscular Hawaiian warrior holds back a pack of ravening pit bulls, with the caption "TRADITION." A local high school teacher with an interest in graphic arts told me that the designers are motivated by creative inspiration and a desire to innovate. They go to swap meets to get a feel for the latest ideas, and then they try to go a little further

Figure 8.4. Two pogs. (Photo by Jocelyn Linnekin)

in their own designs. Identity fashions first appeared at swap meets and neighborhood discount stores and later were adopted by more mainstream retailers.

As the examples above illustrate, the identity designs are highly eclectic even as they assert primordial and essentialized ethnic identities. The profit incentive drives rapid innovation in graphic representations, and there is no room for ethnohistorical pedantry. Designers experiment to see what merchandise will sell and make the transition to high-volume outlets. The Lono Maku shirt (Figure 8.2) exemplifies the dynamism of this creative play. To my knowledge, the god Lono is not particularly associated with fire, and there is no Hawaiian word *maku*. An informant suggested that the designer had lopped off the word *makua* (parent) because it looked better. The Ikaika Bodyware line in which this appears has been very successful, as indicated by the fact that the Lono Maku shirt was purchased in a J. C. Penney store, a relatively upscale outlet for identity fashions.

Figure 8.5. Filipino, Samoan. (Photo by Jocelyn Linnekin)

Identity designs aimed at other groups in Hawaii draw on the same conventional elements, but use small, contrasting details to index ethnic distinctiveness. All of the muscular bodies in these designs are more or less the same; one needs the text and a few artifactual clues to identify the particular ethnicity that is targeted. The Filipino and Samoan Strength shirt logos (see Figure 8.5) are nearly identical except for the posture and weaponry of the figure, which is drawn in the style of a Hawaiian petroglyph. The corresponding Hawaiian Strength logo features a warrior helmet in the center. The Filipino Strength design (see Figure 8.6) depicts ethnic "spirit" in terms of bodybuilder muscularity, with the pit bull dog adding to the macho symbolism. Importantly, the word *pinoy* means a Filipino born in the Philippines. Thus Filipinos in migrant communities are exhorted to identify their spirit with a primordial cultural homeland. The Filipino's loincloth is very similar to that of Hawaiian warriors on other shirts; only the dagger and the headband signal ethnic difference to the onlooker.

Figure 8.6. Pinoy. (Photo by Jocelyn Linnekin)

I found the best selection of Hawaiian ethnic strength T-shirts in Pago Pago, American Samoa. In the Samoas, unlike Hawaii, young women also wear shirts with strikingly masculine images. It may seem ironic that Hawaiian identity merchandise is popular among Samoan youth. Young Samoans are attracted to these fashions not so much because of the specific messages but because they symbolize a link to modernity and metropolitan centers. Many of them receive the shirts as gifts or buy them abroad. Wearing them conveys the message, "I was in Hawaii," or "I have relatives in Hawaii." But Samoan identity fashions are also becoming increasingly popular (see Figure 8.7). In a design celebrating Samoa's beloved rugby team as "Pride of the Pacific," the muscular figure holds a football instead of a weapon and is depicted with a *pe'a,* a full-body tattoo. The tapa cloth pictured in the background is not stylistically Samoan but suffices to invoke a generic Polynesian identity. Other shirts seen in

Figure 8.7. Manu Samoa. (Photo by Jocelyn Linnekin)

Apia's market stalls and streets explicitly assert a naturalized idea of cultural/ethnic authenticity, with such slogans as: *Tòtò Samoa* (Samoan blood), *Samoa moni* (real Samoan), and *Tòtò Samoa moni* (real Samoan blood).

Even as identity fashions evoke ideas of racial purity combined with cultural distinctiveness, they draw on an increasingly transnational graphic symbolism of political protest. Similar images can be found on apparel sold by street vendors in Washington, D.C. Some Hawaiian, Filipino, and Samoan identity designs now use the color scheme of red, green, and black. Drawn from the Ethiopian flag and once associated with the Black Power movement, these have attained the semiotic status of global liberation colors, invoking the common experience of oppressed peoples. The identity merchandisers are primarily interested in finding designs that sell; few are concerned about potential contradictions in the messages—such as between micronationalism and global class unity. If there is an overall message conveyed by identity fashions, it may be that subordinate peoples draw their strength and their authenticity primarily from their unique ethnic roots, but they can also identify with other oppressed groups.

Tourism, Self-Definition, and Cultural Politics

I have emphasized that tourism forms only part of the historical and economic context in which ethnic identity is commoditized in consumer markets. But the touristic commoditization of culture is a precursor for other venues in which cultural representations have sales appeal. Picard (1990) argued that tourism can no longer be regarded as external to Balinese culture, and that is certainly true for Hawaii. But many anthropologists would argue further, that wherever culture is a visitor attraction, tourism enters into local self-definition. Further, with the growing presence of affluent visitors from outside, local people may come to perceive the distinction between haves and have-nots in increasingly ethnic terms. On a hypothetical scale of economic engagement with tourism, Hawaii and Western Samoa would represent widely separated points. We could posit a parallel gradient of cultural objectification or distancing. At some point on this hypothetical continuum, local people too become cultural consumers—but of artifacts and performances that they believe to be their own. In the course of promoting ethnic and cultural tourism, the state objectifies local customs and portrays the people of a place as exotic tradition bearers. In most developing nations, this process begins with encouraging cultural performances and sales of crafts (what Westerners of another century called "artificial curiosities"). But I have argued that in capitalist settings the state—at whatever governmental level—has a limited role in directing how cultural representations are ultimately designed and marketed. Capitalist consumer markets are relatively unconstrained by the state. For decades Hawaii's dominant ideology celebrating diversity has tended to blunt the political edge of cultural expression. Yet the public prominence and seeming success of the Hawaiian movement has sparked a general resurgence of ethnic assertiveness in Hawaii. The forms that this assertiveness has taken—from community activism to ethnic power messages on consumer merchandise—are minimally controlled by the state. Moreover, many of these expressions run counter to the normative message of ethnic harmony.

Hawaii's near-total economic dependence on tourism has produced sophisticated marketing techniques and a saturation of retail outlets. In the context of Hawaii's social history of ethnic stratification, these economic conditions make for a thriving local market in identity merchandise that is spreading to other Pacific communities that have regular traffic with Hawaii. The State of Hawaii has endeavored to maintain the public ideology of aloha, widely seen as one of Hawaii's key selling points, in the face of increasing local dissent over tourism. The wearing of identity T-shirts, with rather crude naturalistic depictions of ethnic paragons in aggressive poses, conveys an "in-your-face" local (as opposed to haole) assertiveness that counters the values associated with aloha. The identity merchandisers are for the most part individual entrepreneurs; there is no multinational corporation or state agency behind the designers and silkscreen printers, some of whom operate out of garages. The apparel merchandisers have simply picked up and reinterpreted messages that have long been more-or-less explicit in touristic discourse about Hawaii's ethnic groups. They have also responded to a local zeitgeist that now celebrates ethnic boundaries over ethnic cooperation. In effect, the state's marketing of cultural difference to promote tourism has helped to generate an unintended harvest of "locals only" ethnic exclusiveness that contradicts the approved public text of multiracial harmony.

Identity merchandise is a bellwether for the political yearnings and cultural constructions of ordinary people. In Hawaii and in capitalist settings generally, the state has minimal control over the messages that are communicated through the medium of consumer goods. Profit-driven markets respond to public demand, but in dynamic fashion they also generate more demand, for fashion advertises itself, continually and effectively. Indeed, few media disseminate ideas as effectively as apparel, worn in public settings throughout the day. Where consumer markets thrive, the imperatives of fashion and style are far more efficient than the state in publicizing messages about the nature of human groups.

Notes

1. For other analyses and examples of the Western passion for collection, see Clifford 1988, Handler 1985, Macpherson 1962.

2. The tourism budget was raised from $9.5 million to nearly $30 million for 1993–1994. Most of this money is allocated to the Hawaii Visitors Bureau (*Hotel and Motel Management* vol. 208[10]:3, 25 [June 7, 1993]).

3. These descriptors are taken from surveys I administered over several years to undergraduates at the University of Hawai'i.

4. See the Hawaiian Islands supplement to *Sales and Marketing Manage-*

ment 146(6):4–7 (June 1994). One Hawaiian scholar, George Kanahele, has started a business to help hotels incorporate "Hawaiian values and cultural training" into their operations. The trade journal also reports that Hawaii Visitors Bureau staff are now receiving training in Hawaiian values and culture.

References

Adams, Kathleen M.
  1984 Come to Tana Toraja, "Land of the Heavenly Kings": Travel Agents as Brokers in Ethnicity. *Annals of Tourism Research* 11: 469–485.
  1990 Cultural Commoditization in Tana Toraja, Indonesia. *Cultural Survival Quarterly* 14(1):31–34.
Aiavao, Ulafala
  1991 Friendly, Unique but Filthy. *Pacific Islands Monthly* 61 (6):37.
Britton, Steven
  1987 Tourism in Pacific Island States: Constraints and Opportunities. In *Ambiguous Alternative: Tourism in Small Developing Countries,* ed. Steven Britton and William C. Clarke, 113–139. Suva: University of the South Pacific.
Clifford, James
  1988 On Collecting Art and Culture. In *The Predicament of Culture,* 215–251. Cambridge: Harvard University Press.
Connell, John
  1991 Island Microstates: The Mirage of Development. *The Contemporary Pacific* 3:251–287.
Cooper, George, and Gavan Daws
  1985 *Land and Power in Hawaii: The Democratic Years.* Honolulu: Benchmark Books.
Dearden, Philip, and Sylvia Harron
  1992 Tourism and the Hilltribes of Thailand. In *Special Interest Tourism,* ed. Betty Weiler and Colin Michael Hall, 95–104. London: Belhaven Press.
Farrell, Bryan H.
  1982 *Hawaii, the Legend That Sells.* Honolulu: University Press of Hawai'i.
Finney, Ben R., and Karen Ann Watson
  1974 *A New Kind of Sugar: Tourism in the Pacific.* Honolulu: East-West Center.
Greenwood, Davydd J.
  1977 Culture by the Pound: An Anthropological Perspective on Tourism as Cultural Commoditization. In *Hosts and Guests: The Anthro-*

pology of Tourism, ed. Valene L. Smith, 129–138. Philadelphia: University of Pennsylvania Press.

1982 Cultural "Authenticity." *Cultural Survival Quarterly* 6(3):27–28.

Handler, Richard

1985 On Having a Culture: Nationalism and the Preservation of Quebec's *Patrimoine.* In *History of Anthropology.* Vol. 3, *Objects and Others,* ed. George Stocking, 192–217. Madison: University of Wisconsin Press.

Harron, Sylvia, and Betty Weiler

1992 Ethnic Tourism. In *Special Interest Tourism,* ed. Betty Weiler and Colin Michael Hall, 83–94. London: Belhaven Press.

Jameson, Frederic

1979 Reification and Utopia in Mass Culture. *Social Text* 1(1):130–148.

Jolly, Margaret

1982 Birds and Banyans of South Pentecost: Kastom in Anti-Colonial Struggle. *Mankind* 13:338–356.

Kent, Noel J.

1983 *Hawaii: Islands Under the Influence.* New York and London: Monthly Review Press.

Lea, David

1980 Tourism in Papua New Guinea: The Last Resort. In *Of Time and Place,* ed. J. N. Jennings and G. J. R. Linge, 211–231. Canberra: Australian National University Press.

Linnekin, Jocelyn

1982 Selling Hawaiian Culture. *Cultural Survival Quarterly* 6(3):29.

1987 Statistical Analysis of the Great Mahele: Some Preliminary Findings. *Journal of Pacific History* 22:16–33.

1990 The Politics of Culture in the Pacific. In *Cultural Identity and Ethnicity in the Pacific,* ed. Jocelyn Linnekin and Lin Poyer, 149–173. Honolulu: University of Hawai'i Press.

1992 On the Theory and Politics of Cultural Construction in the Pacific. *Oceania* 62:249–263.

Linnekin, Jocelyn, and Lin Poyer, eds.

1990 *Cultural Identity and Ethnicity in the Pacific.* Honolulu: University of Hawai'i Press.

MacCannell, Dean

1976 *The Tourist: A New Theory of the Leisure Class.* New York: Shocken.

1984 Reconstructed Ethnicity: Tourism and Cultural Identity in Third World Communities. *Annals of Tourism Research* 11:375–391.

Macpherson, C. B.

1962 *The Political Theory of Possessive Individualism.* Oxford: Oxford University Press.

Michener, James A.
1959 *Hawaii.* Greenwich, Conn.: Fawcett.
Murayama, Milton
1975 *All I Asking For Is My Body.* San Francisco: Supa Press.
Nordyke, Eleanor C.
1989 *The Peopling of Hawai'i,* 2d ed. Honolulu: University of Hawai'i Press.
Ortner, Sherry
1973 On Key Symbols. *American Anthropologist* 75:1338–1346.
Picard, Michel
1990 "Cultural Tourism" in Bali: Cultural Performances as Tourist Attraction. *Indonesia* 49:37–74.
Reinecke, John E.
1979 *Feigned Necessity: Hawaii's Attempt to Obtain Chinese Contract Labor, 1921–1923.* San Francisco: Chinese Materials Center.
Said, Edward
1978 *Orientalism.* New York: Vintage Books.
Schmitt, Robert C.
1968 *Demographic Statistics of Hawaii: 1778–1965.* Honolulu: University of Hawai'i Press.
Smith, Bernard
1960 *European Vision and the South Pacific 1768–1850.* London: Oxford University Press.
Smith, Valene L., ed.
1989 *Hosts and Guests: The Anthropology of Tourism,* 2d ed. Philadelphia: University of Pennsylvania Press.
Swain, Margaret Byrne
1990 Commoditizing Ethnicity in Southwest China. *Cultural Survival Quarterly* 14(1):26–29.
Takaki, Ronald
1983 *Pau Hana: Plantation Life and Labor in Hawaii 1835–1920.* Honolulu: University of Hawai'i Press.
Volkman, Toby Alice
1982 Tana Toraja: A Decade of Tourism. *Cultural Survival Quarterly* 6(3):30–31.
1984 Great Performances: Toraja Cultural Identity in the 1970s. *American Ethnologist* 11:152–169.
Volkman, Toby Alice
1990 Visions and Revisions: Toraja Culture and the Tourist Gaze. *American Ethnologist* 17:91–110.
Wallerstein, Immanuel
1974 *The Modern World-System.* New York: Academic Press.
1979 *The Capitalist World-Economy.* Cambridge: Cambridge University Press.

Weiler, Betty, and Colin Michael Hall, eds.

1992   *Special Interest Tourism.* London: Belhaven Press.

Wood, Robert E.

1984   Ethnic Tourism, the State, and Cultural Change in Southeast Asia. *Annals of Tourism Research* 11:353–374.

1993   Tourism, Culture and the Sociology of Development. In *Tourism in South-East Asia,* ed. Michael Hitchcock, Victor King, and Michael Parnwell, 48–70. London and New York: Routledge.

Wood, Robert E., and Monika Deppen

1994   Cultural Tourism: Ethnic Options and Constructed Otherness. Paper presented at the International Sociological Association meetings, Bielefeld, Germany.

Contributors

Kathleen M. Adams is assistant professor of Anthropology at Loyola University of Chicago. She has published articles on the Toraja in a variety of journals, including *Annals of Tourism Research, Ethnology, Cultural Survival Quarterly, Southeast Asian Journal of Social Science,* and *The Kyoto Journal.* She is currently writing a book on the politics of tourism, ethnicity, and the arts in Tana Toraja.

Joel S. Kahn is professor of Anthropology at La Trobe University in Australia. He is the author of *Culture, Multiculture, Post-culture, Constituting the Minangkabau: Peasants, Culture and Modernity in Colonial Indonesia,* and is co-editor of *Fragmented Vision: Culture and Politics in Contemporary Malaysia.*

Laurence Wai-Teng Leong is senior lecturer in Sociology at the National University of Singapore. He received his Ph.D. at the University of California at San Diego and has published in *Critical Studies in Mass Communications, Current Perspectives in Social Theory,* and *Media, Culture and Society.*

Jocelyn Linnekin is professor of Anthropology at the University of Hawai'i. She is the author of *Children of the Land: Exchange and Status in a Hawaiian Community* and *Sacred Queens* *and Women of Consequence: Rank, Gender and Colonialism in the Hawaiian Islands,* the co-editor of *Cultural Identity and Ethnicity in the Pacific,* and the author of numerous articles.

Jean Michaud is lecturer in Thai Language and Culture at the Centre for South-East Asian Studies at the University of Hull, England. As a research fellow he studied montagnards in Thailand, Laos, and Vietnam in collaboration with the International Development Research Centre of Canada and at the Institute of Development Studies in Brighton (U.K.). Before doing fieldwork in Northern Thailand among the Hmong, he did fieldwork in Ladakh, India, and has published articles in *Annals of Tourism Research, Anthropologica, Anthropologie et Societés, International Journal of Comparative Studies on Asia and Africa,* and *Internationales Asienforum.*

Timothy S. Oakes is assistant professor of Geography at the University of Colorado at Boulder. He has published articles in the *Journal of Cultural Geography, Environment and Planning,* and in *Tourism in China,* edited by Alan Lew and Lawrence Yu.

Michel Picard is a researcher at CNRS (French National Center for Scientific Research) in Paris. After investigating at length the local implications of international tourism with the Unité de Recherche en Sociologie due Tourisme International (URESTI), he is currently continuing his research on Balinese society with the Laboratoire Asie du Sud-Est et Monde Austronésien (LASEMA). He is the author of *Bali: Cultural Tourism and Touristic Culture* and co-editor of *Bali, L'ordre Cosmique et la Quotidienneté.*

Robert E. Wood is associate professor of Sociology at Rutgers University, Camden, New Jersey. He was a Fulbright scholar in Thailand and is the author of *From Marshall Plan to Debt Crisis: Foreign Aid and Development Choices in the World Economy* and of numerous articles on development policy and tourism.

Index